# Mirroring and Attunement

*Mirroring and Attunement* offers a new approach to psychoanalysis, artistic creation and religion. Viewing these activities from a relational perspective, Wright proposes that each provides a medium for creative dialogue: the artist discovers himself within his self-created forms, the religious person through an internal dialogue with 'God', and the analysand through the inter-subjective medium of the analysis.

Building on the work of Winnicott, Stern and Langer, the author argues that each activity is rooted in the infant's preverbal relationship with the mother who 'holds' the emerging self in an ambience of mirroring forms, thereby providing a 'place' for the self to 'be'. He suggests that the need for subjective reflection persists throughout the life cycle and that psycho-analysis, artistic creation and religion can be seen as cultural attempts to provide the self with resonant containment. They thus provide renewed opportunities for holding and emotional growth.

*Mirroring and Attunement* will provide essential reading for psychoanalysts, psychotherapists, and art therapists and be of interest to anyone working at the interface between psychoanalysis, art and religion.

**Kenneth Wright** is a psychoanalyst in private practice in Suffolk and a Patron of the Squiggle Foundation. A well known commentator on Winnicott, he lectures nationally and internationally and has published papers on psychoanalysis, the creative arts and religion. His book *Vision and Separation: Between Mother and Baby* (1991) was awarded the Margaret S. Mahler Literature Prize (1992).

# Mirroring and Attunement

## Self-realization in psychoanalysis and art

Kenneth Wright

Routledge
Taylor & Francis Group

LONDON AND NEW YORK

First published 2009
by Routledge
27 Church Road, Hove, East Sussex BN3 2FA

Simultaneously published in the USA and Canada
by Routledge
270 Madison Avenue, New York, NY 10016

*Routledge is an imprint of the Taylor & Francis Group, an informa business*

Typeset in Times by Garfield Morgan, Swansea, West Glamorgan
Printed and bound in Great Britain by TJ International Ltd, Padstow,
Cornwall
Paperback cover design by Hybert Design
Paperback cover image: The Lady and the Unicorn – 'Sight' (tapestry) by
French School (15th century), Musee National du Moyen Age et des Thermes
de Cluny, Paris/The Bridgeman Art Library Nationality/copyright status:
French/out of copyright

This publication has been produced with paper manufactured to strict
environmental standards and with pulp derived from sustainable forests.

*British Library Cataloguing in Publication Data*
A catalogue record for this book is available from the British Library

*Library of Congress Cataloging in Publication Data*
Wright, Kenneth, 1936–
    Mirroring and attunement : self realization in psychoanalysis and art /
Kenneth Wright.
        p. cm.
    Includes index.
    ISBN 978-0-415-46829-9 (hardback) – ISBN 978-0-415-46830-5 (pbk.)
    1. Self-realization. 2. Psychoanalysis. 3. Psychoanalysis and art. I. Title.
    BF637.S4W78 2009
    150.19'5–dc22
                                                          2008047608

ISBN: 978-0-415-46829-9 (hbk)
ISBN: 978-0-415-46830-5 (pbk)

For Alice

This is the creature there has never been.
They never knew it, and yet, none the less
they loved the way it moved, its suppleness,
its neck, its very gaze, mild and serene.

Not there, because they loved it, it behaved
as though it were. They always left some space.
And in that clear unpeopled space they saved
It lightly reared its head, with scarce a trace

of not being there. They fed it, not with corn,
but only with the possibility
of being. And that was able to confer

such strength, its brow put forth a horn. One horn.
Whitely it stole up to a maid, – to *be*
Within the silver mirror and in her.

> Rilke (1960): *Sonnets to Orpheus* 2, iv

# Contents

# Preface

The majority of these papers were given as talks and gradually evolved into the form they take in this book. 'On being in touch' (chapter 1) began as a talk to the Herts and Essex Psychotherapy Forum in March 1995. 'The poetics of interpretation' (chapter 2), was first given at a Westminster Pastoral Foundation conference, Girton College, Cambridge in 1995 and subsequently to the post-congress Section of Psychotherapy meeting (RANZCP), Leura, NSW, Australia, in May 1997.

'Deep calling unto deep' (chapter 3) was presented at a Scientific Meeting of the Psychotherapy Section (Victoria branch) of the RANZCP, Melbourne, Australia in 1997 and later at a Freud Museum Conference in London on the theme 'What is an object?' It was published under the title 'Deep calling unto deep: Artistic creativity and the maternal object' in the *British Journal of Psychotherapy* (1998).

'Making experience sing' (chapter 4) formed a lecture in the 'Psychotherapy and the Arts' series at the Institute of Psychoanalysis, London, 1997. It was published in revised form as 'To make experience sing' in a Winnicott Studies Monograph Series of the Squiggle Foundation, *Art, Creativity, Living*, edited by Lesley Caldwell and published by Karnac Books, 2000.

'Bion and beyond' (chapter 5) was the Enid Balint Memorial Lecture organized by the SCPP (Society of Couple Psychoanalytic Psychotherapists) at the Tavistock Centre, London (2000); it was later revised and published as 'Bion and beyond: projective identification and maternal imperviousness' in the Internet Journal *Funzione Gamma*, and as a chapter in *Studi ed esperienze a partire da Bion*, edited by S. Marinelli and published by Edizioni Borla, Roma, 2008, under the title 'Bion ed oltre. Identificazione proiettiva e impenetrabilità materna' (see Acknowledgements).

'Words, things and Wittgenstein' (chapter 6) was first given as a public Lecture at the Westminster Pastoral Foundation, London, in June 1996, and subsequently presented to the Sydney Institute of Psychoanalysis in June 1997 and the Irish Forum for Psychoanalytic Psychotherapy in April 1999. It was published as 'Las palabras, las cosas y Wittgenstein. Un estudio' in the *Journal of the Madrid Psychoanalytic Association* in 2001 (see Acknowledgements).

'Shaping the inarticulate' (chapter 7) formed the 30th Inaugural Anniversary Lecture at AGIP (Association of Group and Individual Psychotherapy), London, in November 2004 and was published under the title 'The shaping of experience' in the *British Journal of Psychotherapy*, 2005 (see Acknowledgements).

'The search for form' (chapter 9) originated as a parallel contribution with Professor Michael Podro (University of Essex) to an AGIP meeting in October 1995. The topic was 'Looking at pictures – does psychoanalytic understanding help?' It evolved into a more extended paper *Psychic growth and the search for form* which I presented as keynote address to the post-congress Section of Psychotherapy (RANZCP) meeting, Leura, NSW, Australia, in May 1997. Finally, an extensively revised version which forms the basis of the present chapter was presented at the 'Winnicott Today' conference, University College, London in June 2006.

'The intuition of the sacred' (chapter 10) formed a chapter for *Psychoanalysis and Religion in the 21st Century*, edited by D. Black and published by Routledge in 2006 with the title 'Preverbal experience and the intuition of the sacred' (see Acknowledgements); 'Recognition and relatedness' (chapter 11) was my contribution to a conference on 'The Nature of Love' organized by the London Centre for Psychotherapy in April 1997; finally, 'Embodied language' (chapter 8) and 'The silver mirror' (chapter 12) were both written for this collection.

# Acknowledgements

This book owes its existence to the organizations, large and small, who invited me to lecture following the publication of my first book, and even more to the audiences who responded so warmly to my ideas. In particular, I would mention the London Centre for Psychotherapy, the Westminster Pastoral Foundation, the Association for Group and Individual Psychotherapy (AGIP), and the Independent Group of the British Psychoanalytic Society with whom I did my psychoanalytic training. I would also mention the Squiggle Foundation, The Freud Museum, the Society for Couple Psychoanalytic Psychotherapy and the Zeitlyn Trust in conjunction with the Cambridge Young Peoples' Service.

Further afield, I owe a special debt to the organizers of the three International Winnicott Conferences in Milan in 1997, 2000 and 2005, Andreas Giannakoulas and Max Hernandez, who invited me to participate on each occasion, and to Neville Symington and Eng Kong in Sydney, Australia, who between them arranged a lecture tour which provided a major stimulus to develop my ideas.

Among the individuals who have given encouragement, I would mention Josephine Klein whose interest in my work has never flagged; the late Professor Michael Podro for many interesting conversations and his much valued appreciation of my forays into art; Nina Farhi who in the early days was so welcoming at Squiggle meetings; Andreas Giannakoulas who has championed my work in Italy and arranged the Italian translation of my first book; and Jan Abram, not only for her invaluable reference book, *The Language of Winnicott*, but also for her personal support.

I am deeply grateful to my patients, past and present, who unwittingly provided a holding medium and unobtrusive background for my creative efforts; to the individuals who let me know that my ideas spoke to them in a personal way; and to the few artists who felt that I understood in a deep way what they were trying to do.

I would like to thank: Blackwell Publishing and the *British Journal of Psychotherapy* for permission to reprint revised versions of 'Deep calling unto deep: Artistic creativity and the maternal object', *British Journal of Psychotherapy* (1998), 14: 453–67 (now chapter experience', *British Journal of Psychotherapy* chapter 7); Asociación Psicoanalítica de Madrid the English version of 'Las palabras, las cosas y *Revista de Psicoanalisis de la Asociación Psicoanali* 197–216 (which now appears as chapter 6, 'Wo stein'); *Funzione Gamma* (Internet Journal) of Roma, and Edizioni Borla, Roma, for permissi beyond: Projective identification and materna appeared in *Funzione Gamma*, l'edizione on line, *esperienze a partire da Bion* (2008) ed. S. Marinell oltre. Identificazione proiettiva e impenetrabilità pp. 197–216 (now chapter 5). 'To make experience in *Art, Creativity, Living* edited by L. Caldwell (c 2000) and has been reprinted in revised form (as mission of Karnac Books. Finally, 'Preverbal expe of the sacred' in *Psychoanalysis and Religion in petitors or Collaborators?* edited by D. Black and p 2006 (copyright Taylor and Francis Group 2006), i revised form by permission of Taylor and Francis B

I must also thank Random House Group Ltd fo extracts from *Rainer Maria Rilke, Selected Works.* J. B. Leishman, published by Hogarth Press; and London, and Farrar, Straus and Giroux, LLC, for extracts from *Finders Keepers: Selected Prose 1* Heaney (copyright © 2002 by Seamus Heaney).

Thanks are due to my publisher Kate Hawes, se Jane Harris and project editor Nicola Ravenscro making this book possible. Finally, a huge thanks to support and for being so patient when the demands attention.

# Introduction

Most of these papers were written for special occasions and bear the strengths and weaknesses of this origin. They share an underlying theme and since each tackles this from a different angle, the focus sharpens as the work progresses. They appear in roughly chronological order but have been revised and rewritten to a varying degree.

The sequence records an emerging, and possibly obsessive preoccupation, for although I approached each project as a new and interesting venture, it would always come back to the same questions, precisely the ones I had explored in my first book (Wright 1991) and even my first paper (Wright 1976). It is possible that every writer has a 'territory' of this kind to which he feels compelled to return, and if that is so, it is surely the *terra*, always *incognita*, of his own subjectivity.

In my first book I considered the role of vision, and also separation from the object (mother) in the development of symbols. In the present work, symbolic development remains a critical issue, but I now place more emphasis on earlier stages of the process. I thus focus on two functions provided by the preverbal mother, namely *holding* (Winnicott 1960a) and *containing* (Bion 1962a, 1962b, 1965), which most analysts would see as fundamental to the psychoanalytic enterprise and linked to the development of symbolic understanding. Both terms refer to aspects of the mother–infant relationship but by extension can be applied to other situations: for example, the way the analyst, or analytic situation 'holds' the patient, or the way some mental content is 'held' or 'contained' in the mind. Clearly, the ability to hold something in mind is inextricably entangled with the development and use of symbols, and the growth of self-awareness and understanding in psychoanalysis can also be thought of in terms of symbolic development.

The concepts of holding and containing are now an established part of psychoanalytic discourse, but while the sense of the terms can be felt, and intuitively understood within particular contexts, it can often seem that their operational meaning is less than clearly defined. Even though analytic technique has evolved significantly and now places greater emphasis on holding and containing, most writing on the subject continues to privilege 'interpretation' over other analytic activities. As with 'projective identi-fication', the meaning of the term has expanded in portmanteau fashion and this hinders, rather than facilitates, understanding of the issues at stake. In the chapters which follow, I use the term 'interpretation' in a more restricted sense in order to differentiate it from 'holding' and 'containing'.

Bion (1962a, 1962b, 1965) discussed containment (the 'container-contained') in terms of a maternal process ('$\alpha$-function') which transformed the infant's 'raw experience' ($\beta$-elements) into more manageable (contained) form. In ordinary language, this seemed to mean that through her 'reverie' the mother transformed the infant's overwhelming *bodily* experience into something that could be dealt with in a *mental* way. In other words, she helped the infant to create *mental* objects out of raw physical sensations, thus making possible the *mental* manipulation of experience (incipient thought) in place of more primitive, quasi-physical methods of dealing with it – for example, in Kleinian theory, by 'projective identification' or 'evacuation'.

From this perspective, the 'mind', which is formed through $\alpha$-function processing, is the sphere of *symbolic* objects and a 'mental' object is an aspect of experience that has been symbolized; it consists of 'experience' that at least in a rudimentary way is 'held' or 'contained' in symbolic form. Thus far Bion is clear; in my view, however, he did not clearly explain *how* the mother's containment of infant experience actually led to its *mental* containment by the infant – in other words, to containment in symbolic or pre-symbolic forms. Although his major outline of the process was entirely plausible, the finer details remained obscure.[1]

This makes it a challenge to define the mother's contribution in a more operational way. If mental development involves a growing ability to contain experience in symbols, then the study of containment offers a new way of approaching symbolic development.

In speaking about subjective life, the term 'experience' has an unavoid-able ambiguity. On the one hand, it refers to that which transpires within the individual, the entire gamut of inner (sensory) events that impinge on consciousness; on the other, it refers to something more specifically mental,

---

1  Lecours (2007: 909) noted that 'an important phase is missing in Bion's interpersonal model of $\alpha$-function building'. He suggests it is not so much the analyst's (mother's) *reverie* that is internalized in cases where the patient (baby) is overwhelmed by un-symbolized, concretely experienced $\beta$-element material. It is rather the analyst/mother's *soothing* function that is made possible by *her* ability to contain and process material. If this is so, the beneficial effect is not mediated directly by the symbolic process, but indirectly, and it therefore remains an enigma how the processing function itself would come to be internalized.

to that which can be grasped and reflected on, recalled and felt, somewhat in the manner of Wordsworth's 'recollections in tranquility'. If we think of the first meaning as referring to 'raw' experience' – to that which impinges directly on consciousness and is 'suffered', the second meaning could be reserved for something more processed – a distillate from raw experience that has passed through the refining fire of containment and symbolization. Experience in this sense is 'transformed immediacy', the result of processing 'raw' experience. This is synonymous with 'mental content' – it forms part of the mind's tools, or part of its furniture, depending how you look at it. From this angle, symbolic processing – the containment of 'raw experience' in symbols – *generates* 'experience as mental content'; without symbols, experience as mental content cannot exist.

All the papers in this collection are concerned in some way with symbolic processing and its roots in the field of mother–infant relatedness. In what follows, I argue that the link between *maternal* containment (a maternal provision) and *mental* containment (containment in the mind) can be illuminated through the idea of *containing forms*. These are patterned maternal responses to infant states which have the potential to become symbols if and when they are internalized by the infant. I suggest that such forms are created by the mother during certain kinds of interaction in which she is so intensely identified with her baby that she enacts, or in other ways demonstrates what it is like, to *be* the baby in that moment. Such enactments constitute external images of the baby's purported experience, and if internalized could provide the baby with a means of creating mental structure. From this perspective, the baby's internalization of maternal forms would be an essential phase of early symbol-formation, at least in so far as this involved the containment of subjective experience. This way of thinking is compatible with the widely held view that mental structure arises from the internalization of previously external interactions (Hobson 2000; Target and Fonagy 1996) but it leaves undefined the specific nature of these maternal forms.[2] In the chapters which follow I address this question in different ways.

The present line of enquiry complements my earlier study of symbolic development (Wright 1991). This was linked to an exploration of certain

---

2 Target and Fonagy (1996: 472) write: 'Linking his internal state to a perception of that outside state offers a representation (a symbol) of the internal state: it corresponds to, yet is not equivalent to, that state. The attitude of the parent is crucial. The child's mental state must be represented sufficiently clearly and accurately for the child to recognize it, yet sufficiently playfully for the child not to be overwhelmed by its realness; in this way he can ultimately use the parent's representation of his internal reality as the seed of his own symbolic thought, his representation of his own representations.' This aptly describes the mother's attuning responses as depicted in Stern (1985).

narcissistic states of mind in which a person's *subjective* sense of self was felt to be obliterated by the look of another person, so that, momentarily at least, the person experienced himself as defined and transformed by the other's view. In a metaphorical way, I thought of this as being turned into stone by the 'look' of the Gorgon.

Clearly, however, such catastrophic transformation is not the norm. Only certain individuals react in this way and most are more resilient, being able to relate to an external view without a sense of imminent subjective collapse. This leads to the idea that such resilience is linked to critical differences in level of symbolic functioning and in what follows I attempt to clarify what this difference might be.

In considering the question, it has to be remembered that symbolic development is a gradual affair, with the potential to miscarry at any stage. In essence, the formation of a symbol involves the linking of an external form with an inner experience – in other words, a relationship between an externally derived form and an element of experience embedded in sensory memory; in a later phase this could be thought of in Freud's terms as a 'word presentation' linking with a 'thing presentation' (Freud 1915), but *pre*verbally it includes both mirroring (Winnicott 1967a) and attunement (Stern 1985) in which image-based forms are fashioned by the mother at a time before the infant is clearly differentiated from her. In both mirroring and attunement, each element of infant experience can be seen as *inhabiting* a maternally provided form which has been adapted, or tailored to the experience by the mother's imaginative identification. The end-product of such a process would be a coupled structure, the maternal form being linked to an infant experiential substrate in a way that could be similar to Bion's conception of the 'container-contained' (Bion 1965). Within each structure of this kind, an element of infant experience would be 'held' (Winnicott 1960a) within an adapted (i.e. matching) maternal form, and such 'holding' of experience could be seen as an early stage of symbol-formation, furnishing the substrate for later symbolic developments, particularly language.

Language can be thought of as a part of reality that brings infant experience under the jurisdiction of the word. Being external to the infant, and thus un-adapted and 'other', language has unlimited potential to shape infant experience to its *own* forms rather than adapting itself to what is brought by the infant. In relation to this, I shall argue two things, however: first, that a prior 'holding' of raw experience in maternal 'forms' is itself generative of early experience (in the sense defined above) – it constitutes a transitional realm (Winnicott 1953) in which the infant is beginning to 'have' his own experience; second, that such holding is a major factor in protecting experience against the defining pressures of the word.

In these terms, the coupled structures which derive from maternal holding would provide an experiential matrix strong enough to keep the word at a distance and resist its defining power.[3] Individuals who experience subjective collapse at the interface with the other's view would be lacking in such structures and according to my thesis, this would stem from an early deficiency in maternal holding, with consequent impairment of an inner holding function in adult life.

It is easy to see how this protective function of maternal forms could be highly dependent on the accuracy of the maternal reflecting process. If mirroring and attunement (see below) were 'off beam' or deficient – as, for example, where the needs of a narcissistic mother were uppermost – the provided maternal forms would no longer 'hold' infant experience but 'impinge' upon it, and even provide a substitute for it (Winnicott 1960a). In such cases, the infant might try to inhabit (adapt to) the proffered 'alien' forms despite their poor 'fit', and the infant's own experience, lacking a safe enclave, would then be annihilated. Rather than generating a life enhancing 'container-contained' structure, the maternal process would now result in 'colonization' of the infant mind by alien forms filled with maternally imputed and spurious experience (by 'spurious', I mean 'not rooted in the subject's own psyche-soma'). Such a distorted process would create split off, alienated self elements in which the seeds of genuine experience would remain dormant. Winnicott's concept of the 'true' and 'false self' (Winnicott 1960b) is clearly applicable in this context.

I now regard this as the core narcissistic dynamic that underpins the scenario of my earlier study. In other words, only a subjective element that is safeguarded *within* a holding maternal structure (dyadic and isomorphic) can survive the defining impact of a separate and/or poorly attuned view (triangulated and heteromorphic); and only in these circumstances can an external symbol (e.g. the other's view) be experienced as a reflection *on* experience rather than a traumatic transformation *of* it. In the absence of inner maternal holding, every contact with an external form (symbol, view, interpretation) risks repeating the original trauma of impingement, a dynamic I explore further in relation to Wittgenstein in chapter 6, and clinically, through a case study, in chapter 8.

It follows from what I have said that a person's ability to use symbols in a triangulated way (i.e. as exploratory tools rather than omnipotent definitions) depends on their earlier history. Only when the quality of early relatedness has been adaptive enough – in Winnicott's terms, 'good enough'

---

3 Somewhat fancifully, one could visualize the structure created by maternal holding in the following way: an experiential inner core that is the infant's own registration of experience, surrounded by an isomorphic maternal pattern that resonates with it. In the normal process of language acquisition, this bipartite structure would engage with the word, to form a reversible and loosely constituted three part structure – namely word plus the earlier dyadic structure. It is easy to imagine that without the consolidating maternal pattern, experience would be more vulnerable to the defining power of the word. Experience being less available, and less robust, the word could more easily usurp its place.

(Winnicott 1987: 38) – to foster the development of attuned and resonant dyadic ('container-contained') structures, will the subject be able to confront a world of separate views and opinions (symbols) without trauma.

Throughout these papers, Winnicott's work with its relational perspective has been an enduring reference point. Putting himself to an unusual degree into the world of the baby, he created a paradigm of early development that differed significantly from that of Klein. In Klein, the baby is relatively alone, and struggling with primary aggression; in Winnicott, he is bathed in relation from the start and continuously protected from impingement by the adaptive mother. Klein's mother stands on the margin of the infant's phantasy world; Winnicott's mother constitutes the primal environment protecting the infant from unmediated reality. The two paradigms are separated by the concept of the 'good enough mother' (see above); they differ radically in tenor and feel, and profoundly influence the ambience and detail of clinical practice.[4]

The concept of the 'good enough mother' permeates Winnicott's work but one paper – a variation on the theme of the adaptive mother – has been a source of inspiration. 'Mirror role of mother and family in child development' (Winnicott 1967a) breaks new ground by shifting focus from the body-based paradigm of baby at breast (instinctual satisfaction) to a more social realm in which the mother's facial expressions are critically important as a source of mirroring and feedback to the infant. This shift gives a central role to non-verbal communication in emotional development and thus introduces a new dimension into psychoanalytic theorizing.

Winnicott's mirroring paradigm links to a second inspirational source – Stern's work on maternal attunement (Stern 1985). Like Winnicott, Stern emphasizes the importance of mother–infant non-verbal communication in development, and by putting this at the centre of the frame he changes our conception of infant life in a number of ways. Moving beyond the traditional focus on major *categorical affects* to the *vitality affects* (the infant's background 'feeling states'),[5] Stern, like Winnicott (1971) in relation to

---

4 Every analyst chooses between such paradigms and they influence both his clinical work and his understanding of human nature. We could thus contrast the emphasis on primary aggression and primitive defences (e.g. projective identification) in Kleinian theory and practice with the emphasis on the environment and the facilitating role of the mother (and analyst) in Winnicott and some of the other Independents. Likewise we could contrast a theory of symbol formation that is linked to the vicissitudes of instinctual drives and the depressive position (Klein/Segal) with one that is inextricably entwined with maternal provision/transitional phenomena (Winnicott).

5 In speaking of an infant's 'feeling state', the same considerations apply as in the case of 'experience' (discussed pp. 2–3). The infant's immediate feeling state is an ongoing affair of shifting psychosomatic arousal, but a 'feeling state' which can be grasped or sensed by the infant, and potentially recalled, must first be captured and contained within a maternal form and fed back to the infant in this way.

play, makes us realize that infant experience is not confined to peak moments of bodily satisfaction and distress. It includes much besides and in detailing the unbroken thread of the mother's attuned responsiveness, he highlights a field of microcosmic events that, arguably, contribute to the development of the infant mind. I keep returning to Stern's work for this reason – that it offers a model of how *maternal responses*, through internalization, could become the rudiments of *mental structure* in the infant.

In the context of this study, the significance of Stern's work lies in his detailed descriptions of mother–infant communication (attunement) and the way this is mediated by non-verbal perceptual forms. He defines attunement as the 'recasting . . . of an affective state' (1985: 161) and means by this that the mother portrays the 'shape', or essence of the infant's affective state, as she experiences it, within the intuitively created form that she enacts for her baby. This gives the baby the possibility of seeing his own subjective state portrayed within the 'shape', or 'objective' pattern that the mother provides.

'Objective' is a relative term that in this context implies a subject able to sense the 'otherness' (separateness) of the other person. Within this constraint (at this early stage, it is only the mother who is capable of such separateness), it will be seen that attunement offers an ongoing portrayal of the patterns of infant experience and the possibility of the infant using these in phase appropriate ways. At what point, and in what way, the infant will stumble on the link between such enacted patterns and his own psycho-somatic feeling states is unclear, but even before the advent of such rudimentary self-awareness and its relative separateness, he is likely to *feel* a connection with the mother's forms by means of *resonance*.

The concept of resonance is central to my argument and these papers reflect my growing appreciation of its role in preverbal and non-verbal experience. By resonance, I mean the felt recognition of vital resemblances – like resonates with like. Resonance generates a feeling of affinity between related forms and a sense of mutual recognition and even communication between them. The concept thus offers a communicational way of thinking about *primary process* functioning, which is usually thought of mechan-istically as a primary and given form of mental life.[6] Likewise, we can think of resonance as underlying the intuitive sense of affinity that people often

---

6 If we approach mental phenomena in a more radically relational way, it is possible to see all mental forms as in some sense 'communicating' with each other, or as refusing to do so. There is some logic in this perspective if we regard the mind as constituted by the internalization of external forms (e.g. the forms of attunement) which communicate non-verbally with the substrate of infant experience. Seen in this way, the mind is a residue of earlier interpersonal relatedness (mother and infant), not an organization of impersonal mechanisms.

feel for each other, and less dramatically, the sense of affective contact between persons that we term *rapport* (chapter 1).

In the course of these papers, I have come to realize that resonance is the key to understanding non-verbal communication. While language conveys 'objective' meaning through the medium of conventional words (each word mediates the same learned meaning to each of us), non-verbal forms arouse a direct and 'sympathetic' response (resonance) in the recipient by calling forth related but idiosyncratic non-verbal patterns. By this means, resonance creates the illusion of *direct* communication between separate individuals, and in chapter 5, I attempt to understand certain aspects of *projective identification* in these terms.

Communication through non-verbal forms brings me to a third inspirational figure – the philosopher Susanne Langer. I owe much of my understanding of symbols to the clarity of her expositions and when I first discovered her writings on art (Langer 1942, 1953), I *knew*, in a certain and immediate way (perhaps through resonance), that her work had enormous relevance for psychoanalysis. It seemed to offer a new perspective from which to view the analytic task, and I read her account of the artist's activity with great excitement, seeing in it an extended metaphor for the analytic process.

Langer's ideas were forged against a background of positivism and behaviourism in which art was seen as an *expression* of emotion little different from a grunt or cry. In this context, her thesis that art portrayed the 'shapes' of human feeling through a complex structure of non-verbal *symbols* was radical and revolutionary. It led her to a detailed analysis of non-verbal symbols and how they differed from language, perhaps most importantly in the way they lacked conventional and socially agreed referents. Thus, while words invariably refer to a *specific* and agreed 'something', having a *fixed* consensual meaning, the symbols of art, like those of dreams, have no such agreed meaning but *depict* what they portray through similarity of form. Non-verbal representations of feeling are thus protean: for example, in music, a specific *emotional* contour can generate unlimited musical depictions, all loosely linked through formal similarity. From Langer's perspective, such *formal* connection between emotional contour and artistic 'shape' is the key to understanding the expressive potential of art.

For Langer, then, the work of art is a complex symbolic rendering of emotional life in a form that enables *apprehension of its being* rather than *comprehension of its meaning*. Its non-verbal symbols articulate the shapes and textures of living experience rather than its cognitive definition, and because they present this *semblance* in analogical form, she called them *presentational symbols*. Art does not, in the manner of language, *describe* experience but offers it directly to our senses through iconic forms. It is not an alternative means of *expressing* emotion but *a means of revealing its forms* in a concrete, yet quasi-abstracted way.

Langer contrasted *presentational* (non-verbal) symbols with the forms of language which build up and convey their sense through sequences of *discursive or representational symbols* whose meanings are conventionally agreed. Words enable us to *comprehend* experience – to refer to it and talk *about* it – but they only show us what it is *like* when language shifts into more poetic mode (see chapters 2, 4 and 8). Non-verbal symbols (Langer was mainly concerned with the symbols of art) reveal the *forms* of experience rather than simply referring to it, and *portray* it much as the mother's attuned enactments portray the shape of the infant's feeling states. Langer's (1942, 1953) theory of artistic creation and Stern's (1985) account of attunement thus echo each other in remarkable ways. The similarity was noted but not explored by Stern, and it raises the possibility of more fundamental linkage which I explore in some detail in chapters 3, 4 and 9.

Langer's work also casts light on the analytic process, for if one conceives of the analyst as seeking to provide containing forms for unrealized elements of the patient's emotional life, his engagement with the patient can be seen as similar to that of the artist with his landscape, or the mother with her baby – each identifies with their 'object' (subject) and recreates it within the forms engendered by the encounter. From this perspective, the analyst emerges in the mould of artist, though such a view deviates from conventional wisdom which emphasizes his cognitive and 'scientific' skills. *Explaining* the patient's material – talking *about* it and *understanding* it – are the more familiar parts of his task, while conceiving of the work as iconic – as a process of creative image-making – evokes the less explicit maternal function of containment.

From this point of view, analysis, like art, can be seen as a process of finding 'forms' for human feeling – forms that resonate with the patient's experience, allowing it to be contained, and eventually appropriated. Within such a framework, the containing 'images' engendered in the analytic encounter can be seen as analogues of the mother's attuned enactments or the artist's creations – a far cry from the discourse of explanatory interpretation. In chapters 2, 7 and 8, I consider the changes that follow from such an altered view, especially in relation to the analyst's use of language. Logical *clarity* becomes less important than vividness of expression, while the need for a resonant and metaphorical language becomes more apparent. In discussing this aspect of the analytic task I have found it helpful to consider poetry and the way poets think about their work.

Langer's work highlights the capacity of non-verbal symbols to operate in their own right as a medium of communication. Because of their capacity to evoke resonant responses in the recipient, they provide a direct emotional link between subjects: *my* non-verbal form arouses in *you* an emotional 'structure' comparable to that which gave birth to it in me. Music furnishes a good example: when I listen to a piece of music, the shape of the musical form (rhythm and melody) and its varying textures (tonal colour, timbre of different musical instruments, etc.) combine to arouse a certain experience. According to the present thesis, this experience *corresponds* in important ways to that which the composer trans-formed, or recast (Stern), in creating his music. In these terms, it can be seen that the created musical form (non-verbal) provides a bridge between composer and listener: it straddles their separate sensibilities and unites them through its capacity to resonate with each.

In attunement, a similar situation prevails. First the mother identifies with the baby's experience (emotion), then recasts it in her own idiom and replays it to the baby. If the baby can experience the mother's enactment in a resonant way (i.e. as corresponding to something in the infant), at that moment, baby and mother, like artist and audience, will be momentarily linked through the created (maternal) form.

Such a link differs from that made through ordinary language because the sense of contact is more direct: although *in fact* mediated by a non-verbal form and therefore symbolic, it creates the illusion of *un*mediated contact, so that your experience *seems* to resonate directly with mine. While the language link takes time and is made discursively between subjects through objective words whose meaning they share, the non-verbal link sparks instantaneously across the bridge of imagery and engenders a sense of subjective contact.[7] While in the case of ordinary language, I know that you *understand* what I am talking *about*, with non-verbal connection, I know that you *feel* my experience in your heart. What underpins this difference is the shared feeling of resonance created by the bridging form.

This way of thinking enables one to make clearer differentiation between two modes of analytic activity. If I talk to the patient *about* his experience, he will know that I have listened to him, and in some degree *understand* him. If, on the other hand, I offer him a form or *image* that *resonates* with his experience, he will *sense* that I am *in touch* with him. The resonating form achieves what the ordinary word cannot – a direct bridge between two sensibilities. I discuss this more fully in chapters 7 and 8.

## Chapter synopsis

I conclude this introduction with an overview of the chapters and how they relate to the central theme.

1   'On being in touch' is an attempt to understand what it means to be in touch with another person. I discuss the non-verbal processes of

---

7 Examples of such immediate understanding in analysis would be when the patient recounts a dream and the analyst understands in a flash the import of the images. Another example would be the use by the patient of a vivid metaphor to explain what his experience was 'like'. Such an image yields 'direct' access to experience that talking *about* it never quite provides.

mirroring (Winnicott 1967a) and attunement (Stern 1985) and attempt to show that contact and communication between mother and baby in the preverbal period involves resonance between related patterns or images. I argue that in adult life the experience of being in touch involves a similar process. Whenever a form offered by one person 'fits' the form of the other person's experience there is a glimmer of resonance, a sense of being touched and recognized. One person's proffered form may then go on to become the container of the other person's experience. Developing this idea, I discuss how mental structure can be regarded as a 'precipitate' (Freud's word) of earlier modes of relatedness, the internal containment of experience being created from earlier maternal forms.

2    'The poetics of interpretation' is a first attempt to apply these ideas to the analytic situation and consider how they could alter the way an analyst thinks about his task and his way of talking to the patient. I compare interpretation, with its distanced language of explanation, with 'holding' that seems to require words of a more embodied kind. I suggest that the language of holding is closer to the language of poetry because it creates a sense of being in touch with experience and, equally, in touch with the therapist who 'holds' the experience in such an embodied way.

3    In 'Deep calling unto deep', I discuss artistic creativity from a Winnicottian perspective, suggesting that this offers an alternative to Kleinian conceptions of art with their emphasis on destruction, guilt and reparation (Segal 1991). I argue that art is a form of empathic engagement with the self through which the artist generates for himself the containing forms he so desperately needs. From this perspective, the creative process involves a heightening of non-verbal dialogue and thus looks back to the early mother–infant relationship. I argue that the artist's creativity provides a means of furthering containment and self-realization for both himself and his audience, this being a necessary precursor of personal integration.

4    'Making experience sing' continues the critique of Segal's essentially Kleinian approach to art (Segal 1991) and offers a deeper analysis of transitional phenomena and attunement. It further develops the theory of art that I sketched in chapter 3, and illustrates this through the work of the Austrian poet, Rainer Maria Rilke.

5    In 'Bion and beyond', I discuss the concept of projective identification and examine the clinical material that led Bion to revise Klein's original theory. Approaching the concept from a Winnicottian perspective, I suggest that the process may be less fundamental to infant life than is often claimed, and can be understood, at least in part, as a reaction to maternal imperviousness. I question the view that it forms the basic mode of communication between infant and mother, and suggest that

early communication is better understood in terms of emotional signs which are integral to the infant's emotional arousal. I argue that such signs are not *projected into* the mother by the baby but have an innate communicative intent, and are '*read*' by an attuned mother who then *imagines herself into* the baby's situation – a process mediated by symbols. According to this view, the use of projective identification in adult life stems from earlier maternal failure rather than persistence of, or regression to, primitive defences.

6   'Words, things and Wittgenstein' is a case study of the philosopher Wittgenstein and provides a basis for discussing the effect of language on the developing self. Wittgenstein was arguably the most influential linguistic philosopher of the twentieth century, yet astonishingly did not begin to speak until he was four years old. I attempt to understand this fact in the light of his early history, and formulate a core difficulty that may have interfered with his ability to integrate words and experience. I use this understanding to reflect on his stormy life and philosophical concerns and to make observations on the normal process of language acquisition. In this sense, the chapter continues my examination of the relation between preverbal and later verbal modes of relating, and further explores the protective, containing function of preverbal maternal forms.

7   'Shaping the inarticulate' develops the argument put forward in chapter 2 that a 'holding', 'containing' language has much in common with the language of poetry. It explores how we sometimes manage, and often fail, to communicate (contain) the 'feel' of live experience and how this may depend in subtle ways on our use of words. I try to illuminate this through the way poets think about their work, and show how the idea of *containing forms* can act as a bridge between poetry and psychoanalysis. My argument owes much to Winnicott (1953), Bion (1965), Stern (1985) and Langer (1942, 1953) in ways already outlined, and I use Langer's (1942) distinction between *presentational* and *discursive* symbols to explore different therapeutic ways of talking to patients.

8   In 'Embodied language', I enlarge on this theme. I contrast the explanatory language of interpretation, which sets experience at a distance, with a more embodied, poetic kind of language that reflects experience and offers it containing forms. I suggest that finding a voice is a primary analytic goal for both analyst and patient and requires developing a capacity for spontaneous play. Because language is the primary medium of analysis, the notion of 'voice' includes the ability to express oneself in images, and embody experience in metaphorical language. For the patient, finding a voice is synonymous with self-realization; for the analyst, it involves more exposure than traditional interpretation and fewer opportunities to hide behind a professional

façade. The chapter contains several clinical examples and further develops the theoretical argument.

9   'The search for form' develops out of chapters 3 and 4, and continues my attempt to develop a Winnicottian theory of art. Building on an idea of the art critic, Peter Fuller, I argue that the canvas surface in painting is a derivative, or analogue, of the mother's expressive face in infancy, and functions in a similar way: as responsive and mirroring extension of the self (Fuller 1980). From this perspective, the artist's medium can be seen as a surrogate adaptive mother, allowing itself (like the early mother) to be moulded by the artist's emotional gesture. In these terms, his creative activity is driven by the need to make good an earlier deficit, and through it he attempts to realize and 'hold' his contemporary emotional self within the containing forms of his own making. The chapter provides a further critique of Segal's theory of art (Segal 1991) which sees the creative process in Kleinian terms as a form of reparation for earlier destructiveness.

10  In 'The intuition of the sacred' I look at religion through the lens of preverbal experience and attempt to understand its maternal roots. Since *The Future of an Illusion* (Freud 1927), psychoanalysis was mainly concerned with religion's paternal aspect, putting emphasis on a father god who upheld the moral law by threat of punishment. By contrast, this chapter explores the maternal roots of religion in pre-oedipal experience, thus linking it to a longing for recognition and containment rather than to guilt and forgiveness from sin. I argue that from this point of view, the religious quest is closely related to the project of art (chapters 3, 4 and 9), and more concerned with a search for wholeness than with making reparation for earlier destructiveness.

11  'Recognition and relatedness' was my contribution to a symposium on the nature of love and I used the freedom it gave me to explore the topic in a personal way. In this chapter, I stake out a relational view of loving, somewhat at variance with traditional psychoanalytic theory, but compatible with attachment theory and more recent views of infant development based on empirical infant research. I further discuss the concepts of attunement and resonance and their importance in emotional communication.

12  In 'The silver mirror' I attempt to draw together the themes which run through this book. Although schematic, and by no means comprehensive, it summarizes a way of thinking that places greater emphasis on the interpersonal than most psychoanalytic writing. The chapter title is taken from one of Rilke's *Sonnets to Orpheus*, reproduced in the front of the book, in which he describes how a 'creature there has never been' is drawn into existence by giving it a space in which 'the possibility of [its] being' is kept alive (Rilke 1960: 270). Those nurturing this possibility lovingly imagine what the creature will be like, and in

this facilitating environment it gradually becomes real. The poem provides an apt image of Winnicott's holding environment, upon which the book is an extended reflection.

# Chapter 1

# On being in touch

## The sense of connection

Feeling in touch with other people is integral to the sense of being alive. We usually take it for granted and it only becomes an issue when we start to feel disconnected. In this regard, a variable sense of involvement with the world is quite normal, but more noticeable and lasting changes are the province of mental illness. Psychiatric patients quite often complain of an altered feeling of relatedness to the world and sometimes report a pervasive sense of being 'cut off' and 'out of contact'. When this happens, things feel flat and two-dimensional – neither world nor self feels fully real.

*Depersonalization* and *de-realization*, as these states are called, represent major alterations in the sense of reality though minor degrees are quite common. In this chapter, however, I shall only consider the subtle, continuous variations in sense of relatedness that form the background to ordinary living.

In considering pathological shifts in the sense of reality, it is reasonable to invoke deranged physical mechanisms – the toxic effects of drugs and alcohol on the brain are a case in point. When it comes to the less dramatic variations, this sort of explanation is no longer compelling and it seems more relevant to seek psychological explanations. From this perspective, my sense of being in touch with another person is not so much defined by the state of my physiology as by what is going on between me and him. According to this view, there is a substratum of *non-verbal communication* underlying the experience of connectedness, even though this can be hard to pinpoint and describe.

Psychoanalysis has not always been the best place to turn for an understanding of such issues, for in spite of the value it placed on interpersonal relationships, it privileged a view which took the individual as the unit of analysis. From this perspective, the baby was born solitary (you could say 'out of touch') and only gradually acquired connection with others ('being in touch' with them). Recently, however, a more relational view has gained ground. From this perspective, the human infant is bathed in relationship (i.e. is 'in touch') from the start, while separation and individuation are developmental processes which emerge later (Balint 1968; Mahler *et al.* 1975; Winnicott 1953). From this perspective, 'being in touch' is the norm, while distance and separation only gradually appear in the infant's experience. Many years before this relational trend in psychoanalysis, the philosopher Martin Buber had put forward a similar view, declaring that 'in the beginning is relation' (Buber 1937: 18). Winnicott was one of the first to take such a relational stand within contemporary psychoanalytic thinking, a position often associated with his remark: 'There is no such thing as a baby . . .' (only baby with mother, or mother-and-baby as a unit) (Winnicott 1958: 99). His view owed little to philosophy but arose from extensive work with mothers and babies; at the time, it was radical and counter-culture and caused many disagreements – for example, with Melanie Klein. He was convinced, however, that the baby was immersed in relationship (with the 'environment mother') from the start, and he had no doubt that the processes of psychological development needed to be rethought from this new perspective.

## The nature of the process

Being in touch describes a basic modality of relations with other people. Each person knows from his own experience what it feels like and the same is true of feeling out of touch. However, knowing what it is like is not the same as being able to describe it, and in this chapter I want to develop a language for talking about such feelings.[1] It will help if I start with some brief clinical examples.

### Example 1

A patient in three times weekly psychotherapy walked into the consulting room and started her session as follows: 'As I was walking here I could feel myself cutting off from my feelings. The nearer I got the less I seemed to feel. I just wanted to leave all my feelings outside.' This woman is frightened of her emotions and has found it difficult to cope with them in

---

1 It may seem naive to speak of *developing* a language when the issue of being in touch is centrally important in psychotherapy and so much has been written about it in terms of empathy, projective identification and countertransference reactions. However, my stance is deliberate as I like to approach a topic with relatively uncluttered vision – in other words, without the encumbrance of familiar theoretical concepts. Although theoretical mapping enables knowledge to be codified, it can be a hindrance if brought to bear at too early a stage. In this sense, my approach is loosely phenomenological (Merleau-Ponty 1962) and attempts to create distance between theory and the experienced world in order to make room for fresh perceptions of it.

sessions. She alternates between subdued accounts of her experience and sudden upsurges of uncontrolled sobbing which leave her unable to speak. For long stretches she is detached and cut off from her feelings, and then suddenly she is overwhelmed by them. My own experience seems to mirror this alternation: for much of the time I feel cut off and prone to sleepiness and boredom, but when her emotions come to the fore, I feel more engaged. At such times, I may not be able to understand what her sobbing is about, but it *touches* me directly.

## Example 2

The next patient, a man, comes across as more consistently out of touch, though not in the same way as the first patient. He speaks in a dull, monotonous voice and has a grey, depressing effect on me. He describes his life as though speaking of someone else and frequently applies complicated theories to his experience. On this intellectual level he can sometimes be interesting, but on an emotional level he is deadening. He frustrates my wish to share his experience and somehow prevents all emotional contact. It is hard to say whether he wants to hide his feelings from me or whether he is out of touch with them in himself, but I have a sense that he experiences his life in a cold and distanced way. I have come to think that my experience of being an outsider with him reproduces his own experience of being an outsider in his original family. It seems then that he cannot accept his own emotional self because he has never had the experience of another person relating to him in such an accepting way.

## Example 3

My next example adds further complexity to the question of emotional contact. This patient is a woman who at first seems controlled and 'together' but in time it becomes clear that this is only part of the picture – her close relationships are in a mess. In sessions she will get upset about this but somehow, in spite of the emotion, I feel excluded; in contrast to the previous patient with whom I felt in contact when she cried, I now feel like a spectator. My lack of warmth troubles me and I feel I am hard and unsympathetic. Rationally, however, I suspect that there is something which makes it hard for me to be empathic; I can *see* what she feels but cannot *feel* my way into it. I surmise that I might be enacting a part that she unconsciously expects of me and in some way moulds me to adopt.

These examples illustrate the fact that expressing an emotion does not guarantee an experience of contact. The feeling of connection may also depend on *how* the person expresses their emotion and *to whom* they feel they are expressing it. Thus, patient 1 may have anticipated a soothing, comforting response from me, while patient 3 may unconsciously have expected distance and lack of involvement. According to this notion, each person moulds the other into realizing their unconscious expectations.[2]

### Example 4

My fourth case illustrates a more complex experience of being in touch. Like patient 3, this woman gives the impression of an organized and constructive life, though attempts at intimacy are problematic and constrained. During the sessions she speaks in a thoughtful, reflective way and I sense that she is in touch with her feelings and wants me to share them. A range of expressions play on her face and her intonation varies; there is fluidity and emotional depth and her finely tuned expression engages me in its moods like a good play. I feel close to this patient and enjoy my contact with her; when derailments occur, they take place against this background of good rapport.

In each of these cases the clinical picture could be unravelled in greater depth but I merely want to exemplify the concept of being in touch and tease out some of its parameters. Thus, we have seen that patients can seem to be cut off from their emotions or swallowed up in them, outside them or involved in them, looking at themselves from the outside or participating in their own experience. In considering my own responses as a therapist, I have spoken of feeling 'cut off' or 'involved', 'distant' or 'close', 'in touch in a deep way' or 'coldly looking on'. Such metaphors capture two things: first, a sense of the patient's varying relation to his own feelings; and second, a sense of the therapist's shifting emotional contact with the patient. Experienced *location* and *distance* in relation to feeling emerge as important: inside or outside, in touch (i.e. very close) or watching from further away (i.e. from outside). Linked to this is a further distinction between *expressing* emotion, as, for example, when a baby cries, and *conveying* an emotion in a less immediate way. For example, patient 1, who sobbed uncontrollably, expressed emotion directly, while patient 4 conveyed her experience in more sophisticated, indirect ways. Patients 2 and 4, who both seemed cut off from their feelings, neither expressed them nor conveyed them. They talked *about* their lives but failed to convey the feel of actual experience.

Analysis of such experiences seems to suggest an emotional spectrum: at one end is the person with no distance from his emotional states who swamps himself and others with them; at the other is the person far removed from his own emotion, who feels cut off from it in the same way that others feel cut off from him. From this perspective there would seem to be an *optimal* distance in relation to emotional arousal (Akhtar 1991) but

---

2 This is a familiar notion in psychoanalysis. Sandler (1988) spoke in this context of 'role induction'.

almost certainly the situation is more complicated than this model suggests. The linear image of *distance* may well be misleading, and optimal relations with emotion would then involve a different kind of ability. From this perspective, the capacity to feel in touch with another's experience, and equally the capacity to share one's own, requires a different ability from straightforward expression. This is the ability to *represent* an emotion, to *hold it in mind* and *convey* it in quasi-symbolic ways. From this point of view, an optimal relation to emotion would not simply involve the 'right' amount of emotional *expression* but rather the ability to convey its 'sense' or 'feel'. This requires a different stance in relation to oneself and one's experience, an ability to stand back from it in order to *apprehend* it. It implies a different psychological 'space' (a space for reflection) from that in which raw emotional signals are transmitted (a space of action) – in short, a space in which emotion can be sensed and communicated rather than simply expressed.

In summary, I am suggesting that *expressed* emotion is raw and unmediated: the expression is biologically given, a direct manifestation of the emotional arousal itself. In effect it is a special form of action that is read through its signs. In contrast to this, 'conveying' an emotion is a form of indirect communication; it involves the capacity to 'hold' an emotion in mind and operates through learned non-verbal symbols such as intonation, tone of voice and nuanced facial expression. 'Expressions' of this kind involve symbolic representation rather than expressive signs.

In discussing symbols and signs, I follow the usage of Susanne Langer (1953: 26) which she adopted from Morris (1946). According to this, a sign or signal indicates the *presence* of an object in the immediate behavioural field, while a symbol *represents* the (idea of the) object and occupies a purely semantic (i.e. mental) field of meaning. A symbol relates to an absent object, a 'no-object', and, unlike the sign, has no essential *indicative* function. If I *convey* that I am angry with you in the more subtle ways I have described, I am sending you a symbolic message *about* my emotional state rather than bombarding you directly with it.

## The language of feeling

Before further discussing the mediation of feeling through symbols, I want to consider the notion of being in touch from a different angle and ask why language has thrown up this phrase to describe the experience. Why does it refer us to *touch* when no actual touching is involved?

I think this depends on the fact that experience can never be described directly but only approached by saying what it is 'like'. In other words, feeling and experience can only be grasped in metaphorical mode. 'Being in touch' is one such metaphor – this experience, it says, is '*like*' touching: when we are 'in touch' with someone, it is as *though* we could touch their inner being. In a similar way, the experience of 'feeling cut off' is grasped metaphorically through the idea of unbridgeable distance: we feel *as though* we can no longer touch the other's sensibility but only regard it from afar. The analogical link between 'touching' and 'feeling in touch', 'looking' and 'feeling cut off (from touch)', illuminates the respective experience, but this explanation has other dimensions. I allude to Winnicott's views on early development mentioned above.

In the early months, infant care is focused on the baby's bodily wellbeing. Touch is central to this core situation and thus pivotal in the baby's experience of the 'adaptive mother' (Winnicott 1958). However, such activities are mediated by a mother who also relates to her baby as a person: she smiles at him, talks to him, plays with him, imagines what he is feeling, and this fosters the infant's emotional and mental growth.[3] It follows that when the baby is *literally* in touch with the mother – being held and ministered to by her – he is simultaneously learning what it is like to be 'in touch' with a responsive and adaptive person. It seems likely that this is the experiential reference point for all later experiences of being in touch.

As separation from the mother gains ground both physically and mentally, and the baby's mobility imports physical distance into the *contiguity* (Latin root: touching together) of early touch experience, the communicative relationship with the mother becomes more important as a means of staying 'in touch' with her (Wright 1991). Long before words become meaningful, non-verbal communication supplements physical closeness (actual touch) as a line of connection. I refer here to Mahler's account of *separation-individuation* (Mahler *et al.* 1975), with its cycles of distance and return; and in a different framework, to Winnicott's account of transitional processes which keep the experience of the 'touch mother' alive during periods of maternal absence (Winnicott 1953).

## Non-verbal communication and symbolic containment

Between the communication of raw emotion (e.g. baby crying) and the full development of symbolic expression ('I am sharing my feelings and experiences with you') lies Winnicott's transitional area (Winnicott 1953). Transitional functioning allows an emotional experience to be 'held' (contained) within a sensory form or concrete object; the particular object is emotionally invested because it *evokes* the needed experience through its analogical structure. Thus, an observer can see that the baby's comforting bit of blanket is *like* the mother's skin in being soft and warm. For the baby, it creates the illusion of the mother's skin, and thus facilitates the *illusion* of

---

3 The fact that the mother relates to the baby in this way creates a potential 'space' in which the baby's emotional life can begin to take shape.

the object's presence *while not confronting the reality of its absence*. Such transitional concrete 'symbols' provide a first means of holding on to experience in its absence by re-creating a simulacrum of it; the object 'holds' the missing experience, obliterating or 'softening' its absence. In this sense the transitional object is a primitive form of mental containment.

Two tentative conclusions can be drawn from this: first, it is only possible to feel *in touch* with feelings that have been contained within a form or an object; and second, feelings can only be *contained* in so far as the means to grasp them symbolically, or pre-symbolically (transitionally), are available. *Transitional* containment is the key to emotional survival; *symbolic* containment is the key to holding feelings in mind and getting to know what they are like.

Transitional containment falls short of being fully symbolic because the absence of the missing object cannot yet be tolerated. A transitional container *re*-presents and *re*-creates the missing object; it does not yet *represent* it.[4] Through illusion, it enables the baby to revive the needed experience of being physically in touch with the mother, and in this sense it 'holds' and 'holds on to' the missing experience.

However, being 'in touch' with one's feelings – being able to symbolize them – implies an ability to take up a stance towards them and be at a distance from them. This developmental achievement derives, at least in part, from the experience of others, originally the mother, taking a similar stance towards oneself. This kind of development, in which an external relationship becomes an internal function, has long been familiar in the psychological literature and was recently reviewed by Hobson (2000).

How then does the mother demonstrate her 'attitude' or stance towards her baby's feelings? What does she actually do, and how does the baby 'know' that she is in touch? This is part of a more general question concerning the way mother and baby *keep* in touch with each other as separation proceeds.

Keeping in touch is such an important human need that many different strands are likely to be involved. At first, physical touch may be paramount, but as new capacities develop, they too will be drawn into the process. We can imagine, for example, a baby pointing at an entrancing object and the mother following the infant's gaze and sharing his pleasure: perhaps this is a moment of being in touch (experiencing something together). Or we could imagine the eye contact and mutual smiling between mother and baby bridging the distance between them – even in adult life,

4 There are similarities between Segal's concept of *symbolic equivalence* and Winnicott's idea of transitional objects and function (Segal 1986: 53). The interpretation of the two writers is different, however, in that while Winnicott sees a positive, creative value in the transitional object, Segal regards symbolic equivalence as indicating pathology (psychotic functioning).

eye contact (eyes 'touching together') has the effect of reducing interpersonal distance. Later, language enters the scene and words will bridge the gap between mother and child. This creates a new potential for feeling in touch – but also for feeling separated and out of touch if the process of putting experience *into* words breaks down.

## Attunement

I will consider language in later chapters (chapters 2, 6, 7 and 8). I will focus here on the pre-language period when communication and sharing are achieved by non-verbal means. Among such means is the type of interaction described by Stern as *attunement* (Stern 1985: 138–61). Stern derived his concept from detailed observation of mothers and infants and, like Winnicott's concept of mirroring (Winnicott 1967a), with which it has much in common, it enriches thinking about early experience by moving beyond traditional psychoanalytic paradigms.

In Stern's account, attunement refers to certain processes by which a mother tracks, and then reflects back to her infant, her sense of having shared in her infant's feeling state. It can be regarded as an extension of mirroring, and Stern distinguishes it from empathy which makes greater use of cognitive and verbal responses. Attunement is essentially non-verbal and spontaneous, and relatively outside the mother's awareness. It forms part of her intuitive response to the baby, and equally important, is more or less continuous so long as the infant is active. The attuned mother does not merely respond to major episodes of infant arousal but in a more ongoing way to what she senses as the baby's changing 'experience'. Stern thinks that in attunement the mother *tracks the changing contour of the infant's feeling state* and through her responses provides a background of resonant feedback. Her activity is not related to instinctual arousal, does not relieve instinctual tensions and is subtly different from the type of behaviour that Winnicott attributes to the adaptive mother (e.g. being available to hold and feed in appropriately responsive ways). It is more continuous and communicative than these and appears to attend to relational rather than physical needs.

What then is this changing contour of the baby's feeling state that the mother responds to in such an ongoing way? Stern calls it the infant's *vitality affect*, thus differentiating it from those discrete feeling states normally implied by the word 'emotion'. Such affect states – happiness, sadness, fear, anger, disgust and so on – are traditionally referred to as the *categorical affects* and tend to occur as discontinuous episodes which move centre stage and then subside in response to environmental events. For example, a baby is frustrated, gets angry, screams, and then again subsides into quiescence – this constitutes an episode of frustration and anger. By contrast, *vitality affects* are more continuous, forming a background feeling tone to whatever the baby is doing. They are an aspect of how the baby goes about things – for example, with excitement, pleasure or suspense – and are manifest in the visible and audible *signs* (not symbols) that reflect the tensions and energies of the infant's moment by moment way of being.

Attunement is an ongoing process and creates in the viewer a cumulative impression. Thus the mother identifies with the baby and spontaneously enacts her version of what the baby is 'feeling'. For example, an infant may try to get hold of something which has taken his interest but finds it is just beyond his grasp. He pulls himself up on a piece of furniture and reaches towards the object. While doing this, he holds his breath in concentration, then suddenly lets go of the object and falls back, making a sharp exhalation. The sequence is repeated until he gets hold of the desired object. As the mother watches this, she senses the baby's anticipation as he strains towards the object, his frustration as he loses his hold of it and finally his satisfaction as he grasps it and puts it in his mouth.

Attunement refers to the intuitive way in which the mother identifies with the baby and responds to the mini drama. Perhaps she makes a sequence of sounds that match the rise and fall of the baby's effort, or perhaps through a sequence of movements and gestures she recreates the sense of drawn out effort and pleasurable feeling of relief. But crucially, although matching the contour of infant *activity*, she does not imitate this in an external way but goes for the 'inner' state, as she has experienced it through identification. The baby reveals the contour of its 'feeling' through shifts of posture and tension, vocalizations and changes in pattern of breathing, and the mother renders this in external form, *capturing* it in her mini-performance. However, while the maternal sequence follows and reflects the infant 'experience' (as sensed by the mother), it is at the same time significantly different – for example, it may be transposed into a different sensory modality, or exaggerated and made more emphatic. There is thus difference as well as similarity in the mother's portrayal – as Stern says: 'An attunement is a recasting, a restatement of a subjective state' (Stern 1985: 161).

Although Stern's description is based on the observation of mothers and infants, he believes that attunement remains important throughout life. In this way, his concept illuminates what I have called the feeling of 'being in touch'. He writes:

> Tracking and attuning with vitality affects permits one human to 'be with' another in the sense of sharing likely inner experiences on an almost continuous basis. This is exactly our experience of feeling-connectedness, of being in attunement with another. It feels like an unbroken line. It seeks out the activation contour that is momentarily going on in any and every behaviour and uses that contour to keep the thread of communion unbroken.
>
> (ibid.: 157)

## Mirroring and attunement

It may be useful to wonder about the experience of a baby who is being attuned to and compare this with other forms of mirroring. Winnicott (1967a) made the innovative suggestion that the mother's face is the child's first mirror: if the baby is happy and smiles, the mother picks up on the child's happiness and smiles back; if the baby is sad, the mother's expressive response is again resonant. However, he suggests that the baby does not merely experience the smile as a smile, the sad face as a sad face, but as a reflection of his own state: like an emotional mirror, the mother's face shows him a picture of his own feeling state. Winnicott supposes that the baby feels enhanced and confirmed by this kind of response which offers a *visual analogue* of its internal state (for a fuller description of mirroring see chapter 2 pp. 33–4).

Mirroring is most relevant in the realm of categorical affects. Stern's ideas are complementary – the mother's attuning responses, occurring later in the preverbal period, involve a wider range of infant experience and behaviour. They too offer external analogues of infant feeling states but the range of feeling now responded to, and thus 'imaged', is far greater than in the early months. Potentially it is the whole of the infant's experience. Likewise, the variety of means employed is more diverse: no longer just facial expression, but patterns of voice and bodily gesture, of rhythm and tempo of response in different channels – all are now drawn into the mother's repertoire and become available to the infant as a kind of external phase of his own experience.

Seen in this way, attunement constitutes an early phase of preverbal symbolic development, and provides a model of how maternally reflected forms could eventually be internalized as containing symbols. From this perspective, attunement can be seen as facilitating the development of mind. The mother's resonating response, first perceived 'out there' as an answering form, has the potential to be taken back (internalized) by the infant as a container, within which to 'hold', and manipulate 'experience' within an emerging 'mental' space. Such forms, however, can only be as containing and confirmatory of infant experience as the mother's capacity for identification with the infant allows; where she imposes her own interpretations on the baby's experience, a different story will unfold.[5]

## Sharing through resonant forms

While in the longer term, attunement may lie on the path to symbol-formation, on a shorter time scale, it almost certainly mediates experiences

---

5 There are clearly links between the interactive process of attunement and the cycle of projective identification and maternal reverie described by Bion. There are, however, important differences between the two models as I discuss in chapter 5.

of being in touch. Because the patterned form the mother enacts is engendered by her empathic response to the infant's 'feeling state', it bridges the baby's feeling state and her own. Her feeling 'resonates' with the baby's feeling and the pattern is a bridge between them, a 'pattern that connects' (Bateson 1985: 16). In this way the enacted maternal form straddles two selves and connects two subjects. This is the crux of experiential sharing (see Introduction pp. 9–10).

Stern stressed that the maternal form does not merely reflect the externals of infant behaviour as in mimicry, but captures the shape of the 'lived experience'. It thus points the infant to a new kind of space in which 'feeling' and 'experience' can be apprehended within a world of 'forms'. It marks out a mental space *between* mother and baby (Winnicott's 'potential space') and opens the way towards the further development of 'mind' *within* the baby. (In this sense, 'mind' is a 'space' or area of awareness, of mental 'forms'.)

## Concluding remarks

My account suggests that feeling in touch with another person depends on a certain kind of symbolic capability, at least in one member of the interacting pair.[6] For an experience to be apprehended, it has to be held in a form (ultimately a symbolic form) that allows its realization. The expression of raw emotion (anger, for example) requires no symbolic mediation; it is emotional *action*, with direct and unmediated effects on the other person. Thus in the animal kingdom, hostility (the expression of aggression) provokes fight or flight – reciprocal *action* in the recipient; not for a moment do we suppose that either party 'knows' what is going on, nor do we imagine the event will be recalled once it has run its course. In other words, it may influence future behaviour (by modifying nervous pathways) but will

6 The discovery of *mirroring neurons* (Gallese *et al.* 1996, 2007) suggests that some *awareness* of the inner state of another person *might* be possible without symbolic mediation. In essence, these authors have shown that in monkeys, the observation by one monkey, of another engaged in a particular motor activity, activates in the observing monkey a group of neurons in an area of cortex adjacent to the corresponding motor area of the active monkey. Thus, if the *active* monkey makes an intentional arm movement, there is activation of *mirror neurons* in the cortex of the *observing* monkey, adjacent to its own motor arm area. This suggests there is wiring at the hardware level that in certain circumstances (A is watching B) results in linked firing of neuronal circuits between the members of the dyad. It is possible that this facilitates prediction: if one animal A 'knows' (through neurological mirroring) the state of animal B, he will be better placed to predict B's next move. Mirror neuron activity might thus prepare the observing animal for more appropriate responsive action but it seems unlikely that this would lead to awareness of the other animal's *experience*. I make the assumption that being able to apprehend another's feeling state – to hold their feeling in mind – is only possible with *symbolic* mediation.

not be 'held in mind'. Knowledge and recall are mental events; they require symbolic mediation, a means of holding experience in mind in its absence.

In this chapter, I have taken the view that mental functioning is built on the structural imprint of earlier interpersonal relationships. Thus, a person's capacity to be in touch with himself or herself is built on the earlier experience of another person (originally the mother, or other care giver) being in touch with them. I explored certain aspects of this preverbal relationship and showed how experiences of contact might develop out of interactions in which the mother's responses presented the infant with external 'forms' (analogues) of his own experience. I argued that the feeling of contact depended on resonance between external form and corresponding inner state, and suggested that the external relationship might be internalized, thus providing the basis of inner containment. In effect, this would constitute a preverbal structuring of experience in the infant, and thus a step in the early development of mind.

This way of thinking not only casts light on the shadowy processes of non-verbal mental life but also has implications for the practice of psychotherapy, in which finding forms for experience plays an important part. While analysts have traditionally concerned themselves with the 'what' of an interpretation –the content of experience and what it means – the early relationship between mother and infant invites attention to its form. For if it is the *form* of the mother's response that creates moments of contact – of 'being together' between baby and mother – it could equally be the *form* of the analyst's interpretation that determines whether it 'touches' the patient's experience or passes it by. I explore this idea further in the next chapter.

# Chapter 2

# The poetics of interpretation

Aristotle's *Poetics* (350 BC/1983) was a major work of the classical era and is still discussed by philosophers and classical scholars. Among other things, it sets out the figures of speech a poet can use with their differing poetic effects. My aim in this chapter is related though less ambitious, namely to consider different forms of language that analysts use in talking to their patients. I shall discuss this topic further in chapters 7 and 8.

Clinical discussions usually revolve around issues of *content* and consider which aspects of a patient's material should be interpreted. Less often discussed is the *way* the therapist speaks and in what follows I shall argue that this is equally important. In a poem much of the effect depends on how something is said and when it is paraphrased its magical essence disappears. It is possible, therefore, that interpretations too are voice and language sensitive and, in a similar way to a poem, may lose their efficacy if the choice of language is 'wrong'.

This idea is hardly contentious and therapists intuitively take it into account. Considerations of timing are familiar, and most therapists would acknowledge that tone of voice, facial expression and verbal intonation are important qualifiers of the 'content message' that is being conveyed. The real question, however, is this: Are such non-verbal qualifiers merely desirable additions to what is said, making it more acceptable or palatable, or do they have a value in their own right which transcends this secondary function? In the first case we would be justified in taking such elements for granted as a background of good practice; in the second, we would need to develop a theoretical approach within which they could be seen as more precise elements of technique.

As normally used, the term 'technique' refers mainly to the *content* of interpretations: Should the therapist interpret something or not? Should he make links to the past or only interpret in the here and now? Should he offer reconstructions or is that more or less irrelevant? Should he only interpret in the transference or make extra-transference interpretations as well? All these are issues of content and they constitute the principal subject matter of clinical discussion. The question boils down to this: What does the material mean and what aspect of it should be taken up?

Considerations of this kind are clearly important but they overshadow the question of *how* an interpretation is actually made. While the content issue – 'what the patient is *really* talking about' – is grounded and tangible, questions of style and form are more difficult to pin down.

Concern with 'content' has a long tradition and is rooted in classical analysis; this typically dealt with neurotic patients who formed classical neurotic transferences. It was predominantly the *content* of such transferences – what was being transferred on to whom – that occupied the analyst's attention. In this kind of work other matters could often be taken for granted, including the existence of analyst and patient as stable objects and all the details of the setting itself. In classical analysis there seemed to be a *stable core* that did not need to be analysed; it constituted the invisible *container* within which the 'real' analytic work of exploring meaning could proceed unhindered.

In the last few decades, under pressure of a more disturbed type of patient, this model has proved insufficient and analytic technique has evolved to take more account of the containing function.[1] There is no longer a background of stable containment, whether in society or the personality of the patient himself, and increasingly patients come to therapy because containment itself is the problem. For such narcissistic/borderline personalities neither object constancy nor the constancy of the self can be relied on, and even the analytic setting is liable to be challenged. In this regard, both society and patient are more *psychotic*,[2] and the basic fabric that contains, and holds things together, has itself become the problem.

This is the context in which a theory of *style* is needed – a theory of the way the analyst talks to the patient, the way he actually uses words. It is no longer a matter of simply undoing defences and bringing excluded elements back into consciousness. It is now a question of whether emotional life can be contained at all – whether it can be reached or symbolized.[3] The basic

---

1  In this chapter I use the terms 'holding', 'containing' and their derivatives in a loose way, not far removed from their use in ordinary language. This leaves their more technical meanings in the work of Winnicott (holding) and Bion (container/contained) in the background as a set of meanings that can be recruited as and when the reader wants. See Ogden (2004) for a detailed definition of the terms as used by Winnicott and Bion.

2  I am using the term 'psychotic' in the way analysts often use it – as a way of pointing to disturbance of mental function that stems from developmentally early levels.

3  The notion of contained experience is a complex one to which I will often return. There is a sense in which emotional *experience* does not really exist until after it has been transformed and symbolically contained. This does not mean, however, that emotional arousal and expression are subject to such limitations; they are there from the beginning and part of our biological equipment.

material is still the same in that patients continue to have problems with relationships, sexuality and aggression, but the core problem now lies in the containing function.

It is here that a link can be made with poetics because poetry, like analysis, is concerned with containing experience; since both must find 'forms for human feeling' (Langer 1953), it would not be surprising if the expressiveness of language, so important in poetry – its ability to evoke and contain experience – were also an aspect of analysis that needed to be taken seriously. However, to hold such a view shifts attention from the content of the analytic dialogue – its 'prose' – to its form or 'poetry', its articulation of metaphor and image, the cadence of its emotional rhythms, and all those things that determine the success or failure of words in conveying the texture of emotional life.

## Interpretation and holding

Classical analysis emphasizes insight – the 'content' the patient learns to 'see' and know about himself – because it is this that frees him from the bondage of unknowing and repetitive behaviour. That at least is the classical story. It is insight that enlarges conscious choice, and the vehicle of insight is interpretation. Interpretation explains; it clarifies previously unknown connections between elements of behaviour and feeling: 'You are doing this because you are afraid that X will happen if you don't.' 'You feel this person to be your mother, and you treat her in ways that may have worked with her, but are inappropriate in the present context' etc. (I am describing the *structure* of a classical interpretation, not necessarily the way it is given).

This conception of analytic interpretation has sometimes been taken to extremes. Ezriel, at the Tavistock Clinic, for example, often argued that the analyst should not speak until he could give the patient a 'complete' interpretation (explanation) of what he was doing: 'You are doing this (what Ezriel called "the required relationship") in order to protect yourself from something else ("the avoided relationship"), which you feel would have catastrophic consequences ("the catastrophe")' (Ezriel 1956).[4]

Interpretations of this type articulate content. They involve *standing back* and *looking at* one's emotional life, and gradually *seeing* it more clearly. Self-deception and defence are *seen through* as the clear lines of vision (looking from a distance) are brought to bear on the patient's 'undisciplined squads of emotion', as Eliot called them (Eliot 1944: 31). In this sense, the

4 It may be unfair to suggest that Ezriel always operated in this way as the paper cited documents a research project. However, I have little doubt that the position that he spells out in pure form was a major determinant of his analytic style.

analyst clarifies and demystifies. His task is to make plain the underlying emotional structures and in order to do this he must put things clearly, without embellishment or ornamentation. In this task, it is not poetics that matter but unambiguous prose.

This tough position is informed by a kind of work ethic: analysis is seen as a work task which pursues self-knowledge – as in Bion's (1959a) 'work group', for example – and its view of truth is 'scientific' in the broadest sense. There is little to provide comfort, and the bottom line is stoicism, with acceptance of that which cannot be changed.[5]

Set against this is a more intuitive view that is closer to the immediacy of the patient's feelings; sharing, empathy, attunement and 'being with' are the terms that come to mind in connection with it. In this approach, the pursuit of insight is down-played and more emphasis is placed on *providing the conditions* within which self-discovery can be fostered. An analyst of this persuasion is more likely to see himself as emotional facilitator than workshop foreman, and the balance in his work between identification and more distanced 'looking' is likely to be skewed towards the former (see e.g. Winnicott 1967a/1971: 117). He is also less likely to see himself in a 'scientific' mould, his 'truth' being closer to the imagination and 'the holiness of the heart's affections'.[6]

The Independent tradition is particularly associated with such an approach. Starting with Ferenczi, who claimed that the therapist's love cured the patient, it continued down through the Balints, Winnicott, Milner, Little, Rycroft, Guntrip, Khan and Bollas. Such therapists, among whom I include myself, lean towards a 'holding', maternal stance. This does not exclude interpretative work but such therapists are more likely to explore non-interpretative ways of engaging with the patient when confronted by an impasse. This tendency is less apparent in the work of Kleinian analysts – for example, Rosenfeld, Bion, Segal, Joseph, Rey, Steiner and Britton – who generally adopt a tougher stance and believe that interpretation (explanation) remains the principal analytic tool in all circumstances.[7]

These contrasting strands of thinking and practice may well be linked to personality organization (Wright 1991). New analytic techniques are usually seen as responses to therapeutic challenges (see p. 28) but it seems likely that on a deeper level, the personality of the innovator may be equally or more

---

5 This conception of psychoanalysis goes back to the very beginning when Freud conceptualized the 'cure' of hysterical symptoms as involving the replacement of neurotic suffering with ordinary everyday suffering. It is not particularly comforting to learn that this is the best that can be hoped for.

6 'I am certain of nothing but the holiness of the heart's affections and the truth of the imagination' (John Keats: Letter to Benjamin Bailey, 22nd November 1817).

7 The flavour of the Independent tradition can be gleaned from Rayner (1991) and that of Contemporary Kleinians from Spillius (1988).

important. For example, it is not hard to see that Winnicott's personality was organized around a more maternal axis than Freud's (Rodman 2003); and where psycho-biographies have been written, the close intertwining of personality structure and innovative theory becomes even clearer, as in the case of Guntrip (Hazell 1996) and also Khan (Hopkins 2006).

Rycroft (1958/1968) was one of the first to draw attention to non-verbal elements in the analyst's behaviour in his paper: 'The nature and function of the analyst's communication to the patient.' He underlined the fact that what the analyst said (his actual reference to content) was only a part of the total picture. It was always underpinned by something else that was non-verbal and merely implied. Thus he wrote:

> In addition to an explicit statement about, say, the patient's phan-tasies or defences, [an interpretation] contains a statement about the analyst himself and his attitude towards the patient. It says in effect: 'I am still here. I have been listening to you. I understand what you are talking about. I remember what you said yesterday, last week, last month, last year. I have been sufficiently interested to listen, and remember, and understand.' Also 'You are not the only person to have felt this way. You are not incomprehensible. I am not shocked. I am not admonishing you or trying to get you to conform to any ideas of my own as to how you should feel or behave.' . . . [These implicit statements tell] the patient the one thing that he needs to know about the analyst, and it is the analyst's major contribution to making the relationship between himself and the patient a real and not an illusory relationship.
>
> (1958/1968: 67)

Rycroft wanted to widen awareness of non-verbal events in the analytic relationship but his focus was limited. For him, the non-verbal elements were relatively fixed components of the analyst's communication and not something which could be varied in response to what the patient brought. It was not until Winnicott (1960a) formulated the concept of 'holding' that a theoretical place was found for such adaptable elements, and the possibility of 'using' them in more deliberate and conscious fashion.

Winnicott contrasted 'holding' with 'interpretation': 'interpretation' is the verbal message that conveys information and fosters insight; 'holding' is a more subtle process that is less dependent on the clarifying and explanatory use of words. Thus he wrote that 'every analyst knows that along with the content of interpretations the attitude is reflected in the nuances and the timing in a thousand ways that compare with the infinite variety of poetry' (Winnicott 1968a: 95). He saw holding as a maternal function originating in the mother's holding of the baby. It included her literal holding, but also her capacity to stay with the baby emotionally and physically, no matter what transpired. Analytic 'holding' was linked to this maternal function.

It is perhaps surprising that Winnicott made no explicit connection between interpreting and three-person, 'paternal' modes of relating. However, in differentiating two analytic functions which could be drawn on independently (though often intuitively) to suit the needs of the patient, he opened up new technical possibilities. Thus, in relation to schizoid patients, he believed that holding should be pre-eminent and spoke of 'refraining from being side tracked into doing [interpretative] work that is inappropriate *because the main need is for an unclever ego-support, or holding*' (1965: 241, italics mine). In Winnicott's hands, technique was becoming less rigid and more adaptive to changing needs of the patient.

## Interpretation as trauma

Implicit in this view is the idea that patients must have a capacity to separate and stand alone if they are to use interpretation without trauma. Winnicott understood that while most patients feel exposed in some degree by interpretation, a significant number are overwhelmed by the process. In such circumstances, he felt there was little point in continuing to interpret; it was better for the analyst to shift into a different gear and foster the patient's development through some form of holding. To persist with interpretation merely recapitulated earlier traumas of impingement and separation; it provoked alienation of the patient from his own sense of 'going on being' – or 'continuity of being' (Winnicott 1960a) – and often a feeling of being catastrophically exposed to the other's critical regard. I recall one patient of this type (described in more detail in chapter 8) who experienced all my interpretations as dangerous attacks; and while I saw what I was doing as an invitation to insight, she experienced me as destructively critical. At these times she would block her ears so as not to hear me. At other times, perhaps when my voice was less 'hard' and explanatory, she seemed to enjoy listening to me but would then treat the content of what I said as irrelevant. I often felt that she responded more to my tone of voice (the non-verbal aspect emphasized by Rycroft) than to what I actually said (the content).

A patient of this kind has an intense need to feel 'held' – if this is not forthcoming, or disappears, it creates a sense of imminent collapse. There is rupture in what Winnicott calls the sense of 'going on being', a feeling that subjective experience is draining away. Instead of experiencing oneself as unfolding from within, there is a sense of being metamorphosed into a 'him' or a 'her', an *object* defined from the outside by the other person.

Sartre (1957) regarded this 'fall' into objectivity as a basic structure of human existence, and while there is some truth in his contention that such an occurrence (the recognition of objectivity) is inevitable, the horrific feeling tone with which he imbues the moment, and the sense of profound catastrophe that it heralds, suggest that he is describing a pathological form, perhaps of his own experience, and elevating this to a universal status it does not deserve (Wright 1991). Since many people do not experience objectification in such a traumatic way, it is reasonable to suppose that something in normal development protects against it. Sufficient holding and attunement in infancy are likely contenders, cushioning against impingement and allowing the passage into objectivity to be smoothly negotiated. This is in keeping with Winnicott's theory of a transitional stage in which separation from the mother is not experienced as a separation (i.e. as a painful rift), but as an imperceptible phase in the progress towards independence.

## Maternal mirroring and attunement

What does it mean to provide holding? As a way of answering this, I want to consider one of Winnicott's most important papers: 'Mirror role of mother and family in child development' (Winnicott 1967a). In this paper, he implicitly enlarges the concept of holding beyond its roots in bodily cradling and draws it into a framework of communication. In so doing, he shifts the analytic paradigm from object relating (body) to inter-subjective relating (mind). Whereas psychoanalysis since Freud had conceived of the infant as relating to early objects[8] in a purely concrete way – doing things to the object or getting things from the object – this paper makes the quality of communication with the object decisive for emotional development. According to this view, the infant has communicative needs that in their way are just as important as bodily satisfaction, and in the first few months of life these centre on the mother's face.

The critical importance of maternal responsiveness runs through all of Winnicott's work, but whereas in earlier formulations he emphasized the mother's *physical* response – the adaptive bodily dialogue between her and the infant – he now focuses on adaptive *communication*, thus shifting attention from interaction between baby and breast to a non-verbal dialogue with the mother's face.

He likens the mother's face to an emotional mirror and suggests that the infant sees, and begins to experience himself, through the medium of the mother's responsive expressions. This means that the rudiments of 'self' are formed within this dialogical matrix, and the quality of future experience will depend on good enough experience in this area. With a glance at

8 Confusingly, the term 'object' in psychoanalysis also refers to subjects. For the infant, the mother, or some part of her, is the most important 'object'.

Descartes, and perhaps also at Bishop Berkeley, Winnicott defined this formative moment with the phrase: 'When I look I am seen, therefore I exist' (ibid.: 114).[9]

Existentially, mirroring confirms the infant's sense of being and agency, but in terms of theory, the process enlarges the concept of holding into the social arena. It could thus be said that the infant's embryonic sense of self is 'held' within the envelope of the mother's mirroring responses;[10] or that the mother's response provides an incipient objectification – not yet objective enough to be a symbol – of the infant's feeling state. In other words, from the infant's point of view: 'what you (mother's facial expression) look like (proto-symbol) is how I (baby) feel (proto-referent)'.

Winnicott's theory of mirroring breaks new analytic ground. The currency of transactions between mother and infant is no longer confined to physical exchange; it now includes visual signals that carry affective messages, and these pre-symbolic non-verbal exchanges form the essential building blocks for psychic structure.[11]

Towards the end of this paper, Winnicott applies his new insight to the clinical situation with the following statement:

> This glimpse of the baby's and child's seeing the self in the mother's face . . . gives a way of looking at analysis and the psychotherapeutic task. Psychotherapy is not making clever and apt interpretations; by and large it is a long term giving back what the patient brings. It is a complex derivative of the face that reflects what is there to be seen. *I like to think of my work this way and to think that if I do it well enough the patient will find his or her own self, and will be able to exist and to feel real.* Feeling real is more than existing; it is finding a way to exist as oneself, and to relate to objects as oneself, and to have a self into which to retreat for relaxation.
>
> (1971: 117, italics mine)

---

9  To be preoccupied, as both these philosophers were, with the question: 'How do I know that I exist?' surely suggests a less than securely established sense of self and identity. Descartes' answer in his '*Discourse on method*' (1637) was the famous *cogito*: 'I think, therefore I am'. Berkeley's answer in '*A treatise concerning the principles of human knowledge*' (1710) was less solipsistic, and somewhat closer to Winnicott's position. It was the equally famous dictum: *Esse est percipi* – 'To be is to be perceived.' Whereas for Winnicott, the infant only (feels that he) exists in the mother's reflection, Berkeley was led by his thinking to the view that we only exist in the mind of God.

10  As Diamond and Marrone (2003) have pointed out, this way of thinking was anticipated by the phenomenologist Merleau-Ponty (1962: 146) who wrote: 'I live in the facial expressions of the other.'

11  I am assuming that the mother's reflective forms become internalized and provide a substrate for preverbal symbolic containment of infant experience. I discuss this further in chapter 12.

This quotation gives some idea of what it means to 'hold' the patient through a non-interpretative analytic technique. In Winnicott's new image of analysis, analyst and patient no longer stand back and objectively view together the content of the patient's inner world but engage in a more immediate dialogical exchange. The analyst feels his way into the patient's world through identification and gives back to the patient his 'reflection' of it. Analysis in this mode does not involve describing and explaining but generates 'reflections' or 'forms' ('subjective objects') that in some way *embody* the essence of the patient's experience in its living reality. Such reflections not only enhance and affirm experience but in a real sense bring it into being for the first time. In this new way of thinking, insight takes second place; what is more important is creating a 'place' (a certain kind of symbolic location) in which the patient can 'be', a containing 'place' in which the patient can discover and 'hold' their own experience.

This new view of therapy is more comprehensive than the classical one, and within it, interpretation as normally understood no longer holds pride of place. With its tendency towards objective description (creating 'objective objects') rather than evocative embodiment (creating 'subjective objects'), interpretation constitutes a highly differentiated form of reflection that assumes considerable maturity in the patient. It can be regarded as a post-separation mode of giving something back to the patient.

Stern's (1985) attunement, which I discussed in chapter 1, builds on mirroring and can be seen as an extension of it. While sharing important characteristics with the earlier process – both are spontaneous preverbal forms of reflection based on affective identification – attunement provides a richer variety of forms. While mirroring is confined to the mother's facial expressions and a single modality (vision), attunement generates a variety of forms across the sensory modalities. Its patterns are more differentiated than facial expressions and can thus track the 'shape' of infant experience in a more detailed way. This greatly increases the range of preverbal forms available to the infant and thus the range of potential containers (preverbal symbols) for inner feeling states.

## Embodied language

I began this chapter with the idea that language could be used in a number of ways, and that psychoanalysis had traditionally privileged a somewhat detached way of speaking to patients which has come to be known as 'interpreting'. I suggested that poetry exemplifies a more evocative mode of speech whose forms are capable of embodying experience in a vivid way. I then addressed more recent changes in analytic practice and contrasted 'interpretation' – a post-separation way of communicating – with 'holding', a more maternal, less separating type of intervention. Winnicott's original metaphor referred to the mother's provision of background security by holding the baby in her arms, but as his work developed he began to use a model based on communication, in which specific mirroring of infant feeling states was centrally important. I then discussed how in the second half of the preverbal period, the range of such reflecting processes increased to include a more differentiated type of maternal response that Stern called attunement.

I have taken the view that by furnishing symbolic precursors, these processes are quite literally generative of the infant mind. This potential rests on the fact that each reflecting form provides an objective, but subjectively resonant, analogue of a corresponding infant feeling state, as sensed by the mother. However, in addition to this, such forms provide potential bridges between infant and mother, mother and infant, and make possible moments of affective connection, or of 'being together', as Stern would describe it.

It is important to note that because such responses are intuitively forged out of the mother's close identification with the baby and shaped by her experience of him, the infant's emotional development (the development of the infant mind) is totally dependent on the accuracy of the mother's reading of him. It has to be 'good enough', in Winnicott's terms, and failure at this stage will result in distortion of the infant's sense of self and identity.

This understanding of maternal reflective behaviour offers a way of thinking about 'holding' responses in analysis and their difference from explanatory interpretation. In terms of the analyst's words, this lies principally in the use to which language is put. In holding, the aim is to shape language in a resonant way that embodies experience; in interpretation, it is clarity of explanation. In the first case, the analyst's words must 'carry' the feel of living experience; in the second, the structure must support the logic of 'why' and 'because'.

By its nature, the language of resonance (holding) is more spontaneous than the language of explanation; to throw light on passing experience, it must 'catch the moment as it flies'. It is also more sensual and evocative and works through images rather than ideas. It carries conviction through felt correspondences of form ('right' when it connects, 'wrong' when it does not) and in this respect is similar to poetry. If the expression 'works', we take it on board; if it fails to 'work', we ignore it.

There is, however, a proviso in connection with forms that do not 'fit', and this includes interpretations that the analyst 'imposes' on the patient. The outcome of over-zealous interpretation hinges on the patient's ability to reject what the analyst says, and like the ability to tolerate objectification, this probably depends on already having a secure sense of self. This is precisely what is missing in vulnerable narcissistic individuals who are thus at risk from the analyst's activity. If a 'wrong' interpretation cannot be warded off, the patient may compliantly attempt to inhabit its meaning, leading to an element of false self structure.[12] This is exactly the reverse of what is needed, and simply repeats the trauma of earlier attunement failure.

The concept of holding crept into analysis through working with a new kind of patient for whom interpretative work seemed out of place; it now offers itself as a variation on technique for any patient in need of holding and regression. This increased relevance poses a question for every analysis, and perhaps for every session: What is this patient's major need, and what does he most need from the analyst at this particular moment? Is it a thoroughgoing explanation of the *reasons* for how he is, or a resonating form in which to discover his own experience, and capture its shape and feel? In more general terms it raises a larger question: How much is analysis a science and how much an art, and is it closer to the sobriety of prose or the inspiration of poetry?

It is a feature of poetry and all the arts that they have the power to *reveal* experiences never fully known, and arguably both attunement and analysis have a similar potential. It is true that in attunement the process *follows* the infant – the mother responds to that which her infant brings. In a similar way, the analyst follows the patient, but as in attunement, everything depends on the nature of the response. If the analyst uses explanatory language *before* there is any experience to interpret, his words will be empty of real meaning; only after experience has been brought into being (given a body) by providing appropriate images to hold it (evocative language), is there anything substantial to be explained.[13] In this sense, holding precedes understanding in both development and analysis.

Classical analysis differentiated between talking and doing and drew an excluding boundary round doing. It stuck rigidly to an interpretative stance, as though afraid of opening the door to doing. Winnicott's approach suggested a third way: not simply a choice between words and actions, but also between words that explain (interpretation) and words that embody

---

12 By 'wrong' interpretation, I do not necessarily mean an interpretation completely at odds with the patient's material and barking up the wrong tree. It may simply be an interpretation at the wrong time, or one that fails to engage with the 'feel' of the patient's experience. It is possible to imagine a 'right' interpretation that nevertheless leads to a false self structure because it fails to make links with felt experience.

13 Some analysts might argue that what brings experience into being is principally the revival of transference feelings. There is no doubt truth in this contention but it has to be subject to qualification. The idea that the transference is the locus of all significance and that only transference interpretation is truly mutative, has become an article of faith, with the attendant dangers of such a notion. Among these is the possibility of the analyst interpreting the transference whenever he perceives the slightest suggestion of its presence (in my view, a common occurrence). Even if he were usually correct in such a view – and this is at least open to doubt – the chances are high that he would interpret the transference *before* the patient had experienced it. This would mean at best that the patient is given empty words, at worst, that he risks indoctrination.

and evoke (holding). Evocative language, like the transitional object, lies *between* absence and presence, and, like Stern's attunements, *creates* experience rather than simply naming it. In chapter 4, I discuss this creative function of words in relation to the poet Rilke, while in chapters 7 and 8, I explore its clinical implications in greater detail.

# Chapter 3

# Deep calling unto deep

Transitional phenomena occupy a central place in the thought of Donald Winnicott and from such early beginnings he sketched a path to the world of culture and religion (Winnicott 1953, 1967b). In the present chapter I shall build on this schema and draw out its implications for a theory of art. I grapple further with the topic in chapters 4 and 9.

According to Winnicott, transitional phenomena are constituted in the first year of life when certain ordinary objects become endowed by the baby with special significance. He regarded them as occupying a *transitional* place in symbolic development: though not yet separate enough to be fully fledged symbols, they were nevertheless more than mere objects, having been endowed by the infant with personal meaning.

Typically, the transitional object is the comforting bit of blanket that the infant mouths and caresses. Winnicott called this the 'first *not-me* possession' but he also saw it as a special object which the infant had imaginatively *created*. This root of creativity is central to his theory of personal development for in his view it underpins the quality of later experience. Only when the baby is allowed such an early experience can the world be endowed with personal meaning, and only then can there be creative involvement with it in later life.

It was not Winnicott but another psychoanalyst, Michael Balint, who coined the phrase 'harmonious mix-up' to capture this interpenetration of subject and object in early experience (Balint, M. 1959: 62). Balint's term referred to the early relationship with the mother but equally could have applied to the transitional object. Indeed, Winnicott often called this a *subjective object* because of the mix-up of subjective and objective elements in its constitution. In the bit of blanket, for example, the sensory properties of the object – its softness, warmth and smell – appear to embody an earlier subjective experience with the mother. In this sense, the 'created' object is like a shrine within which certain needed qualities of experience have been preserved.

In Winnicott's understanding, subjective (created) objects could only be formed under favourable conditions, most important of which was the attitude of the mother, who had to be able to mediate the world to the infant in a way that corresponded to infant anticipation. The infant's 'spontaneous gesture', as he called it, thus needed to be met and completed by the mother's response: only then could the crucial mix-up of subjective and objective occur. He believed that if the mother failed in this task, the baby would experience her caring (originally her presentation of the breast) as alien and imposed (entirely 'not-me'). In other words, if the breast was not imbued with the infant's hallucinated anticipation, it remained foreign and external to the infant's experience.

Maternal adaptation is thus central to Winnicott's view of normal creative development. Without its mediating influence, objects *impinge* on infant experience and assault the baby with their alien demands (Winnicott 1960b). In such circumstances the baby is deprived of the experience of moulding the object to subjective anticipation because the mother's needs and schedules dominate the situation.

In Winnicott's terminology, an impinging object is thus the reverse of a created object – being unrelated to the baby's needs, the baby must submit to its unmediated reality. In contrast, an object mediated by maternal adaptation (prototypically the breast) can be infused with the baby's feelings and subjectively transformed by them. The object so adapted thus becomes a subjective object.

From this perspective, the derivation of the word 'object' takes on a new significance. Its literal meaning (Latin root, *OED*) of 'something thrown across the path as an obstacle' is precisely the way the impinging object presents itself to the infant. By contrast, the created object, 'softened' by the mother's mediation, gives the infant a sense of potency in relation to it. In the first case, the infant must deal with what the world throws at it; in the second, there is a sense of finding – indeed creating – what is needed. The maternally adapted object becomes a creation of the infant self.

Winnicott's thinking in this area throws up two ideas which contribute to an understanding of the *art object* from a psychoanalytic perspective: first, that an object can be a 'mix-up' of subjective experience and actual physical object; second, that objects of this kind facilitate self-development. I return to both notions later in the chapter but first need to examine the relationship between *language* and infant experience. In my view, the development of language recapitulates in important ways the earlier relationship between the infant and his first objects (see also chapter 6).

## Subjective and objective language

The social behaviourist, George Herbert Mead (1934), believed that 'mind' and 'self' were products of the social process. He did not subscribe to the prevailing view that they were primary structures that existed independently of the social process; on the contrary, he believed they were formed within, and arose out of this process, and were fundamentally social in their constitution. Mead and Winnicott approached questions of mind and self from different directions but converged on one point: they both realized that human subjects (and objects) were socially created. For Winnicott, the crucial medium was the mother–baby mix-up; for Mead it was the social environment.

For Mead, language too was a socially created object which like 'mind' and 'self' was rooted in the concrete world. Notwithstanding its eventual distance from bodily, interactive experience (see below), it nevertheless maintained connection with it. Thus, in one memorable phrase he described a word as a 'truncated act', implying that language was derived from action, even though its relationship with the concrete world had become attenuated. Winnicott, for his part, did not specifically approach words in this way, yet if we compare language to that earlier symbolic creation, the transitional object,[1] we can see that the balance between materiality and meaning in its constitution has shifted further from the concrete pole. Unlike the transitional object, the essence of language no longer lies in its sensual qualities (its visual and auditory forms) but in its *meaning* which is now set apart from its concrete reality. As Bion (1962b) realized, for the meaning of a word to be understood, it must be related to in a new way – not as a thing, but as a 'no-thing'. From this point of view, a word is insubstantial and transparent – its meaning is seen *through* its sensual qualities and could be said to lie in a different 'place'. Unlike the baby's bit of blanket whose meaning lies *within* its sensory reality, the meaning of a word lies somewhere else, in a 'place' beyond the renunciation of physical possession.

Mead was not greatly concerned with the experiential aspects of words but this did concern another investigator of language, the philosopher Ludwig Wittgenstein (see chapter 6). In his early philosophy, adumbrated in the *Tractatus Logico-Philosophicus*, Wittgenstein conceived of language as an instrument external to the individual, a tool that could be brought up to experience from the outside (Wittgenstein 1922). In his later philosophy, however, he reneged on this radically separate view of language and became intrigued by a more existential type of understanding. Language, in this later view, was more embodied: it was 'a form of life' and a means of expression rather than an external tool, a part of experience rather than a label attached to it. From this perspective, words were no longer alien, external structures but arose directly out of our involvement with objects and fulfilled our expressive intentions in relation to them.

---

1 Strictly speaking the transitional object falls short of full symbolic status in that it does not merely stand for the object but re-creates it. In this sense it is similar to Segal's 'symbolic equivalent'; in Winnicott's terms it lies on the 'journey towards symbols'.

From this point of view they were subjective creations, and in a way that resonates with Balint and Winnicott, he now saw them as infused with experience and thoroughly 'mixed up' with the process of living (Wittgenstein 1953).

Wittgenstein's philosophy suggests that words, as well as objects, can present (or be presented) to us in different ways, a view compatible with developmental psychology (Hobson 2000); it would also make sense from a Winnicottian perspective. Not just objects, but words, too, can be experienced as alien and impinging, or adaptive and containing of experience, and while at times we have to submit to their measure and comply with their meaning, at others they seem to adapt to us, springing up in response to an expressive need, and providing an answer to it.

From this perspective, the relation of language to experience is dual: at times it is external and prescriptive, at others internal and part of the experience itself. At times it impinges as part of a fixed reality, at others it allows itself to be moulded by experience, becoming in Winnicott's terms a subjective object. In the first case, we have to mould experience to fit its categories; in the second, it can be infused with our own meanings and made to fit our need. Language in this adaptive mode satisfies 'a speechless want', as Merleau-Ponty (1964b) puts it, and feels 'in touch with' experience (see chapter 1), just as the adaptive mother feels 'in touch with' the infant. Operating in this way, it is created and re-created, subjectively transformed like the breast in Winnicott's account, or the bit of blanket that 'contains' a soothing experience of the mother. When such transformation occurs, the word becomes a subjective creation and tends towards the Humpty-Dumpty sense of language in *Alice Through the Looking Glass*, where Humpty says that when he uses a word it means 'just what he chooses it to mean, neither more nor less'.

I recently watched my two-year-old great-nephew as he struggled to pack his intense experience into a limited vocabulary. He seemed to have just two words: *that*, which he accompanied by an urgent movement of his whole body towards the object that he wanted; and *more*, which indicated how much he wanted to repeat the experience. As he struggled to convey his intentions, one could sense how he re-created these words again and again, each time infusing them anew with his entire being. Through the passion of his need, he stretched his two word vocabulary to accommodate the entirety of his intentions, and each time the word expressed that need in a vivid way.

## Verbal and preverbal symbols

In considering an infant's transition into language, it has to be remembered that words will need to be integrated with earlier organizations of experience (meanings), however inchoate these may be.[2] Even though these preverbal organizations are bound to objects and thoroughly mixed up with the infant's concrete world, they are still *his* meanings, and delineate a world uniquely created from the flux of his own experience. The transitional object exemplifies such object-rooted meaning which can also be thought of as a realm of preverbal symbols.

Since the experience of such a child is already inscribed within the register of his 'created' concrete objects, the arrival of language marks a momentous transition, almost a second birth, for while his preverbal structuring of the world is unique, it now faces restructuring by a language that carries alien meanings. As Bakhtin (1981) puts it:

> The word in language is half someone else's. It becomes 'one's own' only when the speaker populates it with his own intention, his own accent, when he appropriates the word, adapting it to his own expressive intention. Prior to this moment of appropriation, the word does not exist in a neutral and impersonal language (it is not after all out of a dictionary that the speaker gets his words!), but rather it exists in other people's mouths, in other people's contexts, serving other people's intentions: it is from here that one must take the word and make it one's own . . . Language is not a neutral medium that passes freely and easily into the private property of the speaker's intentions; it is populated – overpopulated – with the intentions of others. Expropriating it, forcing it to submit to one's own intentions and accents, is a difficult and complex process.
>
> (ibid.: 293–4)

While it would be hard to find a more eloquent expression of the habitual struggle between expressive need and available language, the child in the period of language acquisition is even more at the mercy of others' meanings, his experience of words being entirely dependent on the sensitivity of

---

2 There is an excellent review of this period of development in Vivona (2006) in which she contrasts two radically different theories of language acquisition. The first is that of Hans Loewald (1978/1980), who sees language as developing within, and alongside, the object world in a syntonic way, presumably mediated by an adaptive mother who intuitively feels her task to be the transformation of the child's experience into words. The second theory is that of Stern (1985) for whom preverbal experience and language are radically disjoined. Though Stern sees such disjunction as inevitable, and while from a structural point of view it may be so, the *experience* of disjunction may well be contingent. An attuned mother will negotiate a smooth transition into language, while a poorly attuned mother will not achieve this. In the first case, the 'translation' into language will be relatively complete, in the second there will be a 'black hole' of unmarked experience.

those who mediate them to him. It is here that the mother's ability to provide the 'right' (i.e. fitting) word to the child is crucially important and another example of maternal adaptation. I explore this further in chapter 6 in relation to the philosopher Witttgenstein.

How much of the infant's experience will make the passage into language is uncertain, for although the infant may struggle to infuse language with his own meaning, this tendency is in dialectic with an opposite process – the capacity of the word to bring its preordained meaning into *him*, to restructure *him* with the meaning of the other person. It can thus be seen, that if the mother of the *preverbal* infant could facilitate or hinder a creative relation with the concrete forms of the *object* world, she now has a similar power in relation to language; and just as previously she could usurp the rhythms of infant desire with the patterns of her own needs, so now the word provides control over increasingly specific elements of infant experience and provides potential access to the child's inner self.[3] First posed on the preverbal level of *object*-relations (for example, in relation to the breast), the question of 'whose meaning' is now fought out on the level of language where words belong to the other person before they belong to the infant.

This Janus-faced feature of language differentiates it from the register of preverbal symbols. Preverbal symbols (or pre-symbols, like the transitional object) look one way – they belong to the self and are unequivocally rooted in *self*-experience. Language, on the other hand, looks two ways – it belongs first to the other person and is already 'populated' with their meanings and intentions (Bakhtin 1981).

This distinction is linked with important differences of function. Whereas from the beginning the verbal function looks outwards towards communication with the other person and requires consensual meanings, the preverbal capability centres on the self, and from the start serves inner need. Its symbolic forms do not need to be consensually validated – they function as containers for personal experience and are idiosyncratic and personal.

---

3  There is a sense in which the analyst's task and responsibility in relation to the patient is similar to the task of the mother in relation to the preverbal child on the threshold of speech. Both infant and patient are learning to speak: the child is learning to speak for the first time; the patient is trying to find a language for the often extensive parts of his experience which have never yet been spoken. The patient is thus an *infans* (without words) in relation to much of his life of feeling. This idea underpins my argument that the ability to speak an embodied language (chapter 8) is a vital part of analytic work: the patient must first discover words *for* his experience before he can use words to talk *about* it. If the stage of embodying experience (literally putting it into words) is glossed over, the patient may finish up inhabiting the words of others and thus remain alien to himself. I have discussed this in the previous chapter and explore it further in chapters 8 and 12.

## Non-verbal symbols and the art object

Since my aim in this chapter is to throw new light on the art object, and since, as Langer (1942, 1953) has persuasively argued, such objects are structures of non-verbal or *presentational* symbols, I shall summarize the salient features of such symbols as a preliminary to more detailed discussion.

First, they are constituted from sensory forms which more or less closely reflect the forms (contours, textures, shapes) of actual experience. The transitional object, for example, is related through textural and tactile similarities to sensory experience with the mother. Later preverbal symbols make use of a wider range of sensory modalities, but always in iconic fashion. Thus vision, the prime distance sense, may become important as the infant develops a more distanced relationship with the object, while the mother's attuning forms with their greater sensory diversity may provide a rich ground for preverbal symbol formation.[4]

Second, and following from the first point, the relation between non-verbal symbol and object is one of formal similarity or isomorphism. This contrasts with the relation between word and object which has no such formal similarity and is based on convention. Clearly the similarity of 'shape' between an experience and its non-verbal representation enables such symbols to *portray* experience in a way that verbal symbols seldom achieve. A verbal representation is typically more distant from experience – it *points* to experience but is less likely to conjure it up (see however previous section, and chapters 2 and 8 on different ways of using language).

Third, while non-verbal symbols may sometimes be shared and conventional (for example, the symbols on a map), this is the exception; basically they are idiosyncratic – formed out of, and relating to, individual experience. Such idiographic representations are significant to their creator (e.g. dream

---

4  Since, according to the theory put forward here, preverbal symbols have their origin in maternal reflections, they too may be poorly fitting and out of tune with actual experience. There are, however, two points which might render the misfit of early reflections less lethal than the later misidentifications of language. First, maternal reflections (in attunement, for example) are by nature an *offering*; there is little sense in which a mother could *impose* them on the infant – they are just there for the infant to notice or not, as the case may be. Second, and related to the first point, the infant is only likely to engage with the maternal display if it is imbued with the buzz of resonance – in other words, if it offers a sufficient degree of fit. I am making the assumption that resonance, or some early precursor of it, is the means by which likeness, or even identity, is recognized. Such considerations refer to a situation (probably the 'normal' one) in which the mother's reflection is 'patchy' – sometimes right, sometimes wrong. In cases of more persistent failure (failure to respond, or consistent misrepresentation), the consequences for the infant would be more serious: the sense of aliveness and self-feeling would be undermined, with damage to the core self and the capacity for creative living. In these circumstances, personal experience would be in danger of disappearing, or atrophying, through a dearth of resonant forms to support it.

symbols) but, having no shared meaning, they are poorly suited to inter-personal communication. As we shall see, however, this state of affairs is transcended in art, which may be one of the reasons we value it so highly.

In summary then, if language first arose in the interpersonal field as a way of meeting the needs of separate subjects for communication about shared *external* objects, it is reasonable to suppose that non-verbal symbols are *inner* determined and originally served the needs of the self. As inward looking symbols, they enable the subject to key into and 'hold on to' his own experience and like the transitional object, they look after the self in a way that resembles the mother's earlier care of the baby (mirroring, attunement). Verbal symbols, on the other hand, are rooted in separateness of self and other, and can more readily be linked to the father and requirements of the outside world (Lacan 1953/1977; Wright 1991).

## Creativity and maternal responsiveness

I can now make a bridge between non-verbal symbols and the art object, for if such symbols originate in the matrix of mother–infant relatedness and perpetuate an earlier nurturing function of the mother, it is probable that the art object too will partake of such characteristics.

There is, however, a difficulty with this approach. If the art object shares the characteristics of non-verbal symbols (Langer 1953), it might suggest that artistic creation itself is a self-enclosed activity. This would mean that the artist, in the act of creation, was simply looking after himself, the whole procedure being merely a form of self-communion. There may be an element of truth in this idea but it goes counter to common experience in which art frequently succeeds in communicating significant import to others. In so doing it reaches out beyond the confines of the artist's self, and with greater potential than the word to move the emotions, it makes contact with the inwardness of others, who in turn resonate to its expressive forms.

The apparent opposition disappears if we think of private (non-verbal) symbols as forged in the matrix of mother–infant relatedness (i.e. originally through attunement and related processes). For in this case, the non-verbal prototype originates in preverbal communication between mother and infant, whereby the mother 'touches' the infant's subjectivity through an attuned or mirroring form that she has created. We can imagine such a form resonating with infant experience in a way that prefigures the reson-ance of the *artist's* form with his own subjectivity and that of others (Stern 1985; Hobson 2000). From this perspective, the artist's symbol is *essentially* communicative since its *apparently* self-contained nature results from inter-nalization of an earlier communion with the mother. According to this view, it is such communion, now on a sophisticated and complex level, that underlies the power of art to move its audience. I explore this further in chapter 9.

If the artist in non-verbal forms has found a way of reaching others by means of his private symbols, the artist in words has a different task. Although his motive may be similar, he sets out from a different place. Starting with language as a practical instrument, he must turn it inwards, bending its outer-directed and limiting forms and forcing them to adapt to his inner needs. In his hands, they acquire an expressive function which was not their primary nature and become infused with personal feeling and experience. Through this transformation they give form to the artist's self, and simultaneously touch the deep in other people.

I can now link back to the beginning of my chapter and sketch an account of artistic creation from a Winnicottian perspective. I shall start with a series of statements.

The artist's *medium* corresponds to the 'not-me' world out of which the infant 'creates' his first objects – the baby's transitional object is a paradigm. The first 'creation' is the mother's breast, made possible by the mother allowing *herself* to become a medium that is moulded by the infant's need. On this foundation, the infant then 'creates' his comforting bit of blanket (his subjective object) from a new compliant medium – a part of the physical world that lies to hand. As in the earlier experience, the object 'complies' – experientially, it allows itself to be transformed. And so it continues: the creative person transforms the object world into *his* world (i.e. a world infused with *his* meanings) because he has learned from the adaptive mother that such moulding is possible.

We can now consider the artist facing his medium and ask in what frame of mind he might relate to it. It would not, I suggest, be with the despair of one who had complied with an impinging, unyielding world/mother but rather with the faith, hope and determination of one who believes that the medium *will* provide what he needs. In this sense, the artist's medium is heir to the adaptive mother: in the same way that the infant 'created' the breast out of the adaptive mother, so the artist creates his forms out of the raw medium by making it conform to the pattern of his emerging sensibility.

From this perspective, the artist is supplicant *and* provider, baby *and* mother. In the intensity of his creative passion, he resembles the baby in a state of subjective need; through his medium, which he coaxes and attacks, cajoles and forces to expression, he is the more or less adaptive mother. When the medium refuses him, he relives the primitive anxiety of not being held and responded to; when it gives him what he needs, he experiences the joy of self-realization. As Winnicott stressed in relation to play, the story of art in this account concerns neither instinctual passion and its satisfaction, nor the pleasure principle, but a more 'spiritual' quality that psychoanalysis is only beginning to take seriously – the joy of being recognized and responded to, of being confirmed as a self, and of being gathered, or re-gathered, into a maternal 'object' which allows itself to become a fitting container for the self.

From this perspective, the project of art has little to do with guilt and reparation which Kleinian writers, notably Segal (1991), consider the mainsprings of creativity. More important than this is the quest to re-find, or discover for the first time, a malleable and adaptive object (medium) which like the transitional mother will provide holding and containing forms. From this perspective, the artist struggles to wrest from his medium the never yet realized forms of his own sensibility. Within the holding of his medium the self can be gathered in; and only then, and only in that place, can the work of integration be accomplished. Guilt and reparation may be part of this process but are not sufficient motives for the artist's endeavour (see also chapters 4 and 9).

## Personal integration and the art object

I shall now discuss the object that the artist creates, and taking as my paradigm the visual arts, consider the nature of a *visual* object. I have suggested that the art object is formed through a kind of dialogue between the artist and his chosen medium, and that this medium is some part of the sensory world which he manipulates in order to bring the shapes and forms of his own sentience to realization. In thus persuading the medium to respond to his technique, he obliges it in an almost literal sense to *be* the adaptive mother of infancy. This idea is the core of my thesis but before I elaborate it, a further question needs to be addressed. If dialogue with a (maternal) medium/object is central to the creative process, what kind of dialogue might be constitutive of a specifically *visual* object such as a painting or piece of sculpture?

In an earlier publication (Wright 1991) I developed a view of symbol formation that depended on two things: a progressive uncoupling of looking from doing/having, and correlatively, an increasing dominance of visual forms over proprioceptive and kinaesthetic modes of experience. My formulation made some sense in relation to physical objects in the child's world, it being possible to imagine that later visual schemata of objects might subsume earlier bodily ones, at the same time offering them a containing and organizing envelope. Extrapolating from this, one can think of the visual art object as an integrated structure whose visual envelope and sensory-somatic elements form a single unit. This approach might begin to explain the tactile values in a visual artefact, a good visual depiction carrying within it the capacity to evoke multi-sensorial involvement.[5]

Symbolic representation of the *self* poses a more complicated problem, however, for while personal experience can be known in a sensual and

5 This way of thinking is particularly relevant to sculpture in which tactile and spatial experience are so keenly aroused.

bodily way from the *inside*, the only way of obtaining *external* knowledge of it is through some form of mirroring. Lacan (1949) believed that this necessity created an *essential* disjunction between visual and bodily experience of the self; he argued that the infant's perception of his own image in the mirror led to a permanent disjunction in a previously unitary state of being. Sartre described the effect of the other's look as even more catastrophic for subjective experience; he saw it as totally destructive of subjectivity, reducing the subject to *nothing but* this object that the other sees (Sartre 1957: 252–302).

Winnicott's (1967a) account of maternal mirroring was more sanguine, for in effect, he described the other's view, epitomized by the mother's facial expression, as vital to the *completion* of an infant feeling state and, ultimately, for a secure sense of self. He hypothesized that although coming from the outside and in reality separate from the infant, the external view confirmed self-feeling because it was resonant with it. Stern's attunement can be understood in a similar way as providing resonant images of infant vitality affects. Such maternally adapted forms *reduce* emotional distance and *enhance* subjectivity; they create affective bridges between mother and infant, and in so far as they provide a substrate for creating internal structure, can be seen as providing the foundations of an integrated sense of self.

Deficiency of mirroring (and attunement) could thus be expected to have serious consequences and in Winnicott's view this was indeed the case. If the mother's face failed to reflect infant mood, the infant's 'creative capacity [would begin] to atrophy, and in some way or other they [would] look around for some other way of getting something of themselves back from the environment' (ibid.: 112). However, since such deficiencies of response are inevitable, and even the good enough mother will at times be too tired or depressed to get it right, it would seem that alternative ways of 'getting something back' might be universal. I suggest that artistic activity is one such way of making good the original deficit; by creating his own containing forms, the artist is saying: 'What I couldn't get from the other person, I am now making for myself.' From this perspective, artistic activity is a means of fashioning mirroring and containing forms, and thus a way of realizing and restoring the self.

## Non-verbal contact

Resonant inter-subjective reflection is based on identification – I put myself in your place and sense how that feels. But when this happens, how do I, the recipient of the process, know that you really understand me? It is no good for you merely to *say* that you love me, know me, recognize me; you have got to *show* it in some way for me to believe you. In other words, I need to *feel* your understanding in my heart, rather than hearing it in words that could be merely saying it.

To convey such deep understanding requires a mediation that carries the message *directly* to the other person. For me to be convinced you must *demonstrate* your knowledge of my experience, and for this a direct bridge between two sensibilities is required.

Ordinary words (discursive symbols) are inadequate to this task because they merely *refer* to experience but fail to *evoke* it. To bridge the gap between us (i.e. to let me know that you *really* understand what I am feeling), you must find a form (symbol) that *presents* me with the experience we are trying to share. More than this, your symbol must evoke my experience in such a way that I *know* you are in touch with it, and therefore with me (see chapter 1). Langer (1942, 1953) called symbols with this capability '*presentational* symbols' and although her focus was the symbolic nature of the art object, her work also illuminates the nature of non-verbal communication.

The word *symbol* is derived from the Greek word *symbollein* (OED) which means literally to throw together, the word having its origins in the practices of a secret society.[6] Members of this group carried a medallion which had been broken in two halves. When they met, each showed their half medallion to the other, and if the two matched up, each knew that the other was a *bona fide* member of the group. The recognition by each of the other's cipher generated the needed sense of certainty.

Something similar lies at the core of non-verbal attunement because it involves you showing me something, saying something, or doing something which convinces me that your claim is authentic. I feel certain that you love me, recognize me and above all know me, because you are able to *show* me the necessary correspondence: in an attuned response there is close 'fit' between my experience (the bit that comes from me) and your cipher (the bit that comes from you). The fact that the two halves fit (resonate) together convinces me that your experience is in tune with mine.

Such affective recognition is self-justifying. It is also part of a larger integrative task that in the beginning necessarily involves another person. It does not only involve the integration of all the bits, as in putting together a jigsaw puzzle. It requires in addition that you (the other person) recognize these bits, because only then will they feel alive, and only then can they have a place within my consciousness. I am speaking primarily from the point of view of the baby, and the baby's need for the mother's recognition, but am also assuming that the task is never complete. Even in adult life, we yearn for a state of more complete acceptance and continue to search for ways of achieving it (see above, and chapter 10).

It could be said that every single piece of the child's inner life must negotiate a contact of this kind with the mother's view. Just as the mother

6 See Laplanche and Pontalis (1973) p. 445, footnote $\beta$.

herself is the first medium out of which the rudiments of self are created, so now the mother's recognition is the medium out of which the self will be made. Each piece of the infant's subjectivity must reach out into it, and either be embraced and given a maternal form, or clash with this view, and because of the child's extreme dependence on the mother, be disallowed from being.

All this could be put less poetically in terms of the conditions that are necessary for the formation of mental content, or indeed of mind itself. At least this is the case if we think of the mind as a 'location' of reflected forms and a 'place' in which such reflections can be used to 'hold' and contemplate experience. Without the mother's early reflective activity, the development of mind in this sense is stunted, and symbolic activity becomes an operational affair in which symbols merely refer to external objects.

From this perspective, one could write an equation for the development of mind (as the location of personal experience) in which 'element of psychosomatic being' + 'maternal reflection of that element' = 'element of mind'. This element of mind is perhaps similar to Bion's 'container-contained' structure, in which case one could say that only those elements which have been contained (reflected) will have a continuing mental existence.

In a different language, it is clear that my formula refers to the symbolic transformation of experience, in which attuned and mirroring reflections by the mother provide a first means of apprehending its shapes and rhythms. I am not suggesting that we remain completely dependent on other people for such reflected forms; if the process gets off to a good start, it will be internalized so that we are able to transform our own experience into symbolic form.

Normal life, however, lies between dependence and independence, and this may be where the arts are important. Every cultural artefact is a reservoir of reflecting forms, an external phase of the individual mind that in a sense replaces the actual mother.

Again we come to the idea that the work of art is a late derivative of the mirroring, attuning mother, while critical or un-empathic responses, whether generated within or without, hark back to the impinging object-mother to which the self must give way. In either case, the self is formed out of dialogue with an other. The objective self is the product of distanced and sometimes critical appraisal; the subjective self (as the location of personal experience) is created through subjective attunement. Every gesture of the self, or as Winnicott says, each 'spontaneous gesture', must pass through the medium of the mother before it can come to be (i.e. before it can become part of the subjective self) and a self that can live creatively has made this passage through the mother. In each of its parts it has put the question of being to her, and emerged with her stamp of acceptance (a mirroring or attuning form).

## Empathic dialogue and self-realization

Over the past few decades a new chapter of psychoanalytic theory has begun to be written. Faced with the pathology of narcissistic/borderline disorder, psychoanalysis has been forced to place greater emphasis on the role of early empathy and dialogue in the development of the sense of self (e.g. Balint, E. 1963; Searles 1963; Winnicott 1967a; Green 1975).

These newer developments have made possible a view of the self that is fundamentally social. The adaptive mother (the mother capable of accurate identification) provides a resonant medium, and within that medium the infant discovers and becomes the self that potentially he is. Her adaptive breast is the first realization, the infant's first creation. Later, her mirroring expressions provide a more attenuated medium of formative response, and later still attunement provides a repertoire of reflecting forms. Stern's (1985) work enables one to see how confirmation through facial mirroring is amplified and extended through the later preverbal period by providing a richer variety of maternal response.

As I discussed in chapter 1, an attuned mother identifies with her infant's state of being in an ongoing way. She 'reads' in more or less continuous fashion the changing emotional rhythms that accompany the baby's activity (its *vitality affects*), and responds to them with sounds and gestures which portray the contour of the infant's 'experience' and give it shape. Through such portrayals the mother re-creates the baby's experience in an external form.

Attunement thus provides a new and more varied medium (the mother's dramatic responsiveness) within which the infant self can be realized and given form. As in earlier kinds of subjective realization the baby has the illusion of moulding the maternal medium, but this illusion, like the preceding ones, is only possible because the mother lends herself to the process and allows it to happen. She allows herself to be formed and reformed in the baby's image.

## Art as transitional object

It is in this area of the self finding containment and realization within a maternal medium that I place the creation of the art object, and in these terms, the creative process is a struggle on two fronts: first, to create a medium more adaptive and responsive to need than the original mother; and second, through this medium, and using it as a kind of surrogate mother, to create an object that more fully contains and realizes the artist's self.

With the help of his medium, and through the forms he creates, the artist retrieves elements of his subjectivity that were in danger of being lost. Within his new object – the art object in process of formation – he places these retrieved subjective elements within the forms of his own making.

Thus an art work in progress is both maternal extension of the self, and a self in formation, within which the artist attempts integration with all the skill he can muster. The structure that results from this intuitive project (the art object) is in continuity with the fabric of the artist's self and resonates with it. It is a genuine mix-up of artist and object, though now with a separate existence in the real world. It is heir to the transitional object of infancy, though now aspires to comprehensive containment of the self in all its complexity.

I may have implied that an art object is completed and static, but this is not my intention, nor does it represent the experience of the viewer, for whom it is an object replete with tensions and possibilities. For just as the self develops through dialogue with the mother and carries in its structure the marks of that origin, so the art object bears within itself the residue of living dialogue with the artist. Just as the self is not an *object* in the normal sense of the word but a dynamic structure – an interweaving of impulse (spontaneous gesture) and meaning (containing response) – so too is the art object a subjective structure, alive with gestures and answering forms. Both constitute a fabric of *inter-communicating* symbols and the richness of both lies in the reverberation of their forms. However, the fecundity of the art object goes beyond this similarity of structure. Precisely because the work of art is a symbolic object, we are able in certain respects to engage with it as though it were a responsive person. We experience it as evoking and making contact with our own dormant sentience, and through its carefully contrived and resonant forms responding to it.

## Art as communication

I have suggested that the art object is a medium of self-realization for its creator – a complex derivative of the transitional object, or as Winnicott says in his paper on mirroring, 'a complex derivative of the face' (Winnicott 1967a/1971: 117). In this sense it is also heir to the mother whose responsive forms were never quite sufficient, and like the transitional object, a 'not-me' extension of the artist, which contains important elements of his affective being. In this sense, the art object is a narcissistic structure that serves the artist's own need for recognition, containment and integration.

One of the things that determines our judgement of a work of art is the degree to which we experience it as having relevance – by which I mean resonance with the shapes and forms of our own feeling. A work of art is successful in this sense, when it mirrors our own 'forms of feeling' (Langer 1953: 40). In fulfilling this function, it repeats in some measure for the viewer what it performed for the artist in the course of its creation. In the same way that the 'shapes' the artist fashioned were the living substantiation of *his* emotional being, so for the viewer who now relates to them, they become forms that he too can inhabit, and through which he is enabled to become more fully himself.

From this point of view, the art object is a structure that bridges between separate subjects. Even though the artist's primary drive may have been his need to restore himself, the work of art ultimately transcends this self-contained objective and becomes a vehicle of meaningful contact with other human beings.

There is thus a paradox at the heart of the art object: it is both narcissistic and intensely relational. If we emphasize its likeness to a transitional creation, we are thrown back on its self-enclosed and self-serving aspects. If, on the other hand, we stress how the baby's search for such an object arose from its fundamental need for dialogue with the mother – for continuing relatedness that was threatened by her absence – the communicative, dialogic matrix of the object comes into view. Just as the baby reached out, and found, an answering response in the soft piece of blanket (repeating thereby an earlier relation to the mother), so we can see the artist as reaching out for confirmation by others through his creation.

From the viewer's position, we find the same double aspect. On the one hand, we turn to the art object with a narcissistic aim of finding confirmation and containment within its forms; on the other, we never forget that this artefact was the work of another human being – a fact which guarantees its relevance and potential significance. We identify with the *artist* even as we relate to the work he has created.

Winnicott's work, and also that of Stern,[7] underlines the importance of being recognized and responded to. It begins to explain how the sense of inter-subjective communication is achieved and the importance of the non-verbal vehicle (originally the mother's adaptive and resonant response) in bringing this about. The artist is a master in creating non-verbal resonant forms, and this places him in continuity with the mother who confirmed and resonated to his experience (though probably insufficiently) long ago. His artistic activity keeps alive this maternal function, and simultaneously presents to us, the audience, the attuning forms that we search for but do not recognize until they are offered (see chapter 9).

Through the bridge of the artist's form a sense of deep communion is engendered. The artist sounds his 'barbaric yawp' (Whitman 1881/1995) with an unspoken question to the void: 'Is there anybody there who will answer me?' The viewer who responds to this call, and resonates to the artist's work, completes the circle – he becomes the other (mother) who answers and confirms the artist as a vital member of the group.

---

7 I have singled out these two authors because their work is seminal and paradigmatic. There are of course other authors who share and contribute to the relational view, but reviewing the history and development of this would be a different project from the present one in which I aim to probe and understand the relational core.

# Chapter 4

# Making experience sing

When Freud (1908, 1910) addressed the question of artistic creation, he used a method that had yielded rich rewards in the investigation of dreams and neurotic symptoms. The method involved analysing the *content* of a psychic product in order to uncover its unconscious sources, and in this way he had shown, for example, that the *manifest content* of a dream was merely a pointer to the unconscious nexus of wishes (the dream's *latent content*) from which it had arisen, wishes that the dreamer was unable to acknowledge (Freud 1900).

Dream analysis came to occupy a special place in Freud's techniques – a 'royal road to the unconscious' – and the meaning of a dream was discovered by tracing its origin to latent wishes in the unconscious layers of the dreamer's mind. One consequence of this approach was to place the meaning of a dream outside the structure of the dream itself; its meaning did not lie in the dream's story line, but elsewhere, in a *hidden* area of thought and feeling that the dreamer could not access directly.

When he came to examine literary creations, Freud employed a similar approach and treated the writer's productions as variants of the dream. Although he was aware of the simplification, he treated the literary product as a kind of daydream. Putting to one side the conscious elaboration of the literary work, he showed that it too could provide access to unconscious ideas and impulses (Freud 1908). Indeed, he came to the view that a large part of the writer's skill lay in fashioning his daydreams (and ultimately his unconscious wishes) into literary forms that were not only acceptable to others, but could also be enjoyed by them.

The ramifications of this idea were considerable. First, the writer was seen as neurotically impaired – he preferred daydreams to reality. Second, he used his daydreams to obtain alternative satisfactions to those that eluded him in ordinary living. Third, the cultural acceptance of his literary productions, and the vicarious pleasure they gave to his readers, provided ratification of his infantile and repressed wishes. And finally, through the recognition that he got from his audience, he could make up, to some extent, for an earlier lack of success in love and social relationships. The view of the artist that emerges from this account is that of a somewhat pathetic character, gratifying his impulses in a hidden, neurotic way. It fails to do justice to the dedication and sense of vocation that artists so often possess, and equally ignores the high regard in which Freud himself held them.

When he turned his attention to painting and the plastic arts, Freud employed a similar approach. In his treatment of the Leonardo cartoon, for example (Freud 1910), he showed that analysis of certain details of the painting enabled inferences to be drawn about the unconscious fantasy of the artist. Such analyses suggested that paintings too could be treated like other psychic productions, and used to throw light on what had been repressed in the emotional life of the artist.

To summarize Freud's approach in such a schematic way does less than justice to his serious and painstaking investigations of creative activity. Nevertheless, it is fair to say that his method failed to meet the challenge posed by the work of art. However much it gave insights into the life and psychopathology of the artist, its achievement in relation to *aesthetics* was limited. While it showed that works of art *could* be made to provide access to the unconscious psychic life of the artist, it failed to illuminate the special nature of the art object. It failed to address why one artefact should be considered a work of art and another not, just as it could not differentiate between significant works of art and those that failed to make it into the cultural arena.

Freud's approach to art was in many ways contradictory, for while he wrote of art as nothing more than the culturally approved expression of forbidden wishes, he himself held the artist in high regard, and often quoted writers and poets as though they were seers with special insight into the human condition. In a similar way, his understanding of how people reacted to works of art failed to take account of his own response, which was one of admiration and awe. It is hardly convincing to explain such feelings in terms of vicarious wish fulfilment.

Recent psychoanalytic theory has taken up such contradictions and I want to mention particularly the work of Hannah Segal, who from a Kleinian perspective has elaborated her understanding of creativity in a collection entitled *Dream, Phantasy, Art* (Segal 1991). Segal's writing is persuasive; it successfully captures the seriousness of the artistic enterprise, and connects with aesthetic concerns in a way that Freud's failed to do. The success of her approach stems from her adoption of a relational focus. Putting on one side a concern with the isolated details of the work of art, and what these might 'mean' in an unconscious sense, it emphasizes the relation of elements to one another within the work as a whole.[1] It is central

---

1 This has always been a major concern of aesthetics.

to Segal's thinking that artistic creation involves psychological work at emotional depth and a working through that eventuates in complex syntheses of previously scattered and fragmented elements. For Segal, what characterizes those objects ranked as art is precisely the creation or re-creation of *whole* objects – a unification of previously separated elements.

This relational view of creativity enables links to be made with the more formal characteristics of works of art that have been the preoccupation of writers on aesthetics. Form, in this aesthetic sense, is a function of how elements in an art object are disposed in relation to one another. It concerns, for example, the shape or contour of a musical sequence, the grouping and relation of masses within a sculpture, the affinity or clash between blocks of colour in a painting. Form is a relational concept, concerned with wholes that are greater than the sum of their parts.

It is thus hardly surprising that new insights about art came from a mode of psychoanalytic theorizing that emphasized object relations. Although object relations theory is still concerned with drives and impulses, it is more dynamically interactive than earlier theories, and always highlights the relational aspects of intra-psychic phenomena. Thus Kleinian theory gives importance to the capacity to relate to whole, rather than part objects – something closely analogous to the appreciation of form in art, where the aesthetic act involves relating to the entirety of a complex object rather than to its isolated elements.

I shall give just one example of Segal's approach – her understanding of the concept of *significant form*[2] (Segal 1991: 78–9). An important idea in aesthetics since its introduction by Clive Bell (1914), this concept sought to capture what it was in a work of art that aroused *aesthetic*, as opposed to more associative, contingent emotions. It was not, Bell said, our *personal* reactions to a work of art that mattered, but particular combinations of shapes and colours that transcended these personal concerns. It was not the specific *content* of a painting, but a more formal quality that gave rise to the aesthetic response. Bell was primarily concerned with painting, but a later writer, Roger Fry (1924), suggested that Bell's approach had relevance for the whole range of artistic media.

*Significant form* is a concept that transcends the specific content of a work of art, and because it concerns the relations between objects, it may, in principle, be perceived within any arrangement of them. It is not, however, the arrangement *per se* that is important, but what the viewer recognizes in the arrangement as an *inevitable sequence*. The term 'inevitable sequence' was Fry's attempt to capture the quality of arrangement that gave rise to aesthetic pleasure. Aesthetic pleasure, he said, was our response to the apprehension of 'significant form' and arose from the recognition of

2 I discuss the concept of 'significant form' in greater detail in chapter 9.

'inevitable sequences' in the art object. This phrase successfully conjures up the 'rightness' of an aesthetic arrangement, the sense of the elements within a work of art *having to be* the way they are: as though they were felt to match some pre-existing pattern that only now came to be realized. To say this is to go beyond Bell and Fry, but I think such notions are implicit in their language, and make a bridge to Segal's work on aesthetics.

Segal understands the concept of *significant form* in Kleinian terms, but much of what she writes transcends this framework. In her view, artistic creation is inextricably linked with the capacity to symbolize. Art involves representation – not necessarily the representation of the external world, but of inner experience. In this view, she is close to Susanne Langer (1942, 1953), who argued that all art is symbolic – a representation of 'the forms of human feeling'. For Segal, as for Langer, the 'rightness' of a representation, its inevitability, stems from the sense of concordance between a felt inner structure and an external form that successfully captures its 'shape'. It is thus the 'truth' of a representation that arouses the feeling of inevitability.

Segal now presses these insights into a Kleinian mould. Building on the idea that a symbol is constituted on the absence or loss of the object, she argues that the object represented in the creative process is always an object that has been destroyed by the subject's own attacks (i.e. it is missing because destroyed). The creative act is invariably driven by guilt or concern, an attempt to make reparation to the object by restoring it within the mind, and rebuilding it from its scattered and damaged fragments.

In my view, Segal's insistence on reparation makes for unnecessary conceptual constraint and I want to consider an alternative way of thinking about creativity. I shall base my argument on Winnicott (1953), who proposed that creativity first develops within the matrix of mother–infant relatedness, at a time before the mother can be experienced as a fully separate object, and thus at a time before destruction and reparation can have any meaning.

## Preverbal symbols and primary creativity

The art object is never a straight replication of the actual object but a representation of it. It is an imaginative re-creation of the object, an object transformed by subjectivity. The matter could be stated thus: First, object; then passage through subject; finally a transformed object, which partakes of both object and subject. To give an example: Cézanne talked as though he struggled to create an exact replica of the world, but in fact gave us a unique subjective vision of it. When, for example, I look at his paintings, I clearly recognize the Mont St Victoire, but I see it through the prism of Cézanne's imagination – it has become Cézanne's mountain, the world according to Cézanne. We recognize the objective landscape, but we value its subjective transformation. In this sense, landscape painting is a land-scape of the heart as much as a landscape of the world.

Merleau-Ponty (1964a) talked of the artist's subjective transformation of the world as the 'germination of style' at the surface of his painting. It was, he thought, like the poet's 'voice' or the composer's musical idiom. Perhaps it is similar to what Bollas (1989) has called the idiom of the self, that highly personal translation, through objects, and within the medium of the world, of the individual's unique spontaneous gesture. Whatever one calls this phenomenon, it involves an amalgam of subjective and objective – a transformation of the objective medium by the subjective gesture of the individual or artist.

Such melding of subjective and objective was a key element in the thought of Donald Winnicott (see chapter 3). He regarded it as a feature of early symbols and spoke of it in many different ways – as a moment of *primary creativity*, a realm of *illusion*, and the place of *subjective or transitional objects* (Winnicott 1953). His focus was not on *reparation* – what he called the *stage of concern* (Winnicott 1963) – but on a much earlier phase of the infant's experience in which omnipotence still holds sway. I want to explore this phase through his concept of *primary creativity* (Winnicott 1953).

Winnicott asks us to imagine two different scenarios of a hungry baby. In each, the state of need arouses a sensory image of the breast in the baby's mind – in other words, the baby 'hallucinates' the breast. Against this background we have scenario one. The attuned mother knows that her baby is hungry and, intuitively, how the baby likes things to go. She has imagined the whole situation and tries to realize it with her actual baby. As a result of her imaginative work, the baby experiences a realization of its own 'hallucination'. Everything arrives in just the right way. There is a sense of 'rightness' or 'fit' for the baby between anticipation and realization, and the feed goes well.

In scenario two, the mother is less in tune with her baby. Perhaps she has less confidence in herself, or finds it difficult to put herself accurately in the baby's place. She cannot imagine what she needs to do and her actions are less responsive to the baby's changing state and thus more mechanical.[3] So perhaps when the baby gets hold of the nipple, the mother fidgets and the nipple falls out. The baby tries again but the mother is anxious and tries too hard to help the baby. So instead of things getting better, mother and baby get into a vicious circle of things not working out, not being adapted, not fitting properly together. All the ingredients are there for a feeding problem.

3 The imaginative effort required from the mother is not a one off, in advance envisagement. She has to be receptive to changing cues, constantly revising her picture of what is going on. Her identification with the baby is always ongoing and always changing.

Out of such recognizable scenarios, Winnicott constructs an important piece of theory. In the second scenario, in which the mother is unable to hold her baby accurately in mind, he suggests that the breast presents itself to the baby as an alien object. It is foreign to the baby's experience, and the baby is likely to reject it. He calls the object that arrives in this way an *impinging object* – it impinges on the baby's experience. By contrast, where mother and baby fit together, the baby has a different kind of experience: what she provides coincides with what the baby expects or hallucinates – there is good enough 'fit' between the two. Winnicott suggests that when the imagined experience coincides with what the mother actually provides, *the baby feels he has created the breast*. He suggests that this enhances the infant's feeling of (omnipotent) agency so the baby can feel: 'I have created the world' or perhaps, 'The world is a responsive place (medium) that I can transform into what I have imagined' (see below and chapter 3 for further discussion of this idea).

Clearly the baby does not actually think in this way – the experience precedes thought – but Winnicott suggests that events of this kind underpin later creativity. This would include both the capacity for play (transforming things into anything we want), and the capacity to create, in the narrower sense of moulding a medium in order to realize imaginative forms. Both kinds of creativity are made possible by the mother's adaptation and in Winnicott's view, whenever we fashion a world infused with our own subjectivity – whenever, in his terms, we make for ourselves a subjective object – we provide for ourselves what the mother originally provided for us.

Winnicott's focus is on the experience of 'fit', the recognition that something in the environment 'fits' and realizes a vital 'something' in our own experience. Like Segal's theory, it is relational and object-relational, but the emphasis is different. Segal's creativity is driven by guilt and reparative impulses; Winnicott's is concerned with maternal nurturance, the created form (symbol or pre-symbol) fitting and answering an inner need. Segal's creativity reconstructs the destroyed *object* (ultimately the maternal object); Winnicott's helps to establish the integrity of the *self*. Finally, if Segal's creativity looks after and restores the object, Winnicott's more directly looks after the self.

Winnicott's theories move in a broad sweep, from the first scenario of infant at breast, through the realm of transitional objects and phenomena, to the realm of adult creative living that includes the world of artistic creation in its narrower sense (Winnicott 1967b). In each case, creation lies in *subjective transformation:* the finding or making of a needed pattern in a new object. If we now think of this pattern as an 'inevitable sequence' – it had to be this way and no other – we could say that the infant's discovery of maternal patterns in the transitional object is the first aesthetic experience (see pp. 57-8). Winnicott does not make such links, nor does he stress the contribution made by the blanket to the process (its sensory qualities of softness, warmth and smell), but clearly the baby can only use the blanket in this way (i.e. creatively) because it *offers*, like the early mother, the sensory patterns that are needed.

If the bit of blanket is thus a *medium* for the baby that allows itself to be used as a source of needed patterns, it is possible to discern the beginning of a series: first the mother offering herself and her body, then the blanket offering its warmth and textures. Moving on to later creative acts, including the creation of works of art, the model I have elaborated continues to have relevance. It suggests first, that creativity is based on lack, and second, that it involves a search for the pattern of that which is missing. Finally, it involves the discovery (or rendering of) the missing experience/pattern within a new medium or form and the gap is temporarily bridged.

The chosen medium, worked on by the artist, can be seen in this light; it yields the patterns for which the artist is searching and partially reinstates the missing experience. In this sense it occupies the place of the adaptive mother who first provided what the infant lacked and carries within it a memory of maternal recognition.

## Maternal mirroring and facial expression

When Winnicott (1953) first discussed transitional phenomena, it was the breast and bit of blanket that occupied his attention. Here, the mother's empathic responses are implicit, both in the way she feeds her baby and in the baby's creation which commemorates this moment. Later in Winnicott's life, the focal point of his theory changes and his interest shifts to the more social domain of mother and baby interacting – the conversation of smiles and gestures, the mother's face reflecting the mood she sees in her baby, and the baby's lively gestures evoking responses from her (Winnicott 1967a/1971).

In his new way of thinking, the central metaphor is the mother's face as the infant's first mirror. Whereas previously, the mother's responsiveness lay in the way she gave her body, it is now manifested in her facial expressions which 'reflect back what is there to be seen' (ibid.: 117). Attention is focused on preverbal communication, in which the *sensory semblance* of infant experience (its visible 'reflection') is found in the mirror of her face.

Winnicott now thinks of his work in terms of this metaphor – the analyst's words are an attenuated form of the mother's facial mirroring: 'I like to think of my work this way [as a giving back of emotional semblances] and to think that if I do (it) well enough the patient will find his or her own self, and will be able to exist and to feel real' (ibid.: 117). He goes on to say that 'feeling real is more than existing' (ibid.: 117) and clearly believes it is the resonating forms that the mother (or therapist) gives back – almost certainly impaired when there is maternal (or therapist) depression

– that transform existence into living. 'I am seen, so I exist' (ibid.: 114), he says, but this is a special kind of being seen (in the mirror of the mother/ analyst's sensibility) which creates a sense of being alive and real.

Winnicott was aware of Lacan's work on the mirror stage (Lacan 1949), but realized that his own ideas were different. In Lacan's account, the baby feels joy (*jouissance*) about his reflection in the mirror, because it represents an external visual perfection that is beyond his motor grasp. For Winnicott, the baby's '*jouissance*' comes from the aliveness and accuracy of the mother's emotional reflection. There, however, the similarity ends. Whereas for Lacan, the mirror experience is the start of an alienation from oneself that is part of the human condition, for Winnicott, the experience is foundational, underpinning the sense of self and protecting against the fragmentation to which the self is vulnerable. The image in Lacan's mirror may be intriguing and exciting, but only the mother's emotional resonance can hold the self and make experience sing.

## The song of creation

It is central to Winnicott's theory of development that the self has only latent or potential existence until subjectively realized within the responses of another person. Only when self-experience is reflected does the baby/ adult feel fully alive. His understanding of creativity is bound up with this view: only a subject who is alive in this way can be creative, but equally, being creative enhances the feeling of being alive.[4] It is thus implicit that adult creativity involves something analogous to early maternal mirroring, as though the creative person, in the act of creation, performs for himself the activities which the adaptive mother once provided.

Winnicott's theory of mirroring pays attention to a limited repertoire of maternal behaviour (the mother's facial expressions) and in the following section I draw on the observations of empirical infant research to show that maternal responses to infant feeling states are not restricted to such expressiveness. First, however, I want to illustrate the creative coming to life of the self in two ways: first, by quoting from an Aboriginal creation myth; and second, by discussing the work of a poet who was himself deeply concerned with understanding the creative process, and who used it as a means of holding on to a precarious sense of his own existence.

---

4 This idea may seem paradoxical but I think the sense is as follows: only a person who can *anticipate* a responsive medium can be creative – in other words, a person who has experienced such a responsive medium/mother in infancy. But equally, it is only through repeating the act of creation – in everyday life as well as in larger creative acts – that we hold on to the sense of being alive and creative. Being creative is a way of living, a way of looking after the wellbeing of the self.

My first illustration draws on Bruce Chatwin's book about the Australian Aborigines (Chatwin 1987). In the Aboriginal creation story, the Ancestors were old men who lived in a state of suspended animation in the crust of the earth, along with all the other beings that were waiting to be created. 'All the forms of life lay sleeping . . . dormant seeds in the desert that must wait for a wandering shower.' Then the Sun warmed the Ancestors and they slowly came to life. (Each Ancestor was related in a fundamental way to a particular life-form of the natural world.) As he came to life each Ancestor 'felt his body giving birth to children' who would later become the forms of the living world. The Snake Man gave birth to snakes, the Witchetty Grub Man to witchetty grubs, the Cockatoo Man to cockatoos, and so on. Each living thing was born in this way and 'reached up for the light of day'.

All this took place in a twilight zone, with the Ancestors themselves still submerged in the mud. But then the Ancestors cast off the mud that was holding them, and with delight they each saw their children. Each Ancestor called out the name of the creature to which he had given birth, and this calling out – what Chatwin calls 'a primordial act of naming' – was in itself a completion of the act of creation. Every living thing that was part of the natural world received a name in this way. The Ancestors named everything, 'calling all things into being and weaving their names into verses. The Ancients sang their way all over the world . . . (and) wherever their tracks led they left a trail of music. They wrapped the whole world in a web of song' (ibid.: 80–2).

This story beautifully expresses the idea of singing (naming, reflecting) the world into life. *Something* is there, in a state of dormant pre-existence, there, but not yet alive – latent, potential. Only when it is named and sung – only when reflected in the song of the Ancestors (or in the mother's face, the analyst's words) – only then does it spring to life. Winnicott, who saw his work 'as a complex derivative of the face that reflects what is there to be seen' (ibid.: 117), would have understood this story; so too might the poet Seamus Heaney, who said in a television interview (1994) at the time of his Nobel Literature Prize: 'An echo coming back to you – that's what writing a poem is like!'

## Praising the world

Heaney's metaphor offers another glimpse of the importance to the self of being reflected back by something 'out there'. It also provides a bridge to the work of another poet, who even as he struggled to maintain a sense of his own existence, believed that the poet's task was to 'praise the world', and in so doing, to infuse it with life and being. In the *Duino Elegies*, a series of poems written over a ten year period, the Austrian poet, Rainer

Maria Rilke, gave form to a quasi-philosophical understanding of the meaning of life and the part that poetic creation held in it.

> Yes, the Springs had need of you. Many a star
> was waiting for you to perceive it. Many a wave
> would rise in the past towards you; or else, perhaps,
> as you went by an open window, a violin
> would be utterly giving itself. All this was commission.
> But were you equal to it?
>
> (Rilke 1960: 225)

As I read it, the 'commission' Rilke describes lies in the necessity he feels to sing the world into existence – to reflect it, echo it, and make it live. Like a baby, the world is dumb and has no words. But for the poet, it dances when he sings it . . .

> Are we, perhaps, *here* just for saying: House,
> Bridge, Fountain, Gate, Jug, Fruit tree, Window, –
> Possibly: Pillar, Tower? . . . but for *saying*, remember,
> oh, for such saying as never the things themselves
> hoped so intensely to be.
>
> (ibid.: 244)

This passage from the Ninth Elegy is evocative and deeply moving, but how are we to understand the *saying* or *singing* that brings the world and experience into existence? I think Rilke is telling us that whatever medium the artist chooses to work in, whether singing, saying, dancing, painting or sculpting – each of these activities in their own way *create* the artist's experience. For the artist, as for the baby, experience is latent until it finds a form.

> Yes, the springs had need of you. Many a star
> was waiting for you to perceive it.
>
> (ibid.: 225)

He sees the artist responding, out of a kind of love, to what he takes to be the mute need of Earth:

> Earth, is it not this that you want:
> to arise invisibly in us?

And he goes on:

> These things that live on departure
> understand when you praise them: fleeting, they look for
> rescue through something in us, the most fleeting of all.
> Want us to change them entirely, within our invisible hearts,
> into – oh, endlessly – into ourselves! Whosoever we are.
>
> (ibid.: 245)

Rilke, the poet, does not need another of Earth's spring times to win him over – to make him sing its praises, and transform it into a different level of existence within the new and communicable realm of the artist's feelings, for he cries out, as though in ecstasy: 'Earth, you darling, I will!' (ibid.: 245).

These passages give powerful expression to the idea that the poet, and perhaps every artist, is engaged in 'singing' or 'praising' the world in order to bring it to life. He sets about this task by finding forms which, in Winnicott's words, 'reflect what is there to be seen'. But for Rilke this is no passive reflection or saying. It is 'such saying as never the things themselves hoped so intensely to be' (ibid.: 244), a passionate 'saying' that creates a sensory semblance, a living form (symbol) of the thing or experience itself, including the way the world has come alive in the artist's feelings. It is the task of the artist to give back to the world this living semblance, and in so doing, to give it a dimension of life it lacked before. It is thus that the poet or artist sings the world into existence, and as the Aboriginal story puts it, 'wraps the whole world in a web of song'.

## Creating the self

There is circularity in this creative 'singing' or 'saying', an intense dialogue with the world that results in each party (world and self) becoming more alive. As the world is transformed (or so it seems) by the creative utterance ('into – oh, endlessly – into ourselves'), so the artist himself is transformed by the world – through his own visionary seeing and praising of it (i.e. discovering himself within its 'offered' forms).[5] As Susanne Langer (1953) says in her book *Feeling and Form*, the artist creates (out of his medium) forms for human feeling. It is as though the artist said to the world: 'I have felt you, world – the rhythm and pulse of your life – and am singing it, and giving back to you the way you live in me!' We can thus begin to understand how the artist finds his own life and voice in the very moment when he gives life and voice to the mute world. Even as he praises the world, he gives voice (form) to his own feeling self that he sees reflected in the forms

---

5 In the terms of my argument, the poet uses the natural world as a (responsive) medium and, perhaps like a landscape painter, discovers within its forms the forms of his own feeling.

of the world. In his passionate engagement with his medium, he subjectively transforms the object (the object of his poetic 'praise'); in Winnicott's words, he creates a *subjective object*.

This ability of the artist to sing the song of himself – simultaneously the song of the world – lies at the heart of his creativity. In the process of creating the work of art, the objective medium is actively transformed until it becomes expressive of the artist's inner being; he works on it until it yields the resonating forms of his subjective life, and *sings his inner song*. If the mother or Ancestor sang the original song that created self or world, the artist must now sing this song for himself because his life, or sense of liveliness, depends upon it.

There is, of course, a paradox in what I am saying. On the one hand, the artist sings the world into existence; he places himself at the service of the world because he loves the world so much. On the other hand, he ruthlessly forces the world, or that part of it which is his chosen medium, to respond to him in the resonating way he wants. The medium (mother) exists to be at his service; but the artist, which means all of us at one time or another, will not give up until he has forced or coaxed the paint, the musical score, the piece of stone, the words on the bit of paper or the word processing screen, to sing to him his own song. In Walt Whitman's terms, the object must be transformed until it sings the *Song of Myself*.[6]

## The mother's song – attunement

I shall now consider another kind of 'singing' in which the mother's response can be seen as life enhancing. In moving back and forth between the activity of the artist and the early activity of the mother in relation to her baby, I hope to clarify the links that may exist between these two fields.

In speaking of the mother's responsiveness, I have thus far confined myself to Winnicott's formulations: first concerning the adaptive mother who gives to the baby the searched for bodily response; second, concerning the more communicative response mediated by the mother's facial mirroring. However, although both responses are important for the infant, they do not take account of the full variety of behavioural means through which a mother may communicate and 'sing' her baby. The findings of empirical infant research suggest other ways, and I draw attention to one particular idea, maternal attunement, which has been developed by Daniel Stern (Stern 1985: 138–61). I have already discussed this mode of mother–infant relating in chapter 1.

Observational studies have shown that mothers not only respond to their infants' major emotions (sometimes called the *categorical affects*); they also respond, in a moment by moment way, to the smaller changes of excitement

6 Walt Whitman (1881): *Leaves of Grass*.

and arousal that accompany everything the baby does (called by Stern the *vitality affects*). The mother tracks these smaller changes as we track a tennis player during an exciting game – she 'reads' her baby by every possible non-verbal means, and intuitively senses the changing pattern of his feeling state: the contours of arousal, the rhythms of excitement, the urgent strivings and triumphant satisfactions. She follows him with a close, yet barely conscious attention that teaches her the changing pattern of his experience. Stern gives the name *attunement* to this tracking process – attunement to the infant's vitality affects.

In the normal situation, the mother does not merely register the infant's state in an ongoing way; she engages in responsive displays of her own, which in one sensory modality or another reflect the patterns and rhythms of the baby's vitality affects. If, for example, the baby is reaching for a toy, the mother may make a series of movements or sounds that reflect, or resonate to, the baby's changing pattern of excitement. It is as though she plays back to the baby what she has just experienced in her identification with him. Often her response exaggerates the baby's pattern, making it more apparent; or it may be cast in another sensory mode than the baby's display, giving it a difference as well as a similarity. It is this combination of similarity *and* difference – the *transformation* of the baby's pattern – which prompts Stern to describe attunement as 'the recasting, the restatement of an affective state' (ibid.: 161). This mini-enactment or portrayal of the baby's state not only gives back to the baby what the baby has just revealed; equally, it gives back something of the mother's uniquely personal stamp. Her response is like an echo, albeit an echo creatively changed by its passage through her own sensibility.

The link between this and artistic creativity is inescapable – in searching, as he believes, for the essence of the object, the artist finds in the object a reflection of himself. The object becomes his attuning 'other', and in the process both object and self are transformed. Something similar occurs in writing a poem, painting a canvas or composing a symphony – the object that takes form is increasingly a reflection of the artist's self.

In analysis and psychotherapy there is room for a similar process, so that when the patient turns to the analyst, he may discover himself in the analyst's reflecting forms. This will only occur, however, in so far as the analyst perceives his goal in a particular way that privileges the mirroring process. This was a stance that Winnicott increasingly adopted towards the end of his life and expressed in an eloquent way: 'Psychotherapy is not making clever and apt interpretations; by and large it is a long term giving back to the patient what the patient brings. It is a complex derivative of the face that reflects what is there to be seen' (Winnicott 1967a/1971: 117). Only when the analyst is able to become a responsive medium in this way will the patient be able to discover himself in the forms created by the analytic encounter (see chapters 7 and 9).

## Artistic creativity and attunement

Attunement is a key concept in understanding creativity for several reasons: first, it enlarges our conception of what it means to get something back in a transformed and enlivening way; second, it clearly reveals the structure of such an interaction; third, it offers a glimpse of how such an interaction might strengthen the foundations of the self and enhance the sense of personal vitality; and fourth, it offers a model for later kinds of interaction with a similar function, not least the process of artistic creation.

Winnicott understood, however, that creativity was a way of living; it was not simply the province of artists and poets but potentially within reach of all. Although not expressing it in this way, he saw the world itself as a kind of medium that a person approached with an attitude shaped by past experience. When there has been sufficient early experience of an adaptive environment, the adult will be able to approach the world in a creative way; he will be able to expect an adaptive (helpful) response from it, and believe in the possibility of transforming it. When the environment has been impinging, however, the adult will not be able to find within himself a creative attitude. The world will then present as obstacle and resistance, with little potential for creative transformation.

In artistic creation the transformative attitude is seen in its clearest form, and Stern's work extends Winnicott's understanding of it. From this perspective, the fundamental project of art lies in the discovery or making of resonant forms that echo the artist's deepest feelings. Clearly, the roots of such a project are developmentally earlier, and in that sense more basic, than the impulse towards reparation that underpins the Klein/Segal theory of art. The need to find forms that hold and reflect the self is an existential one that must surely precede any question of the self's guilt.

I would go further and argue that the search for holding forms is as basic as the need for bodily satisfaction; the need for the mother's responding face is as powerful as the need for her breast and milk. The search for such forms is rooted in the early relationship with the mother – the dialogue with her face and breast – and continues with increasing complexity through the more social, yet still preverbal experiences of attunement.

Winnicott (1967b) claimed that the earliest transitional phenomena looked back towards the adaptive breast/mother and forwards to later cultural creations, arguing a continuity between earlier and later phenomena. Stern's work suggests that a wider group of maternal responses could be inserted into this path, with the mother's attuned enactments, for example, providing fertile ground for later cultural forms. The transitional object gives to the baby some independence from the actual mother, enabling him to create for himself a sense of her presence and responsiveness during her absence. Artistic creation may fulfil a comparable function for the artist, and indirectly for the audience, by enabling him to look after himself through the aesthetic forms he creates. These provide the 'inevitable sequences' that satisfy his search for life-enhancing recognition, and resonate with his inner being.

## Creativity and maternal deficit

If the artist dedicates his life to the creation of emotionally resonant forms, what is it that leads him to pursue this goal, and often in such a driven way? Is it, as Freud said, that he hopes to achieve the love and recognition he has failed to achieve by ordinary means? Or is it, as Segal suggests, that his destructiveness towards his objects is so great that he has to work ceaselessly to repair them?

By placing the impetus for creativity within the preverbal layers of the mind, it is clear that I do not regard either of these as the case. Is it then that the artist's work is a celebration of the mother of infancy, who attended so closely to his emotional needs? Or is it somehow the reverse of this: that the artist is someone who knows what he wants – has had a taste of attuning experience, but not enough – and now feels that his life depends on creating it for himself? Is he, in short, someone who has suffered a relative deficiency in mirroring and attunement – perhaps a disruptive loss of the mother's responsiveness – which has made him feel that security lies in becoming his own attuning 'other'?

The example of Rilke, whose evocations of the poet's task I have already quoted, may suggest answers to these alternatives. Rilke is a lyrical and sometimes ecstatic poet, whose love of the world, and his need to praise it, knew no bounds. If ever a poet *sang* the world, it was surely Rilke. Yet Rilke had an appallingly unhappy and lonely childhood. His mother was narcissistic and thoroughly self-involved. She had wanted a girl, and for the first few years of his life had virtually brought him up as one. She had curled his hair, dressed him in little girls' clothes, and no doubt discouraged all expression of his masculinity. Even his name, Maria, was a girl's name (Britton 1998). In Winnicott's terms, we could say that Rilke's mother was radically *impinging*, in Stern's terms, unable to attune. To treat him as she did, she must have been impervious to the little boy's experience, caring only about the fulfilment of her own fantasies through him. The small child must have felt in continual doubt about his own reality (something which persisted throughout his life), and there must have been a serious shortfall of containing forms in his mother's responses to him.

Given such disconfirming experience, many children would have given up and died emotionally. But Rilke succeeded in keeping himself alive and discovered in himself a means of creating and finding the forms that he needed. His poetic calling can be seen as recognition that this was his most important task: to create and re-create the responsive mother he had lacked. When, as in the *Duino Elegies*, he sees his task as redeeming the world through singing or praising it, we can see him as trying to be the mother he never had. And when he writes about the mute Earth that is waiting to be recognized, we can see his own mute self, waiting upon the life-giving response of the poet-mother, whom he never ceases striving to become.

This brief outline of Rilke's childhood supports the idea that, at least sometimes, the artist's life struggle is to draw his object/medium (the recalcitrant mother) into an expressive and responsive state. From this perspective, the artist's life problem is not that the object has been damaged or destroyed by his own aggression and needs to be repaired (Klein/Segal), but rather that he struggles with a deficit brought about by maternal failure and lack of maternal response (Winnicott). In this sense, his creative work aims to restore the object's capacity to respond, even to create a responsive object for the first time. Rilke's quest – and perhaps that of every artist – is for a medium that *will* respond, that *cannot* now escape his shaping influence, and that *can* be persuaded (or forced) to yield the expression that is needed. In short, he attempts to create a responsive medium that is now under his own control. As Winnicott understood, it is here that the ruthlessness of the artist comes into play, and the use of omnipotence to *make* the world be what the self desires. In the course of realizing this project, the artist's self is at least partially restored and given life, though the task is never completed. The artist is always poised on the edge of a no-mother (unresponsive mother) space – hence the compulsion to go on creating.

## Conclusion

My aim in this chapter has been to develop a Winnicottian approach to art that differs significantly both from Freud's early essays in the field, and from the more recent Kleinian approach of Segal. Freud's theoretical equipment was too deeply rooted in instinct theory to do justice to the relational aspects of the work of art, while Segal's view paid too little attention to the power and influence of the actual environment in shaping the course of development, and subsequent life of the individual.

I have attempted to build on Winnicott's interest in creativity and its roots in the early mother–infant relationship in order to develop a theory of artistic creativity. In particular, I have used his notion of *primary creativity* which can only be understood in terms of specific kinds of interaction with the mother. I have already noted that Winnicott's ideas evolved significantly, and in his later work included a more social and communicational frame of reference (Winnicott 1967a). This was a major change in his thinking about early development and, although the intra-psychic remains important, he now sees it as shaped and engraved by preverbal communicational events, and complemented by a third area of meaning that lies between the individual and the object.

This new way of thinking allows bridges to be made between his work and the field of empirical infant research – it is here that Stern (1985) has been important to my own understanding. Stern too is concerned with interactive events between mother and infant, and his concept of attunement fills a gap in Winnicott's thinking. It addresses what happens after the period of transitional activity, when the baby is beginning to separate more completely from the mother, the period of Mahler's *separation-individuation* (Mahler *et al.* 1975). This is a time when keeping in touch with the mother acquires a new dimension, such contact having to be maintained across actual space. Facial mirroring goes some way to bridging this gap, but the notion of attunement allows for a more diverse kind of connectedness that covers the whole range of sensory modalities, and is better able to span the increasing physical distance.

It is possible to see attunement as providing the beginnings of a preverbal 'language'[7] between mother and infant ensuring that the infant can still feel at one with the mother during separation. It is a versatile 'language' that passes freely from one sensory channel to another, while being highly supportive and containing of infant experience. It seems well adapted, not only to alleviating the sense of separateness, but also to bridging the passage into language proper. In this regard, Stern stresses that attunement is at its height towards the end of the preverbal period.

It is the notion of a preverbal 'language' supportive of the self that lends itself to a new way of thinking about artistic creativity. Langer (1942, 1953) argues that artistic creation also makes use of non-verbal 'languages' which span a range of sensory modalities and, like attunement, operate with iconic symbols.[8] For Langer, such symbols are not so much symbols in the psychoanalytic sense, of referring to, or embodying, specific unconscious fantasies, as iconic representations that give form to human feeling. This highly suggestive though general formulation points to the shapes, rhythms and textures of human experience rather than to its context-bound details. It is, of course, to just such shapes and rhythms that attunement also refers.

7  The term 'language' in this context is impressionistic rather than correct, for strictly speaking, preverbal and non-verbal forms can never constitute a language in the same manner as words. This is because the meaning of a non-verbal symbol is always personal to the individual – there is no agreed one to one correspondence between form and meaning as there is with words. They do have a different capacity, however – namely to make emotional bridges and create a sense of sharing and close connection. This stems from their capacity to embody in their forms the forms of lived experience and thus to connect with similar shapes and forms in the other person. The non-verbal symbol is the form through which deep calls unto deep (chapter 3).

8  It is probably misrepresenting Langer to use the term 'language' in this context, as she explicitly states that the symbols of art can never create a language in the same way as words. However, the term does make sense as a metaphorical extension that is useful in the present context.

Whether or not this new way of thinking will illuminate the artist's choice of medium remains to be seen and I have not addressed the issue in this chapter. But if the matching of patterns between mother and infant is indeed important in laying the foundations of a secure self, it is probable that the preverbal attunement 'language' that develops between a particular mother and baby will significantly influence that baby's later preferences in the area of reflective self-realization.

Responsive dialogue involves a matching resonance of form and experience. It underpins the development of the self and the core sense of 'aliveness'; it also, I suggest, underpins the work of the creative artist. In this view, the core of creativity lies in the ability to make (or find) forms that fit experience – the artist is someone who has developed this capacity to an extraordinary degree. I have proposed that the artist engages in this activity because he must – as a means of survival in the face of a mother poorly attuned, emotionally absent, or erratic to the point of trauma. The artist may believe he is singing the *world* into existence, as did Rilke, but more cogently, he is singing *to himself* the needed maternal song, and breathing *himself* from existence into life.

# Chapter 5

# Bion and beyond

## Projective identification

For many analysts the concept of projective identification has become a pivotal reference point in their work, for like the older term counter-transference with which it overlaps, it addresses the analyst's often confusing clinical experience. To those who have embraced it, it probably represents the most important advance in theory in the last sixty years. To those more sceptical about its explanatory value, it can seem like a Trojan horse that has taken over the analytic establishment. Its importance can be gauged by the number of publications devoted to it; it has been the subject of conferences (e.g. Sandler 1988) and reviews (e.g. Ogden 1979, 1994).

Since its introduction by Melanie Klein (1946), the concept has been significantly modified and extended (Bion 1959b, 1962a, 1962b; Ogden 1979; Grotstein 1981; Joseph 1987; Rosenfeld 1971, 1987). In this regard, Bion was an important contributor because he transformed the concept from one which referred to a primitive psychic mechanism (something the infant 'did' to an 'other') into one that delineated an *interpersonal* process in which the recipient's role (as receiver of the projections) was critically important. Also in part through Bion's work, the process came to be seen as a primitive form of communication between baby and mother, perhaps, indeed, the only one there was. This and other extensions of the term have tended to make it a portmanteau concept which embraces on the one hand the infant's primitive defence against intolerable distress, on the other, the foundation of normal infant–mother communication.

Where perhaps there is common ground between supporters and critics of the term is in the area of non-verbal emotional communication. This includes both the need to have an account of infant–mother communica-tion during the preverbal period, and the need to understand a non-verbal type of communication between patient and analyst in which some understanding of mental content is conveyed without the mediation of words. I shall touch on both issues in this chapter but my reference to previous work will be focused in the extreme. Rather than summarizing the literature (which has been attempted on many occasions), I will examine one key paper in some detail (Bion 1959b/1988), viewing it in counterpoint with a paper by Enid Balint (1963/1993) from the Independent tradition. Bion's paper included clinical material that led him towards new understanding of the original concept, and in discussing this, I hope to demonstrate a certain confusion of ideas that continues to dog the subject to the present day.

Although the concept of projective identification was introduced by Melanie Klein in 1946, it did not for some time acquire the currency it now possesses. Being embedded in the matrix of Kleinian theory, the term was probably uncongenial to analysts of other persuasions. Winnicott, for example, for whom the mother's contribution was crucial, seems never to have used the term, while the Balints, who also emphasized the importance of the actual mother, preferred a language of non-differentiation to one of projection and identification – e.g. Michael Balint's 'harmonious inter-penetrating mix-up' (Balint, M. 1968: 68). Not only did Independent Group theorists privilege the relationship with the actual mother; they gave the infant a more active capacity for communication than the Kleinians envisaged and this made it difficult to accept that everything was determined by primitive instinctual processes. Thus the entire body of Winnicott's theory rested on the premise of adaptive environmental provision, and while the Balints developed no such comprehensive accounts of early development, their writing is permeated with similar thinking.

## Feedback, mirroring and maternal reverie

In an important paper 'On being empty of oneself', Enid Balint focused on a clinical picture that would now be termed borderline or narcissistic disorder (Balint, E. 1963/1993). As the title suggests, she singled out a particular kind of disturbed experience, the origin of which she placed very early in development. She considered it to be linked, 'both in . . . nature and chronology, *to the importance for the child of communication with his mother*' (ibid.: 40, italics mine). She noted that 'much help in understanding the condition is provided by Kleinian ideas' to do with introjection and envy, but concludes that ultimately such ideas 'seem insufficient, since the patient described . . . was troubled more by the lack of a self than of objects good or bad inside herself' (ibid.: 41). Balint elaborated the view that for satisfactory development, something needs to take place between mother and infant that *precedes* the projective and introjective events discussed by Klein. If this 'something' does not occur, a failure in the sense of self will follow. In other words, Balint believed that if there is no sense of a containing self, there can equally be no sense of anything contained. There can be no primitive sense of 'me' and 'mine', no envy, nothing to project, and nothing to preserve inside. She considered that her patient Sarah existed in this pre-self state.

Reconstructing the patient's development, she noted that while on the surface things developed satisfactorily, 'there was apparently a vitally important area where *there was no reliable understanding between mother and daughter*' (ibid.: 50, italics mine). It seemed to her that the mother 'responded more to her own preconceived ideas' than to what her baby actually felt, and she linked this with Sarah's sense of never feeling recognized. [Perhaps], she wrote, 'Sarah's mother could not bear unhappiness or violence or fear in her child, did not respond to it, and tried to manipulate her so that everything wrong was either put right at once, or denied' (ibid.: 50). She developed this idea as follows:

> Sarah's mother was *impervious* to any communication which was different from the picture she had of her daughter [the concept of imperviousness is one that I shall discuss below.] . . . In consequence, Sarah could not understand her mother's communications and felt that her mother never saw her as she was. Neither found an echo in the other . . . [She refers to Winnicott's (1945) idea of mother and child 'living an experience together', and thinks of this] as the child finding an echo of herself coming from the mother; or as the mother accepting her child's as yet unorganized feelings and emotions and, by her reactions to them, enabling the child to organize them into a self. I propose to call this process a 'feed-back', which starts in the child and acts as a stimulus on the mother, who must accept it and recognize that something has happened. Her recognition results in a kind of integration, and this is then reflected, fed back, to the child . . . *This feed-back process presupposes an interaction between two active partners, which, I think, differentiates it from projection and introjection in which one of them is only a passive object.*
>
> (ibid.: 51, italics mine)

These ideas prefigure – and echo – the writings of two other theoreticians. On the one hand, they resonate with Winnicott's seminal paper of four years later: 'Mirror role of mother and family in child development' (Winnicott 1967a). On the other, they have marked resonance with Bion's earlier reformulation of projective identification (Bion 1959b, 1962a, 1962b), which saw the process in a more interactive way than Klein had envisaged.

Of these two convergences, I shall first consider Winnicott's *mirroring*. Although he did not use the word, Winnicott (1967a) proposed that the mother's face, with its rich variety of emotional responses, was a principal means through which the preverbal infant obtained emotional 'feedback' about himself. The mother's face is the child's first mirror, and what the infant sees in the mother's expression is related to what she perceives as the infant's 'experience'. Like Enid Balint, Winnicott saw this mirroring as essential to growth of the infant self, and without it, he thought, the infant would have little sense of existing at all.

Bion (1959b, 1962a, 1962b), on the other hand, took Klein's theory that the baby 'projected' something in phantasy *into* the mother – a one-way traffic – and transformed it into a two-way or circular transaction, in which the mother's contribution, her 'reverie', was vital. Perhaps influenced by the more relational stance of the Balints and Winnicott, Bion had begun to regard the process he was describing as an interactive form of *communication* between infant and mother, the maternal contribution being vitally important to the infant's emotional growth.

In this sense, the ideas of these three writers show remarkable convergence. One could say that certain ideas were in the air and each picked them up in a different way. It would be wrong, however, to suppose that each writer was saying the same thing in a different way. For while the two Independents, Winnicott and Balint, thought in a similar way, Bion, who was still a Kleinian in spite of his innovations, theorized within a different semantic space. I will consider this difference in greater detail.

## Projective identification and maternal failure

> Mrs Klein thought of projective identification as a phantasy in which bad parts of the self were split off from the rest of the self and, together with bad excrements, were projected into the mother or her breast to control or take possession of her in such a fashion that she was felt to *become* the bad self. Good parts of the self were projected too, she thought, leading to the enhancement of the ego and good object relations, providing the process was not carried to excess.
>
> (Spillius 1988: 81)

From Spillius' account, it is clear that in its original conception projective identification was driven by a sense of threat: that either the self would be overwhelmed by bad objects, or the integrity of good objects would be jeopardized if left in the subject's own keeping. This 'threat/defence' aspect of the concept is carried over into Bion's new formulation and it serves to differentiate it from the processes that Winnicott and Enid Balint had in mind. For them, the transactions that occurred between infant and mother (mirroring, feedback and recognition) were not part of a system of defence. They were not a function of aggression or envy and the infant was not being evacuative, hostile or destructive. On the contrary, they were relatively free from such negative impulses, and if responded to by the mother in a satisfactory way, led to positive developments. The mother's interventions not only relieved the infant's anxiety but bestowed a sense of enhanced aliveness. In short, they met a primary need for communication and (maternal) recognition considered essential for the growth of the self.

There are thus two contrasting accounts of early events between mother and infant and it would be possible to see Bion's enlargement of Klein's conception as offering a kind of synthesis. However, this is only superficially the case, for while in Bion's revised concept the maternal element neutralizes innate destructive potential, in the Independent view of Balint and Winnicott, it serves a primary need of the infant to feel connected with the mother. Their view looks back to a more relational tradition: it recalls Suttie's 'primary need for the mother' (Suttie 1935) and has affinity with Bowlby's concept of attachment (Bowlby 1969) which was being formulated at around the same time. It also prefigures the more experimental work of Trevarthen (1979) who wrote of the infant's need for 'companionship' with the primary carer. By contrast, Bion's account still has a foot in Klein's model in which the primary driving force is the infant's primitive aggression and the need to defend against this.

These differences are crucial and mark a fundamental divergence in the way infancy is conceived. In Bion's view the baby is a bundle of impulses seeking discharge and these threaten the potential cohesion of the self; in the Balint/Winnicott view the baby is object-seeking and attachment-seeking, with a primary need for relatedness to the mother and recognition by her. Within this perspective, the development of the infant depends on adequate fulfilment of this relational need by attuned and mirroring feedback.

As I shall discuss, Bion's model retains a basic conception of the infant in which communication with the mother takes place through projecting, even forcing, emotional experience into her through projective identification. Crucially, infant projection into the mother is *followed by* maternal identification with what is projected. The mother thus discovers what the baby is feeling by *finding herself feeling* in a particular way (cf. the way the analyst finds himself feeling some surprising affect and *then* 'realizes' it 'belongs' to the patient). In Winnicott's model, by contrast, the infant is seen as communicating through emotional *signs*, its affect being displayed in such a way that the attuned mother naturally 'reads' it. To be sure the infant may not 'intend' the mother to do this, yet the display is programmed in a way that seems to anticipate such maternal response. In the first case it could seem that the mother is 'absent minded' – she is not attending to the signs and the baby has to redouble its efforts to make her notice. In the second, the mother is right there searching for the signs, in a state that Winnicott (1956) called *primary maternal preoccupation*. In the first case, the mother does not seem to realize that her baby can communicate; in the second, she constantly scans the situation for communicative signs.

This raises the possibility that when infant (or patient) tries to *force* emotional experience into the mother (analyst), it is already a response to the mother/analyst's failure to 'read' the signs. If this were so, projection of something *into* the mother would not, as Bion argued, be the *primary* means through which the infant gained access to her attention and 'reverie' – the fundamental form of infant–mother communication the Kleinian school asserts – but *a consequence of breakdown in more basic modes of mother–infant relatedness*. Such breakdown would result from failure in attuned response on the part of the mother, though other factors, including impairments in the infant, could also be involved. I use the term 'attuned response' in a general sense to refer to any means through which the mother conveys to her infant that its message has been received and attended to. This often takes the form of appropriate action, though it could be conveyed in the way the mother handles her infant and responds to him. I make the assumption that a mother who can get close to her baby's experience through imaginative identification will respond to that baby in different ways from a mother who cannot make such an emotional leap.

## Maternal imperviousness

If we take this idea seriously, it suggests that attempts to force emotionally aroused parts of the self *into* the mother (projective identification) are an understandable response to maternal failure, rather than a primitive defence mechanism. They can be seen as acts of desperation in the face of *maternal imperviousness*, rather than a fundamental means of preserving endangered parts of the self. From this perspective, it would be as though the baby were saying to the mother: 'I've been "telling" you how I feel but you haven't listened! I will *make* you hear me and *force* you to understand what I'm going through!' There would thus be an *inverse* relation between the need for projective identification and the mother's capacity for attunement. Projective identification would attest to failure of maternal attunement, while the violence of the projective process would correlate with the degree of imperviousness encountered by the infant.

*Maternal imperviousness* is a concept that was current in the scientific literature of the 1960s. It derived from the study of schizophrenic families, and was part of a cluster of terms that included the idea of the *schizophrenogenic mother*. As far as I can ascertain, the term was first defined by Lee (1963),[1] and operationalized by Laing, Phillipson and Lee (1966). It

---

1 Lee (1963) wrote: 'For smooth, adequate interaction to occur, each party must register the other's point of view. . . . Typically the parent fails to register his child's view, while the child does not register that his view has not been (and perhaps cannot be) registered . . . Most often the parent appears to remain *impervious* to the child's view because he feels it is uncomplimentary to him, or because it does not fit his value system . . . The parent insists that the child does believe what the parent feels the child "should" believe . . . *The child feels as if he continuously runs into an invisible, solid glass wall*' (quoted in Watzlawick *et al.* 1968, italics mine).

was important in Enid Balint's paper from which I have already quoted, and Bion refers to something similar (see below) when he describes how he came to reframe the process of projective identification to include the idea of maternal responsiveness and reverie (Bion 1959b/1988). It may be significant that Bion too was working with psychotic and severely border-line patients at this time. It was through such work, and the evidence of maternal deficit in the experience of these patients, that he developed the now familiar idea of the mother as 'container' of the infant's projections. He proposed that a 'normal' mother can take in the infant's 'projections' and work on them in her 'reverie', so that the infant can take them back, or 're-introject' them, in a modified and more manageable form.

## Bion's clinical material

Bion's primary purpose in his 1959 paper was to illustrate the operation of projective identification in borderline psychotic patients and to illustrate how this was used by such patients to attack and destroy any process that made links between objects. This included not only the parental relation-ship and the internal couple but also any linking processes in the mind through which meaning was established. He wrote: 'I shall discuss phan-tasied attacks on the breast as the prototype of all attacks on objects that serve as a link and projective identification as the mechanism employed by the psyche to dispose of the ego fragments produced by its destructiveness' (Bion 1959b/1988: 87). In other words, the paper was to be a demonstration of the usefulness of Klein's concept in his clinical work.

In the second half of his paper, however, he offers material from one patient that seemed to suggest a different kind of understanding. Rather than being in the service of primary aggressive phantasies, projective identification seemed to be reactive to maternal failure. I shall quote Bion in detail, highlighting key phrases, though of necessity I have condensed his account. He writes:

> Throughout the analysis, the patient resorted to projective identifica-tion with a persistence suggesting it was a mechanism *of which he had never been able sufficiently to avail himself*; the analysis afforded him an opportunity for the exercise of a mechanism *of which he had been cheated* . . . There were sessions which led me to suppose that the patient felt *there was some object that denied him the use of projective identification* . . . the patient felt that *parts of his personality that he wished to repose in me were refused entry by me* . . . [Note that Bion does not question here the patient's (infant's) basic need to use projective identification; he merely describes a situation in which the process has been frustrated.] (Earlier associations) showed an increas-ing intensity of emotions in the patient. This originated in what he felt

was *my refusal to accept parts of his personality*. Consequently *he strove to force them into me with increased desperation and violence*. His behaviour, isolated from the context of the analysis, might have appeared to be an expression of primary aggression . . . [as in the earlier cases], but *I quote this series because it shows the patient in a different light, his violence a reaction to what he felt was my hostile defensiveness.*

(ibid.: 95–6, italics mine)

This analytic situation built up in Bion's mind an early scenario:

I felt that the patient had experienced in infancy a mother who dutifully responded to the infant's emotional displays. The dutiful response had in it an element of impatient 'I don't know what's the matter with the child.' My deduction was that in order to understand what the child had wanted the mother should have treated the infant's cry as more than a demand for her presence. From the infant's point of view, *she should have taken into her, and thus experienced, the fear that the child was dying.*[2] *It was this fear that the child could not contain* [and the mother could not recognize. How Bion knows that this was precisely the fear is not explained, but possibly it could be inferred from the clinical material he had at his disposal]. *He* [therefore] *strove to split it off, together with the part of the personality in which it lay, and project it into the mother.* An understanding mother is able to experience the feeling of dread that this baby was trying to deal with by projective identification, and yet retain a balanced outlook. *This patient had had to deal with a mother who could not tolerate experiencing such feelings and reacted . . . by denying their ingress . . .*

(ibid.: 96–7, italics mine)

It is clear from this that Bion is describing a particular kind of maternal failure in which the mother (analyst) seems impervious to the infant's (patient's) mental state and the infant (patient) reacts to this with increasingly violent forms of projective identification. Bion's position here is extremely close to the one I have outlined but a detailed consideration of his argument betrays important differences. These lie in the way he views both the normal role and function of the mother and his characterization of normal processes in the baby – precisely the issues that have always separated Kleinian and Independent groups.

---

2 The fact that Bion speaks of the mother taking *into herself* the baby's state illustrates the point I make below about theoretical bias. Bion could have described the mother (or analyst) as imaginatively *entering into* the baby's (analysand's) experience – what I call '*imaginative* identification' (see footnote 4). But Kleinian theory has already decided that the baby can only communicate through *projection into* the mother (i.e. projective identification), which leaves little room for the mother to *seek out* and *enter into* the baby's experience.

Typically, the Kleinian group gives primacy to the infant's inner world of phantasy, the Independents greater weight to the actual environment. Such differences lead to critical questions: Does the mother *only* become alerted to her infant's state because the infant 'projects' (in phantasy) into her, in which case the infant's inner world and projective defences are the prime movers? Or, does the mother play a more active role, scanning the infant for specific 'signs' of distress in a pre-emptive way, in which case the mother takes the initiative? In the first case, *projection* comes first, and the mother may or may not respond (understand what is the matter, or in Bion's terms, 'process' the projection), depending on her receptivity. In the second case, the mother's scanning is already in place when the baby shows signs of distress, her state being similar to that described by Winnicott as *primary maternal preoccupation*.

It is apparent in the paper I have discussed that clinical Bion is closer to Winnicott than theoretical Bion allows. He understands about maternal (or analytic) failure of receptiveness and sees the infant's (analysand's) desperate rage as reactive to this. He also understands how maternal imperviousness *provokes* phantasies of forcing oneself into the other's attention and emotional holding. Theoretical Bion, however, clings to the older Klein schema: the infant's primary form of communication is 'projective identification' and when this is thwarted, a more hostile and intrusive form of the process supervenes. Thus, '[the patient felt that *projective identification*] was a mechanism *of which he had never been able sufficiently to avail himself*; the analysis afforded him an opportunity for the exercise of a mechanism *of which he had been cheated* . . . There were sessions which led me to suppose that the patient felt *there was some object that denied him the use of projective identification* . . . the patient felt that *parts of his personality that he wished to repose in me were refused entry by me* . . . (ibid.: 96, italics mine).

In conclusion, while it can be said that Bion's thought makes an important leap in realizing that the baby's (patient's) behaviour is often reactive to the mother's (analyst's) failure to understand and respond, he never abandons his earlier view that projective identification is the basic form of infant–mother relatedness. In his new formulation the onus remains with the infant to project into the mother, not on the mother to seek out the infant's (communicative) signs of distress. For Bion, as for Klein, projective identification is *primary*; the baby engages in it *from the beginning*, the mother's contribution merely facilitating or thwarting this fundamental process.

## Primary maternal preoccupation and maternal imperviousness

This account contains two elements and the problem for theory is to state the relationship between them. First, a mother who registers, or fails to register, the specifics of the infant's state through empathy and imaginative identification; and second, a baby who emits specific distress signals while anticipating in some basic way that they will be responded to.

The Kleinian view, even in Bion's 'softer' version, asserts that the *infant* puts the experience of an emotional state into the *mother* through projective identification; the Independent view, represented by Enid Balint and Winnicott, turns this process on its head: it suggests that the mother *anticipates* and *enters into* the *baby's* state proactively through an imaginative process that one might call *imaginative identification*. In the first case, the *baby* initiates and does all the work, 'forcing' entry into the mother through projective identification (a pre-symbolic process); in the second, the *mother* leads, feeling her way into the baby through a *symbolically mediated*, imaginative identification (see below).

Underlying these two accounts are different models of infant development, in particular, an implied disagreement about the degree to which the infant experiences separateness from the mother, and how and when such separateness comes about. It has often been noted that infantile projective identification would only make sense if the baby has a rudimentary sense of separateness from the beginning: how else could a baby project something *into* an object unless that object was felt to be separate (Rosenfeld 1971; Sandler 1988)? The Kleinian view thus implies a sense of separateness from the beginning. By contrast, the Independent view (Winnicott and the Balints) regards the infant as having no clear sense of separateness for a significant period after birth (cf. also Mahler *et al.* 1975; Searles 1973).[3]

From Winnicott's standpoint, the development of separateness is linked to the quality of maternal provision and the key to the baby's unawareness of separateness is *primary maternal preoccupation* (1958) which cushions the impact of 'reality'. Through her adaptive responses, the mother holds at bay the experience of frustration and difference, so that the baby is introduced to them in small and manageable doses. In this way, the separateness of 'reality' is assimilated imperceptibly into experience through graduated maternal failure. It is central to this view that any *sudden* impingement of reality is potentially traumatic and part of the mother's role is to see that this does not happen.

Within this model of infant care, maternal attunement and imperviousness work in opposite directions: attunement shields the baby from the harshness of the object world, while imperviousness throws the baby against it. It obtrusively forces the *object* mother into the frame, and throws the baby into premature object awareness. Maternal attunement delays the emergence of separateness while imperviousness catastrophically provokes it.

---

3 Winnicott spoke of the 'merged in state', Michael Balint of a 'harmonious interpenetrating mix-up', Mahler *et al.* of 'symbiosis' and Searles of 'symbiotic relatedness' to refer to a stage in which self and other were hardly differentiated.

Winnicott was keenly aware that sudden change could be potentially traumatic to the infant, and saw, for example, how damaging it was if the mother became depressed, with loss of maternal adaptation (e.g. Winnicott 1967a). He was less obviously concerned with *consistently* impervious mothers (like those described in psychotic and schizophrenic families), who had never (or seldom) been able to respond accurately to their baby's needs. Sarah's mother, in Enid Balint's case, and many of Bion's cases, seems to have been of this kind, and it may be that Bion's ideas concerning the ubiquity of projective identification were shaped by this skewed sample of clinical experience as much as by the Kleinian theory he inherited.

To summarize, within the framework of maternal adaptation, projective identification can be seen as the infant's attempt to overcome the imperviousness of the maternal object. The mother's insensitivity to infant need and her failure to adapt to it throws the infant into premature awareness of separateness. The infant must then find increasingly aggressive ways of forcing itself into the mother's awareness. From this perspective, each failure of maternal adaptation[4] adds to the infant's desperation and rage, and this culminates in phantasies of entering and/or destroying the frustrating object in ways similar to those described by Klein. Finally, in so far as there may have been earlier experiences of at-oneness (merging, symbiosis etc.) with the mother, however fleeting, it can be seen how intrusive efforts to breach the maternal imperviousness might constitute attempts to regain this lost state.

## The issue of non-verbal communication

Any consideration of projective identification has to address the question of non-verbal communication for two reasons: first clinically, because the concept of projective identification is most often invoked when the analyst in the session 'picks up' on an affect that is not being expressed in a verbal or obvious way; and second theoretically, because the concept is used to explain infant 'communication' of affective states to the mother during the preverbal period. In the first case, the analyst discerns the patient's state through an often incongruous aspect of his own experience in the session, and then 'realizes' that the patient has 'projected it into him'. In a similar way, the mother is only deemed to become aware of what her infant is 'experiencing' when the infant has 'projected' this affect into her.

---

4 It is important to note that in Winnicott's schema, timing is critical when maternal failure is in question. In the beginning, the mother's task is to shield the infant from too much 'reality' and allow the infant the experience of omnipotence. Failure at this stage can be catastrophic. Later, however, her task is to fail, but in a manner proportionate to the infant's capacity to cope with it. Winnicott calls this 'graduated maternal failure' and at this later stage sees it as a necessary stimulus to separation and development.

Such 'explanations' are problematic because they do not *explain* anything at all. To explain a process of this kind we would have to say how it was mediated and on this aspect analysts are usually silent. In so far as such experiences are accurately perceived, however, it is clear that the mediating mechanism must be some kind of non-verbal communication. The fact that the analyst cannot describe this is merely evidence of being taken unawares, such experiences being by nature incongruous and unexpected.

However, in discussing non-verbal communication, one comes upon a more intrinsic difficulty. As normally understood, communication involves the mediation of *symbols* which 'carry' or 'refer to' meanings – the words of language are the clearest example. When it comes to non-verbal processes the situation is more complicated. Affects, for example, are normally mediated by *signs* which are part of the expression of the emotion itself (Darwin 1872). When you look at me and see the expression of anger on my face, for example, you 'read' these signs, even though communicating my affect to you by means of my expression is not part of my intention. My angry expression merely accompanies my hostile intentions towards you and for this reason I cannot be said to be conveying my experience in a symbolic way.

At other times, intentional communication may be operating. For example, if you tell me something that I disapprove of, I might curl my lip in a particular way that conveys distaste. In this case, my expression is a conscious symbol – I intended to convey my distaste to you in this way and curling the lip is a culturally shared *non-verbal* symbol of distaste.

While the expression of affective *signs* (as opposed to symbols) is largely involuntary, however, and at most we may partially suppress them, *reading* them (i.e. symbolically processing them) is not involuntary in the same way. While the potential for recognizing emotional expression (signs) is thought to be innate, the degree to which we are aware of, and respond to, another's feeling is more variable. To be emotionally aware, we must be 'open' to the other's affective signs and on the look out for them. Winnicott's 'good enough mother' is 'open' in this way, 'primary maternal preoccupation' being an accentuation of such normal receptivity. An impervious mother, by contrast, is relatively 'closed' to the recognition of affective signs; she behaves as though they are not occurring, and at best misinterprets them.

Being open to affective signs involves more than simply reading them: it includes the ability to process them in a symbolic way (Bion's $\alpha$-function and 'reverie'). Such processing can be seen as a stage of symbolic elaboration. Thus, for a mother to 'know' what is troubling her baby, she has to *interpret* the affective signs by imagining herself into the baby's situation. She has to be aware of when the baby was last changed and fed, and whether it is teething or suffering with colic. She needs to bear in mind recent upheavals of routine or changes in carer, and she has to synthesize these possibilities into a 'picture' or 'story' about the baby. This is what I refer to as '*imaginative* identification' – it involves symbolically imagining oneself into the other person's situation, and constructing a 'context' in which the perceived signals make sense.[5] *Imaginative* identification is quite different from *projective* identification – it is a way of knowing and understanding the other person, and involves more than being simply disturbed by him.

In order to understand what might be going on when the concept of 'projective identification' is invoked, it is necessary to describe a sequence of interpersonal events. We have to regard the 'projector' as emitting non-verbal affective signals (signs) through tone of voice, posture, and so on, *while not knowing that he is doing so*. We could then say that his 'not knowing' is a form of *imperviousness to his own affective state*. He may be aware of inner 'disturbance' but knows nothing about it because he has not symbolically processed it. This could be understood in terms of the attitude towards himself that he has internalized from his own impervious mother. Thus his imperviousness to his own emotional signals (internal) is a consequence of her imperviousness to his emotional signals in childhood.

The fact that the patient does not 'know' about his own affects – he cannot 'read' them, just as his mother could not – does not affect their underlying development when events set them in motion. Thus the analyst, who is relatively 'open' to the patient, 'picks up' these unacknowledged signals and, although surprised by them, is able to process them symbolically through his reverie. To describe things in this way makes it unnecessary to see the patient as 'projecting' such signals 'into' the analyst in the way that Kleinian theory dictates – the phenomenon can be adequately explained by the analyst's heightened receptivity and emotional openness that allow him to 'pick up' the unacknowledged emotional signals.

It would hardly be contested that the analyst habitually attempts to turn towards the patient in such a receptive way. He holds the patient in his sensory awareness, and also holds him in mind; he is consciously and unconsciously in touch with the body of 'knowledge' he has built up about the patient – with what happened half an hour ago, or in yesterday's session, as well as with what happened in his childhood, and what he imagines might have happened in his earliest relationships. He is on the look out for emotional signals, and scans the field for affective cues. He is thus in a state of 'primary analytic preoccupation' – I use this phrase to relate the analyst's state of mind to that of the mother in a state of 'primary maternal preoccupation' (Winnicott). The analyst relates imaginatively to every aspect of the 'material', and senses what might be the case from all the available cues.

5 Note that the analyst is constantly performing a similar function in relation to the patient – imaginatively contextualizing the patient's utterances, and in those cases where he invokes projective identification, the patient's unacknowledged affective signs.

In this way the unacknowledged affect signals of the patient (in Kleinian terms, 'that which the patient has projected into the analyst') come to be 'contained' (Bion) within the symbolic fabric provided by the analyst (his 'imagined patient').

## Conclusion

By examining Bion's modification of Klein's theory of projective identification in the light of Winnicott's work I have developed a clinical account of the concept which frees it from its Kleinian theoretical matrix. The infant's basic mode of communication with the mother (the emission of emotional signals) does not have to be regarded as a projective phenomenon but merely an affective display linked to an inbuilt expectation of maternal response. Closely following Bion's insights, I have constructed a scenario in which projective and aggressive phantasies can be seen as meaningful reactions to maternal failure. In this context, failure takes the form of maternal imperviousness, by which I mean a lack of receptiveness, and response to, the infant's emotional messages. I have argued that the clinical phenomena in question do not necessitate adherence to Kleinian assumptions of defence against primitive aggression but are more readily understood as the infant's desperate reaction to an object that has failed to respond appropriately to its disturbed state. I am assuming that the infant has an inborn propensity to communicate distress through non-verbal channels, and equally, an inborn expectation that these will be responded to in ways that lessen the disturbance.

That infants engage in communicative and responsive interaction from birth is now attested by a huge volume of infant research (e.g. Stern 1985). Such communication frequently has a mimetic quality and is often structured into complex sequences. Disturbance in expected rhythms and patterns creates confusion and disturbance in the infant, and it seems likely that the maternal input to such sequences contributes to the infant's sense of being held and contained by the mother. I underline the existence of such communicative patterns because it is often stated that projective identification itself is the main pathway of communication in infancy and in my view this is not supported by the available evidence.

# Chapter 6

# Words, things and Wittgenstein

The relation between language and experience was pivotal to Freud's theory of the mind and words played a central part in his account of consciousness and psychological defence (Freud 1915). He clearly understood the role of words in self-knowledge and also realized how they could be used in the service of self-deception.

In a different frame of reference, language was also a major concern of twentieth-century philosophy. This stemmed from the work of the Vienna Circle (Ayer 1936) which paid critical attention to the way the forms of language could mislead the user into false beliefs. Although their emphases were different, psychoanalysis and positivist philosophy were equally sceptical about the capacity of language to portray the truth.

Freud's concern was the truth of embodied and bodily experience which was often unconscious and different from that which a person could put into words. Positivist truth, on the other hand, lay in the structure of language and in making statements that could be empirically verified. Its criteria were so stringent that large areas of life were excluded from philosophical attention; for example, apparently meaningful statements about religion were excluded as mere forms of words that did not refer to substantive facts. Equally, the whole of psychoanalysis and other depth psychologies would have been beyond the pale of meaningful philosophical discourse.

By the end of the twentieth century, however, the concerns of logical positivism seemed hardly relevant. The average academic no longer felt constrained by its narrow definitions of truth and while it would be rash to attribute this freeing up of philosophy to one particular individual, it would be hard to give an account of the period without considering the work of Ludwig Wittgenstein. Although he died in 1951, Wittgenstein's ideas about language have dominated the last half-century of philosophy rather in the way that Freud's dominated the dynamic psychotherapies during the previous fifty years.

Given that linguistic concerns so deeply informed the *zeitgeist* of this period, it is surprising how little attention was given to them by psychoanalysis. There were exceptions: Freud himself pondered the relation between language and consciousness, between *word presentations* and *thing presentations* (Freud 1915); Lacan (1953/1977) approached the mind through Saussurian linguistics and the structure of language forms; and more recently Bion (1959b) explored certain primitive aspects of psychological defence through the quasi-linguistic concept of *attacks on linking*. For the most part, however, the relation between words and experience has been a peripheral concern – psychoanalysts have been more concerned with the content of the patient's utterance than with its specific means of expression.

In this chapter, I shall focus on this neglected area and consider the relationship between words and experience in some detail. It is generally believed that the infant is capable of rich experience *before* the advent of language so that during development, words have to be *introduced* to experience and equally experience to words. In this sense, the infant's birth into language is a major transition and I want to consider its potential effects. In what degree, for example, does it help or hinder communication, clarify or submerge an earlier preverbal patterning, facilitate or obscure the expression of inner experience? I want to ask whether language is friend or foe of the developing self, servant or master; and whether our experience is enhanced or impoverished by its growing involvement with words.

It is scarcely possible to tackle so many questions in any detail. I therefore propose to approach them tangentially through the life and work of the philosopher Ludwig Wittgenstein. In so doing I shall draw heavily on Ray Monk's fascinating and informative biography of the philosopher (Monk 1990).

Monk notes that Wittgenstein did not begin to speak until he was four years old (ibid.: 12), and while he makes very little of this, merely noting it in passing, it seems a remarkable fact that the foremost linguistic philosopher of the twentieth century should have started life in this way. For this reason I make it the starting point of my enquiry. By making links between biographical material and Wittgenstein's philosophical concerns, I hope to offer some understanding of his delay in speaking, and in so doing throw light on certain features of language acquisition.

## Wittgenstein the man

Wittgenstein's delay in speaking suggests a significant emotional problem, and from a psychological perspective, his philosophical pursuits can be seen as part of his lifelong struggle to make sense of a difficulty that had troubled him from an early age. I suggest that one expression of this difficulty involved the relationship between words and things in his own experience – or more accurately, between words, originating from the *other* person, and his own unique view of the world. This view gains support from the fact that his lifelong concern with language appeared less a profession than an existential necessity; it often seemed that his life depended on answering the philosophical questions he posed.

Although he was self-taught, Wittgenstein took to philosophy naturally and few would doubt his philosophical genius. Bertrand Russell recognized it at an early stage and gave him patronage; but in spite of this, he was always in some ways the *enfant terrible* of the philosophical world. Nobody knew quite what to make of him and he fitted uncomfortably with those around him.

His published output was small: just one slim volume at the age of thirty-two, the famous *Tractatus Logico-Philosophicus*[1] (Wittgenstein 1922/1974). The book was abstruse and had a mixed reception; not even Russell was sure that he understood it. Nevertheless, Wittgenstein audaciously claimed that it solved the major problems of philosophy once and for all.

Alongside this arrogance which was typical, Wittgenstein also suffered self-doubt; and just as his philosophical self-valuation swung from one extreme to the other, his life too went through violent gyrations and upheavals. This ensured that his unconventional career was characterized by major breaks and changes of direction, yet in spite of this, he eventually became Professor of Philosophy at Cambridge, the most sought after philosophical Chair at that time. Here too his performance was idiosyncratic and controversial: while he thought much and made voluminous jottings, he completed little; all his later philosophy was published after his death, being compiled from his notebooks by others. Overall, his work was contentious and often cryptic, yet philosophers continue to debate its overall meaning to the present day.

His life makes a fascinating study in which connections can be traced between his early development, the abrupt changes of direction in his adult life, and the forms and themes of his philosophical work. Beyond this, however, the issues of language raised by his particular case are in some degree inherent in the process of language acquisition itself – they are merely writ large in the life of this extraordinary individual. For this reason, his story provides a base camp from which to explore important aspects of the process.

## Biographical details

Ludwig Wittgenstein was born in Vienna in 1889, the youngest of eight children. His parents were extremely wealthy Jews but intent on casting off their Jewish background. His father had a vast business empire and was one of the wealthiest men in Vienna. His mother was cultured and exceptionally

---

1 In the text, I refer to this work as the *Tractatus*.

musical, passing on her musical ability to many of her children, including Ludwig. The home was a centre of cultural activities, supported practically and financially by the father but lived in a more involved way by the mother. Frequent musical evenings were attended by top musicians and composers, Brahms and Mahler among them, and the conductor Bruno Walter remembered 'the all-pervading atmosphere of humanity and culture' which permeated the Wittgenstein establishment (Monk 1990: 8).

The trajectory of Wittgenstein's life was far from conventional. His early education was with private tutors, and if anything he showed a practical bent, apparently happier with lathes and tools than with words. At grammar school – where Adolf Hitler was a pupil, though in a different year – he showed scant promise; in Monk's words, he seemed 'content to feel himself surrounded by genius, rather than possessed of it' (ibid.: 13). When it came to career choice, he opted for engineering, his father's profession, and on leaving school he travelled to England as a research student in aeronautical engineering at Manchester University.

It was there that Wittgenstein became interested in pure mathematics and logic and, with no formal training in philosophy, he read Bertrand Russell's *Principia Mathematica*. This proved a decisive event. It provoked a philosophical passion and he started to plan a book of his own philosophical thoughts. Full of these ideas, he travelled to Jena to see the distinguished mathematician Gottlob Frege, and through Frege, who must have been considerably impressed, he eventually obtained an introduction to Bertrand Russell at Cambridge.

This proved the start of a long and stormy relationship, first as Russell's protégé, later as equal, and even master. Wittgenstein studied under Russell, but the roles of teacher and pupil were frequently blurred. Although officially Russell was mentor, Wittgenstein would attack and criticize his work, caring little that Russell was already widely and internationally acclaimed. At the same time he desperately sought Russell's approval for his own unrecognized ideas. It was certainly not plain sailing, but in spite of frequent quarrels, Russell recognized and fostered Wittgenstein's exceptional gifts, and the first phase of his philosophical development was thus intertwined with their relationship.

It was not until after the interruptions of the 1914–18 war, during which Wittgenstein served on the German front, and was taken prisoner by the Italians, that his first and only book, the *Tractatus*, was published. Although Russell had generously written an introduction to this book, Wittgenstein had by now fallen out with him and wanted to have nothing further to do with philosophy. He believed that in any case he had solved its outstanding problems, displaying in this the grandiose attitude that must have contributed to his difficulties with friends and colleagues.

Wittgenstein now suffered the first of many personal crises which he resolved in a characteristic way with an abrupt change of direction: he took employment as a primary school teacher in a small country village in Austria, and although ill equipped for it, he remained in the post for a number of years. He found relations with staff and pupils difficult and for most of the time was deeply unhappy. However, in what turned out to be an essentially practical (as opposed to intellectual) phase of his life, he also designed and built his own house (which has been compared to a three-dimensional Mondrian painting), had an idealized love affair with a woman (probably the only heterosexual relationship he ever had), and worked as a monastery gardener (while giving serious consideration to the idea of becoming a monk).

In this unstable period it is possible to discern a pattern that recurred frequently during the course of his life. This was an oscillation between esoteric and intellectual interests on the one hand, and practical mundane concerns on the other. It was as though he could not make up his mind as to what kind of person he was, or wanted to be. Was he the practical, down to earth engineer/monastery gardener/primary schoolteacher, or the brilliant philosopher of language, moving within the same league as his mentors at Cambridge, Russell and G. E. Moore? Was it his destiny to be involved with things, or to live in the rarefied world of words and academic philosophy?

Monk refers to this decade of Wittgenstein's post-*Tractatus* phase as his years in the 'wilderness' (ibid.: 234). Academically this was true, but philosophically the period was not completely fallow. Although officially he had abandoned philosophy, he continued to keep notebooks of his thoughts and ideas, and these obsessive ruminations would form the basis of a new approach to the questions that troubled him. Moreover, in the context of his developing philosophical insights he now began to view the *Tractatus* as a flawed book which contained fundamental errors.

Finally, at the end of this long but formative period, Wittgenstein returned to Cambridge as a doctoral student and it must be proof of his extraordinary mind, that even after such a turbulent relationship with philosophy and its eminent Cambridge practitioners, he was able to find his way back. Nevertheless, it is evidence of his disordered personality that not everyone rejoiced at his return. The economist, Maynard Keynes, for example, noted wryly to a friend: 'Well God has arrived. I met him on the 5.15 train!' (ibid.: 254).

I have probably given enough material to convey the turbulence of Wittgenstein's life and the upheavals of identity and lifestyle that went with this. In addition, I have highlighted the abrupt changes between verbal/abstract and practical/embodied concerns that characterized these upheavals. In what follows, I shall argue that these changes constituted a repetition of his early history. They repeated, I believe, the sharp and traumatic transition between a prolonged *preverbal* period – it will be recalled that he did not speak until he was four – and his later childhood, when language eventually became his pre-eminent form of communication.

## Family relationships and personality

In order to develop this thesis, I need to expand on certain aspects of Wittgenstein's early life and relationships. Monk tells us little about his relationship with his mother though she may have been somewhat remote; as was the norm in wealthy upper class families, he was brought up by a series of nannies and nursemaids. His father was a powerful and highly successful man – one of the richest men in Vienna – and he must have been a formidable force to be reckoned with. Running through the family history, there is a theme of rebellion against excessively powerful fathers. In his father's generation, Wittgenstein's father (Karl) had rebelled against *his* father (Hermann) by running off to America and pursuing a contrary career; but while he escaped his father's dominating influence, the remaining siblings succumbed completely and followed the careers their father had chosen for them.

As is so often the case, history repeated itself in the next generation. When Karl, the rebel against paternal authority, became a father, he in turn became ruthless and dominating. This was most apparent in relation to Wittgenstein's four elder brothers whose natural talents he totally disregarded. One brother was markedly artistic, another so musically talented that people compared him to the young Mozart. In spite of this, the father insisted that all his sons should follow him into engineering. The results were disastrous: two of the four committed suicide, including the talented pianist.

Monk believes that these events made a strong impression on Wittgenstein's father who supposedly softened his approach with his four younger children, including Wittgenstein. However, given the overpowering nature of his personality, it seems unlikely that such domination would have stopped so easily. An atmosphere of strict paternal authority must still have enveloped the Wittgenstein household, and Ludwig himself would have internalized an intensely omnipotent parental imago. One has only to recall Keynes' remark that 'God has arrived. I met him on the 5.15 train' (see p. 91), or Wittgenstein's own view that he had solved the outstanding problems of philosophy, to realize that this was the case.

It is hardly surprising, then, that dominance and submission were major issues in Wittgenstein's life. As a small child he was compliant and anxious to please; in adulthood, when he started to assert his own point of view, he was often ruthless and uncompromising. With so powerful a father his choices were limited; either he had to *become* the omnipotent father (as his own father had done before him), or submit, like most of his elder brothers.

In reality, his personality seems to have been a mixture of dominant and submissive traits. Aided by the family fortune that shielded him from many external necessities, he was free to attend obsessively to his inner struggles, and allow his personality to unfold in idiosyncratic ways.

A powerful driving force was the quest for the truth: on one level for philosophical truth, or at least a method that would lead him in that direction; on another level, the truth of himself – of who he was, or who he might become. Both quests he pursued in ruthless and uncompromising ways that made him a difficult friend and colleague. This was graphically attested by a letter from Russell to Lady Ottoline Morrell in which he complained bitterly about Wittgenstein's temperament:

> He [Wittgenstein] raged and stormed and I irritated him more and more by merely smiling . . . The things I say to him are just the things you would say to me if you were not afraid of the avalanche they would produce – and his avalanche is just what mine would be! I feel his lack of civilization and suffer from it – it's odd how little music does to civilize people – it is too apart, too passionate and remote from words [remember that Wittgenstein was very musical like his mother]. *He has not a sufficiently wide curiosity or a sufficient wish for a broad survey of the world* [italics mine]. It won't spoil his work on logic, but it will make him a very narrow specialist and rather too much the champion of a party . . .
>
> (quoted by Monk 1990: 73)

Russell's remarks not only convey the explosive nature of Wittgenstein's temperament but give rise to wider thoughts about his personality. First, there is the uncompromising fight with Russell, his powerful mentor and father figure, to gain recognition for his own way of seeing things. Second, there is Russell's reference to his (Wittgenstein's) passion for music, which reminds one of the pervasive musicality of the Wittgenstein home, and his prolonged *infancy* (being 'without words') in an environment saturated with musical forms. Finally, Russell points to Wittgenstein's narrowness, his insufficient wish 'for a broad survey of the world'. In this sense, he is narrow minded and sees only one thing at a time.

## Dynamic formulation

It seems to me that a link can be made between Wittgenstein's obsessive and narrowly focused interest and a small child's normal relationship with objects in a two-person, dyadic world. Russell's remark about him lacking a broader perspective suggests that Wittgenstein had difficulty in moving beyond the dyadic frame with its intense one to one involvement with objects. It suggests that he has not been able to incorporate the flexibility of the 'third position' that lies beyond the first relationship and is normally facilitated by the father. He is thus locked in the intensity of two-person relating (Wright 1991) and can neither envisage things in a wider, more balanced way, nor make flexible use of multiple perspectives. In so far as he has incorporated the father's 'position' (as third), he has done so in a two-person way: rather than using it to put things in perspective by adopting the father's 'third-ness', he has simply reversed roles within an unmodified two-person structure. He thus *becomes* the oppressive, omnipotent father who obliterates the other person's view. As if to illustrate this idea, Russell comments in another letter: 'He [Wittgenstein] treats infant theories with a ferocity they can only endure when they are grown up' (ibid.: 74). It is hard not to link this verbal 'ferocity' with that of his father towards him at a time when his own 'infant theories' of the world (essentially preverbal) were taking shape.

In attempting to understand Wittgenstein's personality in this way, I have made use of the distinction between two and three person organizations of experience. Although variously delineated, this distinction is basic to psychoanalytic theories of development (Wright 1991; Britton 1998). Essentially, the two person organization, stemming from the earliest relationship with the mother, is more concrete and all-or-none than later triangulated developments; its meanings remain embodied in lived situations and lack the relative detachment of triangulated symbols and meanings.

In these terms, Wittgenstein can be seen as struggling to transcend the concrete, 'all or none' perspective of the two person situation. In attempting to move beyond its confines into the freer world of triangular, mental space (Britton 1998), he fails to find a father capable of helping him with his moderating influence. Instead he confronts a tyrannical father who embodies and confirms the very omnipotence that the son needs to surpass. I am making the assumption that Wittgenstein frequently, perhaps predominantly, experienced his *adult* world from within the confines of this dyadic space. Russell, a later father figure, may or may not have struggled with omnipotence (i.e. with overlapping problems) in his own right, but within the stormy relationship of the two philosophers, Wittgenstein undoubtedly cast him in the place of his own omnipotent father and thus repeatedly tried to destroy him.

In the light of these ideas, it seems reasonable to suppose that Wittgenstein's atypical language development was shaped by this struggle. We can thus imagine that from a prolonged 'infant' state of being without words, he was thrown into the language-world of his omnipotent father. The father's alien and dogmatic words would thus have forcefully *imposed* themselves on the child's fragile *preverbal* experience – 'his [own] infant theories' (see above) – threatening them with destruction. The normally adaptive early relation between words and experience would in this way have been replaced by a struggle between them, reflecting the relation between father and son. In the ensuing mental drama, it would have been as though the father's 'word' said to a more maternal, preverbal 'experience': '*This* is the way the world is! *This* is the way things are! *This* is what you feel!' – in this way creating a dictatorship of the word. Any sense of *personal* experience would thus have been obliterated and (the father's) language would have ruled his mind. This state of affairs can be contrasted with a more normal kind of situation in which words are introduced to the infant in adaptive and maternal ways. They are offered, not imposed, and in Merleau-Ponty's (1964b) phrase would be felt to satisfy 'a speechless want', or in Winnicott's terms, to provide a 'good enough' fit between word and experience. In this scenario, personal experience is enhanced by language which endows it with a means of expression and gives it a sharper reality within the new verbal form.

I am suggesting that in Wittgenstein's case, paternal domination had a major impact on this normal *permeation* of experience by language. Instead of the future philosopher finding 'maternal' words that fitted his experience and drew it to expression, he experienced the onslaught of an impinging, 'paternal' language that separated him from it. However, in these terms, one can see not only how his traumatic induction into language may have contributed to the difficulties that dogged him throughout his life, but also how it simultaneously provided the ground for his most creative achievements.

To summarize: I have sketched an outline of Wittgenstein's personality and early development, thereby creating a platform from which to view his relationship to language and the world. I shall now consider his philosophy in the light of these ideas and this will enable me to further examine the normal integration of language into infant experience.

## Wittgenstein's philosophy

To a psychoanalytic eye, Wittgenstein's philosophy reveals the same oscillating, dichotomous pattern as the rest of his life and seems to have provided a principal arena within which to work out the legacy of his childhood difficulties.

His work falls into two contrasting phases: a youthful period when he discovered his philosophical passion and believed he could solve the problems of philosophy; and a later period, spanning his time as Lecturer, then Professor, at Cambridge, during which he developed a radically new approach to linguistic philosophy.

The first phase culminated in the publication of the *Tractatus* and was followed by near abandonment of philosophy for more than ten years; the second was a period of crippling uncertainty – it involved the relinquishing of any attempt to be comprehensive and a total inability to get his work into shape for publication.

The form of his writings also changed significantly between the two periods. The *Tractatus*, more or less synonymous with the early period, is composed of a series of inter-related logical statements with a complex system of numbering into groups and sub-groups. It gives an impression of tightly knit coherence, each thought interlocking with the others in an intricate way. It creates an effect of aesthetic beauty, like a musical fugue or a spiralling geometric design. In the later period, by contrast, the impression is quite different. His *Philosophical Investigations* (Wittgenstein 1953), for example, which were published posthumously, consists of short passages, organized around particular themes, to which he returns like a dog to a bone. There is little sense of completion or certainty and the tight logical coherence of the earlier work is missing.

These differences seem to reflect a changing attitude towards language. Whereas in the *Tractatus*, language is a tool which confidently carries his logical thought and takes him (as he believes) to his destination, in the later period it becomes a more complex and problematic medium. Certainly it continues to deal with meaning, but that meaning is now inextricably entangled with living situations, and has to be pored over and questioned before it can be drawn out. Unlike the disembodied and imposed logical meaning of the *Tractatus*, the new kind of meaning emerges from the utterance of living, speaking subjects. Rather than existing independently of the subject in the external forms of language, it is now something lived, that eventually you come to *see*.[2] Understanding something, in these terms, involves displaying things in such a way that their inner connections become more visible. Wittgenstein calls this 'perspicuous presentation' which 'makes possible that understanding which consists just in the fact that we "see the connections"' (quoted by Monk 1990: 311).

In a sense, 'perspicuous presentation' *is* the new method of philosophy, a new way of discovering what things mean. Meaning now resides *within* objects or situations, not in the external measure (language) which defines them. As a result, his work consists of jottings which refer to real life situations. He wants to show us the *morphology* of living language, to give us examples of meaning that still lies embedded in its natural environment; like a natural historian, he demonstrates the specimens he has collected in the field. He then arranges and rearranges them – literally cutting and pasting in order to get the 'best' arrangement that reveals the *inherent* meaning in the most 'perspicuous' way. His new philosophy thus consists of endless demonstrations but few conclusions.

While the logical coherence of the *Tractatus* is in keeping with his earlier understanding of meaning as external and given *in* language, his later writing is consonant with his new belief in subjective meaning that can be

---

2  There is a certain similarity between the embodied meaning that Wittgenstein now wants to disengage from lived situations and the kind of embodied meaning (e.g. transference meaning) that the analyst is trying to 'make conscious'.

'seen' *through* the way language is used. Philosophy in this new sense clarifies what ordinary speakers 'mean'; it is a process of questioning, of going back to language as it is lived and spoken, and teasing out meaning from the way words are used in lived situations. Ultimately this provides elucidation of certain confusions into which language leads us.

It is thus clear that Wittgenstein's two philosophical periods are distinguished by markedly different attitudes towards experience. While in the *Tractatus* the stance is observational and disengaged, in the later period it is more existential and involved. In the *Tractatus*, the philosopher is spectator, or detached observer, looking at the world from a distance and defining it with logical patterns of words. In the later period he is more engaged: he listens to the way language is spoken. It is no longer an external instrument imposed on experience and the world but a part of life that springs up between the actors and gives voice to their living perceptions.

## Dynamic understanding of Wittgenstein's philosophy

Wittgenstein's contrasting philosophies of language suggest two radically different ways of being in the world, corresponding, I suggest, to an unresolved conflict about the kind of world he inhabited, or wanted to inhabit. I described previously how this split in his personality propelled him from philosophical prodigy to primary school teacher, and after many twists and turns, back to philosophy as prestigious Cambridge professor.

From a psychoanalytic perspective, his philosophical transformation was merely the latest turn of the screw. So what was the basic problem he was trying to resolve? I have already mooted that it stemmed, at least in part, from difficulties with his autocratic and dominating father. I now want to elaborate on this idea. Thus we might suppose that the observer stance of the *Tractatus* is that of his dominating father, naming the world and decreeing what everything is, while the more involved stance of the later work is that of the mother (or other maternal figure) who offers form and words to experience in a more resonant way.[3] From this perspective, we could see Wittgenstein as engaged in an argument, not least with himself, about the *ownership* of language and experience (see Bakhtin's remarks on this in chapter 3). If language 'belongs to' the father, as it seems to in the *Tractatus*, it ordains a complete picture of the world, which soon becomes a closed system of *facts*. It furnishes a complete inventory of *that which is the case* (the world of natural science and verifiable propositions), and anything that falls outside this lexicon of 'facts' is automatically excluded from existence (and philosophical study). This is indeed the way it is portrayed in the *Tractatus*.

---

3 This implies, of course, an alternating identification with these figures in his inner world.

However, if one reads the book as a psychoanalytic observer, it is possible to discern an ironic twist. This is most apparent at the end of the work and resides in the author's draconian assertions and exclusions. In a group of statements that form his conclusion, Wittgenstein (we might say, in identification with his father) radically dictates the limits of philosophical discourse. However, what he *excludes* in this way is by no means unimportant. On the contrary, it entails practically everything that matters most in life, and certainly what mattered most to Wittgenstein, at least in an emotional sense: religion (he seriously considered becoming a monk), ethics (he was an intensely moral person, deeply concerned with right and wrong), the arts (including music, his first love in the arts), and not least, the domain of traditional philosophy (which included God, Truth, Beauty, etc.). Wittgenstein referred to these excluded things as *the mystical* and *it constituted a domain which cannot be talked about.* Herein lies the ironic twist: he has put 'the mystical' beyond the reach of the father's words. It is as though Wittgenstein is saying to his father: 'You can talk as much as you like about practical, empirical matters (engineering, perhaps); but if you try and speak about the things that *really* matter to me (the world of non-verbal experience, music, religion, art, and architecture), you will (philosophically speaking) be talking nonsense.' It is this that leads me to think that by placing his preverbal (maternally derived) sensibilities out of bounds, he was protecting them from the imagined destructive onslaught of the father's words.

If this is so, the victory of the father that is chronicled in the *Tractatus* – the victory of a rigid, defining language over experience – is ultimately a pyrrhic victory because the paternal domain (the domain of rational discourse) is now severely curtailed. As if in confirmation of this idea, Wittgenstein confides to his notebooks as follows: 'If you have a room which you do not want *certain people* to get into, put a lock on it for which they do not have the key' (Monk 1990: 300, italics mine). In other words, the *father* is to be locked out and kept at bay by a clever argument that radically circumscribes the field of philosophical discourse.

In similar vein, he writes:

> The correct method in philosophy would really be the following: to say nothing except what can be said, i.e. propositions of natural science – i.e. something that has nothing to do with philosophy – and then whenever someone else wanted to say something metaphysical, to demonstrate to him that he had failed to give a meaning to certain signs in his propositions. *Although it would not be satisfying to this other person . . . this method would be the only correct one.*
> (Wittgenstein 1922/1974: 73–4, italics mine)

According to my interpretation, this passage defines Wittgenstein's strategy in relation to his omnipotent father. Through a philosophical sleight of hand, (and at the same time being the omnipotent father), he says to the father: 'I'm getting you off my back for good! I will never let you get hold of my experience, nor will I let you destroy me in the way you destroyed my brothers!'

The *Tractatus* ends with the statement: 'What we cannot speak about we must pass over in silence' (ibid.: 74), and after writing these words, he himself closes the door on philosophy (as the domain of the father) – or so he thinks. Having shut his father out (along with his own identification with him), he returns to a less verbal mode of existence, veering towards a 'maternal' world of things, sensations and emotions, and struggling per-haps, to regain some involvement in embodied living. He teaches small children, builds a house, and considers entering a monastery to devote his life to religion, and perhaps agriculture; he imagines working in the monas-tery garden. Not least, and under guise of not doing philosophy at all, he *plays* (Winnicott) with a new, and more grounded approach to language that will become the basis of his later philosophical work. This will involve returning to a point *before* the trauma of collision with the father's words, and will constitute an attempt to work out the relation between language and preverbal experience in his own way, free from the father's interference.

## Preverbal and verbal experience

For approximately the first two years of life every human being is an *infans* without speech, and most psychoanalytic theories regard this as a formative period during which the basic structure of the person is established. Many attempts have been made to conceive of this preverbal structuring in terms of instinctual processes and unconscious phantasy, but only recently have efforts been made to understand the effect of language on this early organization.

Vivona (2006) in a recent paper has reviewed the field by means of two contrasting paradigms: that of Hans Loewald (1978) on the one hand and Daniel Stern (1985) on the other. She describes how Loewald's account of language acquisition maps a relatively smooth transition from preverbal to verbal, words being there from the beginning and gradually acquiring meaning within the holding matrix of the mother–infant relationship. Stern (1985), on the other hand, sees an essential disjunction between preverbal and verbal, with loss of preverbal experience in even the most favourable transition.

For Stern, the transition to language is really a translation between two 'languages', each dividing the world in different ways. Even though the mother plays a crucial part, the move into verbal meaning is intrinsically divisive and separates the infant from a unitary state of being which preceded it. Translating experience into verbal form situates the child in a new domain which has only tenuous continuity with the earlier one. In Stern's view, it is not possible to be in both domains at once.

As Vivona points out, Loewald and Stern approach language acquisition from different directions, Loewald clinical and Stern research orientated, and while their contrasting views may derive from this, it is possible that personal history and disposition play a part. Thus we might suppose that Loewald describes a relatively normal transition into language with optimal maternal adaptation, while Stern emphasizes a more troubled development in which the advent of language is associated with trauma.[4]

Winnicott's theory of maternal adaptation may serve as a bridge between these two accounts. If words are normally presented to the infant in such a way that they meet an expressive need, they can be seen as a late example of an adaptive maternal provision that started with the breast. Like these earlier provisions, they realize (give form) to pre-existing infant states, in this case, the silent, preverbal organizations of experience. Conceived in this adaptive way, there is little room for dislocation or loss in the process and the (actual) separateness of word and experience will hardly be realized.[5]

If, however, words are pressed on the infant with insufficient regard for expressive need, they could be said, in Winnicott's terms, to *impinge* on experience, causing trauma to the preverbal self. This in turn will lead to splitting of the self: on the one hand a compliant *verbal* self (false self) that speaks the other person's words, on the other, a *preverbal* self (true self) (Winnicott 1960b) that remains hidden and lacks a means of expression.

We can only guess at the maternal element in Wittgenstein's case, though the father's tendency to ferocious domination is well documented. We do

4 It is interesting in this context that Stern (1990: 4) describes how he was hospitalized for a long period around the age of two and felt totally dependent on his ability to read the non-verbal cues of those around him in order to survive. He adduces this fact in order to account for his highly developed sensitivity to non-verbal cues and his chosen field of infancy research. This is the positive aspect. The more negative side might be his association of language acquisition with the trauma of hospitalization as a two year old, in a pre-Robertson era when hospital visiting was severely rationed, and children were regarded as 'doing fine' so long as they were not screaming. I have no biographical data on Loewald so my idea remains speculative – but see Wright (1991: 310–16) for discussion of the idea that psychoanalytic theory is always in some degree autobiography.

5 This is in keeping with the way Winnicott saw the function of the transitional object: it bridged the gap of separation with an illusory semblance of that which was missing. Words can be thought of in a similar way: if they have the power to conjure up the *presence* of the missing object (it should not be forgotten that the symbolic process is *founded* upon absence, or separation) then the gap between word and thing need not be experienced. It is this use of words that I have in mind whenever I discuss a language of holding as opposed to a language of explanation. The language of holding (embodied meaning) is closer to that which interested Wittgenstein during his second philosophical period, while the language of explanation (interpretation) is closer to that of the *Tractatus*, being always separate from experience and to some extent in danger of destroying it.

not know if he suffered a shortfall of maternal care: he could have been well provided for by nannies and other maternal figures. There is no doubt, however, that he suffered from troubling splits in his personality. Arguably, his unsettled relationship to language was a feature of this, his later philosophy being an attempt to restore contact with a partially lost maternal domain.

## Two philosophies, two languages

Wittgenstein's two philosophies of language seem strangely discontinuous, but if my thesis is correct, the disjunction stems from a difficulty in integrating language with preverbal experience. I have suggested that in 'normal' development, language at first interweaves with experience in a relatively seamless way. Beginning as a system of signs within the lived relationship with the mother, as in Loewald's model (see p. 99), its symbolic, separate nature would gradually assert itself, and experience would thus acquire a genuinely linguistic dimension. This would normally coincide with increasing triangulation of experience: the capacity to adopt a third position (formally speaking, the father's) with consequent modulation of two-person extremes (Wright 1991). In this scenario, the father, as representative of that third position, would mediate a more external language to the child and thus provide a bridge to the social world, in which meanings are necessarily more defined and consensual. However, this sharpened and refined (triadic) language would normally interface with the infant's maternally derived language (baby-talk) which would act as a buffer that protected preverbal experience from too powerful an impact of 'reality'.

In Wittgenstein's case, it seems clear that this process miscarried. Perhaps he lacked the buffering of maternally derived language, or perhaps the impact of the father's omnipotence was too much for the earlier organization to cope with. For in Wittgenstein's case, the father's personality and language, at least as presented to the child, was completely lacking in thirdness; apparently the father himself operated in a world of two-person omnipotence in which he and his words *dictated* reality. As Wittgenstein says in the *Tractatus*: 'The world is the totality of facts, not of things . . . The totality of facts determines what is the case, and also whatever is not the case' (1922/1974: 5).

The tone in this passage is decisive and final – Wittgenstein is up against the immovability of paternal 'fact' (while also enacting it): 'The world is the totality of facts', but '*not of things*' (ibid.: 5, italics mine). The 'not of things' is important, marking the exclusion of his father discussed above. It now appears, however, that his strategy for dealing with the father is established in the first few pages: the father can dictate '*facts*', but not '*things*'; the concreteness of experience is excluded: 'I will not let you touch me.' This exclusion provides the door through which he escapes his father at the end of the book, 'telling' him that if he talks about these 'things' ('the things that matter to me, i.e. "the mystical"') he will by definition be talking nonsense.

From this, we can surmise that Wittgenstein's hidden aim was establishing a father-free zone within which he could work out his own meanings, in his own way, thus managing a rebirth into language without the father's interference. It can be argued that such a project underlay the whole later period of his life, beginning with his abandonment of 'philosophy' (i.e. the father's dictatorial, external words), and continuing until his death. In these terms, his later philosophy, with its meditations on ordinary language, was devoted to retrieving the experience (the 'self') he had previously lost to the father's words, by expressing ('saying') it in a way that was truly his own.

From this perspective, his difficulty in publishing anything after the *Tractatus* was probably based on a fear of the father's retaliation. The father he had excluded could well return (in the shape of Russell or other philosophers) and again threaten his 'infant theories'.[6]

In the *Tractatus*, Wittgenstein conceived of language as an external measure that mapped out a *picture* of the world and established 'the totality of facts'. In the later period he speaks of *language games*, and *language as a form of life*. These later images present language as interwoven with experience; it is claimed by, and expresses the meanings of, those involved in actual living (originally the mother and infant), rather than being an instrument of philosophers and observers of living (omnipotent fathers).

Wittgenstein's later philosophy represents a return to lived language in which words and actions form the warp and woof of a single cloth. This is also the way language is normally learned. Mothers talk to their babies about what they are doing, and as babies begin to talk, so their words appear as an integral dimension of interaction. Stern (1985: 171) refers to the 'we-meanings' that develop in the course of mother–infant interaction, which is a way of saying that in the maternal mode, words have agreed meanings within specific contexts, not in isolation and for all time, as in the paternal mode. Moreover, the normal mother, at least early in the language process, tolerates (and enjoys) the baby-words that the infant creates, will use them in talking to him, and feel pride in their creation. I suggest that emotionally speaking, it is this area of experience that Wittgenstein strives to resurrect in his later philosophy.

---

6 Cf. Russell's letter to Lady Ottoline Morrell (see p. 94) in which he speaks of the way Wittgenstein 'treats infant theories with a ferocity they can only endure when they are grown up'. These were the theories of his mentor-father (Russell) which had to be destroyed before they could destroy him. It would be easy to understand this fighting between 'son' and 'father' as oedipally determined, but I think this would miss the point that Wittgenstein is struggling for survival at a more basic level. At the very least, his oedipal struggle is saturated with earlier dyadic elements.

## Meaning and facial expression

Within the searching of his later period, Wittgenstein experimented with one further approach to meaning. Anscombe (quoted in Finch 1995) called this his *physiognomic theory of meaning*. This can be seen as a variant on the notion of language games but refers to the expressive potential of the face rather than the fabric of personal interaction.

Wittgenstein suggested that when we grasp the meaning of an object or situation, the activity is similar to reading the expression on a face. Finch quotes Anscombe as saying that it often seemed for Wittgenstein that the whole world was a face whose expressions he attempted to read.[7]

This idea is important because we often forget that before language achieves dominance, the face is the principal vehicle of meaning (Winnicott 1967a; Wright 1991). The power and precision of language are such that it easily overshadows other means of expression. However, we may some-times recapture traces of preverbal experience when we go to a foreign country and cannot speak the language. In such a situation, non-verbal expression becomes more intense and immediate. We gaze at people's faces for reassuring signals and search their gestures for meanings we cannot discover in any other way. In such situations, we are *infans*, without speech, thrown back on our non-verbal capacity for understanding and making contact.[8]

Wittgenstein's physiognomic theory of meaning – his interest in the expressive potential of the face – lends support to the idea that in his later work, he explored earlier modes of meaning and relatedness which had been eclipsed by the logical and linguistic power of 'objective' language.

## Conclusions

In the course of normal development language does not spring fully fledged into existence. The passage from preverbal communication to more verbal modes is a gradual process, mediated by significant adults in the infant's world, initially the same adults who communicated with the infant by non-verbal means (including the sound and music of language). Within this perspective, it is helpful to think of different *phases* of the language func-tion, and talk of earlier *maternal modes* of language and meaning, followed by later *paternal modes*. We can think of maternal modes as issuing from

---

7 This idea is reminiscent of the artist Natkin's statements about his painting, discussed in chapter 10. He believed that everything he painted, whether figurative or abstract, was in fact a face. He had in mind the expressive qualities of the canvas which in Wittgenstein's terms might be called 'physiognomic'.

8 In this respect, the foreign country situation is similar to Stern's hospital experience at the age of two (see footnote 4).

experience and exchange in the mother–infant dyad (e.g. Winnicott's mirroring, Stern's attunement, the first finding of words for needs etc.), and paternal modes as dependent on later 'triangulated' experience, with its increasing capacity to be separate from the mother and see things from an 'objective' third position (the father's) (Wright 1991; Britton 1998).

In this chapter, I have attempted to view Wittgenstein's life and work in these terms and suggested that many of his problems stemmed from difficulties in negotiating the transition from two-person to three-person modes of functioning. I have suggested that his stormy relationships and chronic unhappiness, the sharp reversals in his career line, the obsessive, yet fractured relation with linguistic philosophy, and above all, his delayed acquisition of speech, begin to make psychological sense in the light of this idea, the normal transition to language having been complicated by the uncompromising omnipotence of his powerful father. Only in so far as he could put this father to one side, both internally and externally, was he able to renegotiate the passage from preverbal to verbal meaning, and begin to find a new way of realizing himself through language. I have discussed the two major periods of his philosophical work in the light of this idea.

My approach to Wittgenstein in this paper is that of a non-philosopher and I may have misunderstood his writing in terms of pure philosophy. Nevertheless, a psychoanalytic look at his life and work is informative, and in my view throws light on the wider difficulties with which he struggled. His delayed speech and his adult concerns with the nature of language invite meditation on the larger issue of language acquisition and the environmental factors that facilitate or hinder this process. In a larger frame, Wittgenstein's preoccupation with the nature and function of language overlaps with Rilke's struggle with the nature and function of poetry (chapter 4) and Natkin's struggle with the nature and function of artistic creativity (chapters 3 and 10). Each is involved with an expressive medium, and each, according to my thesis, seeks redemption through it. Redemption, in this sense, lies in turning the medium towards the expressive needs of the self, in order to find through it a means of self-expression which had hitherto been impossible. In each case, redemption can be seen as the undoing of an earlier trauma.

# Chapter 7

# Shaping the inarticulate

## Feeling and knowing

In an earlier publication (Wright 1991) I explored the idea that *seeing gives form*. At that time, I thought it was the organizing power of vision that first gave form to experience, and reflexively, through *being seen*, to the experiencing self. I now think this focus was too narrow and realize that we grasp at form through any medium that will yield it to us. In this chapter I use the term *shaping* for the processes through which we come to know in a felt way the form or pattern of our own experience. My subject overlaps with existing topics in the psychoanalytic literature, in particular *structuring, holding* and *containing* (Bion 1962a, 1962b, 1965; Ogden 2004; Winnicott 1960a). I shall discuss these, but only in so far as I need to further my argument.

I have used the word 'know' in relation to self-realization but this is different from knowing *about* something. Experiential knowing is not the same as cognitive knowing and the two kinds of knowledge are mediated in different ways.

When experience is talked about in a cognitive way, it often seems that its essence – the way it feels – has escaped the net of words. In such circumstances, it seems that words have failed to *capture, contain* and *hold on to* what is most essential, namely the living quality of the experience. This often occurs in psychotherapy where a patient might say: 'I *understand* what you are talking about, but it doesn't really *touch* me', or 'I *know* all that, but what difference does it make?' When this happens, it is easy for the therapist to think that the patient is being defensive, but at least in theory, the problem may stem from the way the therapist is using language: his words may have been insufficiently 'alive' to touch the patient's experience.

A similar problem can occur with the patient's use of words, and for shorter or longer periods the therapist may feel a lack of engagement with what the patient is saying. He does not feel touched (see chapter 1), and struggles with an atmosphere of deadness and boredom. This kind of countertransference is often understood in terms of projective processes:

thus, the patient may be seen as attacking the therapist's capacity to think, or as lulling him into a stupefied state so that he will not see beyond the surface of what is being said. Less malign reasons are possible, however, including deficiencies in the patient's symbolic capability. In the latter case, feelings of dullness in a session could result from the patient's difficulties in 'packaging up' experience (containing it in symbolic form) rather than from attacks on the therapist's mind. In other words, the patient may have little problem in telling a coherent story, but lacks the resources to bring it alive. He is able to use words in a referring, factual way but not to create structures that resonate with live experience.

In communication about factual matters, words serve principally as pointers. The denoting word and the object to which it refers (the referent) are separate and have little similarity to each other – the referring relation is simply one of convention. Used in this way, language is a device for practical communication; it enables us to talk about *things* – the shared objects of the outside world that we touch, see, hear, taste and smell. When we talk about *inner* objects, however – emotion and experience – the situation is more complex; there is no longer an external focus and what we need to share is intangible and personal. The challenge here is to make language serve this more intimate purpose.

To convey to another person the quality and timbre of my private experience, I have to find a way of describing it that preserves its life. Practical language will not suffice because conventional symbols merely point, and do not re-create. To arouse the vividness and feel of actual experience, a more concrete, sensory medium is needed and this requires a different kind of symbolic vehicle.

From this perspective, sharing an experience with another person is more like dispatching a parcel containing a model of the experience than sending a letter that merely describes it. Thus, when you open my parcel, you participate in my experience directly and vividly; by reading my letter you acquaint yourself with the bare facts. Obviously a parcel cannot contain an experience, but it can recreate a semblance of it in the recipient which leads to resonance between his feelings and mine. The re-created semblance acts as a bridge between us.

I will give an example. One of my earliest analytic patients was a very disturbed girl who would now be described as borderline. Language was often a problem for her and sometimes she would talk about words and the different feelings they gave her. I remember her saying to me one day: '*Childhood* is such a beautiful *round* word!' Her statement evoked imagery and I found myself remembering some poignant lines from a poem by Rilke about childhood. The poem was nostalgic and full of longing for a state that had once been fleetingly glimpsed. On another occasion she spoke of the word 'who', saying how *hollow* it sounded; again, I found this evocative, and it conjured up powerful feelings of absence and loss. 'Round' and 'hollow' were the sensory, metaphorical words within which she 'packaged' these experiences, and through which she evoked in me their idiosyncratic 'feel'.

This patient was also interesting in an opposite way in that she often had difficulty putting her experience into words, and sometimes even in accessing it. Thus, when I was going away on holiday, her actual words would convey indifference to my not being there but at the same time her dreams would portray disasters: being cut off and stranded with terrible things happening to her, telephone lines cut and so on. Here too she vividly conveyed what was going on inside her, but this time she lacked words to *tell* me her experience and communicated instead through unconscious, non-verbal images.

At the time, I tried to make sense of this in terms of classical defences but I now see the matter in a different way. Rather than supposing that she warded off her experience by *refusing* it access to words (an active process of defence), I would be more inclined to see her difficulty in terms of language deficiency. It was clear from her dreams that she had some capacity to symbolize her emotional reactions in non-verbal, iconic ways, but she lacked the means to send these 'packages' either to herself or me. It was as though she had never learned to put her feelings into words, so that her affective core remained dumb.

Daniel Stern has written about different levels, or organizations of the self, preverbal and verbal, and how these are superimposed on each other, with varying degrees of integration, as development proceeds (Stern 1985). This is a helpful concept that leaves room for a *structural* as well as a dynamic unconscious. While the dynamic unconscious results from repression and other defences, the *structural unconscious*, in his terms, would be *a realm of experience that lacks the means of expression* – as perhaps in my patient. Rather than being denied expression in a dynamic way, the latent content simply lacks a voice. Stern's concept thus allows for environmental factors in the genesis of psychological states: in this case a lack of parental empathy during the period of language acquisition is probable (see chapter 6).

## Capturing the feel

Putting experience into verbal form requires a special kind of skill: an ability to draw into the ambience of the word the concrete feel of actual experience. Such skills are nowhere more developed than in literature, especially poetry, and for this reason it is useful to see how poets think about their work (see also chapter 2).

The poet has made a vocation out of what the ordinary person intuitively attempts and at least in some degree has become aware of how the task is to be achieved. He has gained an understanding of what the Canadian poet, Archibald MacLeish, called 'the means to meaning' (MacLeish 1960), which in my terms is the means of getting the quality of lived experience *into* the verbal structure.

MacLeish examines this 'means to meaning' in some detail, introducing a voice from fifteen hundred years ago that reverberates down the centuries and speaks as one poet to another. This resonating voice is that of the Chinese poet, Lu Chi who, in his treatise on poetry, describes the poet as one who 'traps heaven and earth in the cage of form' (ibid.: 16). MacLeish elaborates this remarkable image as follows: 'The poet's task,' he says, 'is to cage, to capture, the whole of experience, experience *as* a whole . . . in meaningful form . . . or shape . . . to which the emotions answer' (ibid.: 16–17).

MacLeish's account not only pinpoints the use of words to 'capture and cage' experience but introduces a further idea to which I shall return. He suggests that the form or shape in which a living experience is captured must somehow engage in *dialogue* with the emotion or experience that is so captured ('to which the emotions answer'). It is not enough that the containing form *points to* an experience; it has to be involved in more active communication with it. Lu Chi says something similar in one of his couplets: 'We poets struggle with Non-being to force it to yield Being; / We knock upon silence for an *answering* music' (ibid.: 17, italics mine). Even though we may not understand Lu Chi completely, we can sense that he too is referring to dialogue. The lines contain an expectation of someone or something responding: 'We knock upon silence for an answering music.'

It is, of course, easy to say that experience must be captured but more difficult to say how it should be done. However, in an essay entitled 'Feeling into words' (Heaney 2002), the Nobel Prize winner, Seamus Heaney, offers some interesting pointers. He suggests that putting feelings into words – the business of capturing them in poetic form – has two aspects: the first is 'craft' – the whole business of imagery, rhyme, rhythm and cadence – which to some extent can be learned from other poets by studying how they do it; the second is what he calls 'technique', a much more difficult achievement. Confusingly, Heaney's 'craft' is closer to what therapists call 'technique', while his 'technique' is a more comprehensive term that includes the quality of the poet's creative involvement in his work for which the therapist has no comparable word. Heaney writes:

> Technique involves not only a poet's way with words [the craft aspect that MacLeish calls 'the means to meaning'], his management of metre, rhythm and verbal texture; it involves also a definition of his stance towards life, a definition of his own reality. It involves the discovery of ways to go out of his normal cognitive bounds and raid the inarticulate [a quote here from Eliot]: a *dynamic alertness* that mediates between the origins of feeling in memory and experience, and the formal ploys [the craft aspect] that express these in a work of art. *Technique entails the*

*watermarking of your essential patterns of perception, voice and thought
into the touch and texture of your lines; it is that whole creative effort of
the mind's and body's resources to bring the meaning of experience within
the jurisdiction of form.*

(Heaney 2002: 19, italics mine)

Although Heaney's emphasis is different from that of MacLeish and
conveys a greater sense of struggle, his account contributes importantly to
what I want to describe. Bringing experience, with its tangible and emotional charge, within the 'jurisdiction of form' is more or less what I mean
by shaping and containing. It is more than simply giving an account of the
experience, dispatching a letter or other verbal construction; it is an act of
the entire being that involves descending inside oneself – 'sinking a shaft',
as Heaney puts it in the same paper – and somehow returning with the
inarticulate 'feel' of experience in one's grasp. Heaney continues:

Technique is what allows that first stirring of the mind round a word or
an image or a memory to grow towards articulation: articulation not
necessarily in terms of argument or explication but in terms of its own
potential for harmonious self-reproduction.

(ibid.: 21)

By self-reproduction, I take Heaney to mean the creation of a semblance
that gives form to the inarticulate experience, thus capturing it and
containing it as in my metaphor of making a model. It is the whole forming
process that brings the inarticulate under 'a new jurisdiction of form'. 'A
poem', he says, 'can survive stylistic blemishes but it cannot survive a still-
birth' (ibid.: 21).[1] It can survive faulty craft, but not a failure to tap the
reservoirs of feeling. The essential act is to cage and capture something
living within the form, or to put it differently, find a form that resonates
with the living creature of experience. Heaney continues:

The crucial action is preverbal, to be able to allow the first alertness or
come-hither, sensed in a blurred or incomplete way, to dilate and
approach as a thought or a theme or a phrase.

(ibid.: 21)

Whereas before he described the active stance of the poet – the poet's
effort to capture the living creature of feeling – he now emphasizes the
striving towards expression of the inarticulate itself. In other words, the

1 The same could be said of the analyst's interpretation, at least from the position that I am
  arguing.

inchoate feeling is active too, and reaches out to discover the words that will bring it into being.

Although Heaney is describing the poetic process, it would be hard to find a better description of the ordinary person's struggle with the inarticulate, whether as patient, therapist or merely as human being. Finding an authentic voice, in this sense, is not only a part of therapy but an aspect of living: 'I like to think,' said Winnicott, '. . . that if I do this work well enough [his particular variety of creative mirroring], the patient will find his or her own self, and will be able to exist and to feel real' (Winnicott 1967a/ 1971: 117). To exist and to feel real is to act from one's creative core and this surely involves creative utterance. Finding one's voice as a therapist is part of the same process.

In the accounts of both MacLeish/Lu Chi and Heaney, the creation of a poem has much in common with Winnicott's description of discovering one's self. In each case a preverbal 'gesture' (Winnicott) is brought 'towards articulation' (Heaney) through the mediation of a containing form. Heaney quotes Robert Frost: 'A poem begins as a lump in the throat, a homesickness, a love-sickness,' and this visceral stirring then '*finds* the thought, and the thought *finds* the words' (ibid.: 21, italics mine). First there is reaching out, then the finding of a form.[2] The discovered form (the container) is the 'answer' that plays the tune, or echoes the pattern of the inchoate searching – the image, or semblance that enables me to see what my experience is really like.

Poetic creation as described by Heaney overlaps significantly with the psychoanalytic enterprise. Both poet and psychoanalyst assert that a person's true being lies 'deep' in the non-verbal strata of the mind. Both, in their different ways, 'sink shafts' into that domain. What is interesting, however, is the means of retrieval. Does it involve, as Eliot implied, and some analysts appear to believe, 'a *raid* on the inarticulate' (Eliot 1944: 22, italics mine), returning, as it were, with a haul of booty, in the sacks (theories, perhaps) we have taken with us? Or does it involve, as Rilke asserted (chapter 4) and Winnicott implied, a process resembling grace, where the needed word – the form that resonates – arrives, if we can wait, from an answering silence? I will discuss this question in relation to therapeutic technique later in the chapter but first, a literary illustration.

---

2  I am placing in the same frame, the forms provided by the adaptive mother – Winnicott's mirroring (chapter 2) and Stern's attunement (chapter 1); the poetic forms with which Rilke gave voice to the dumb creatures (chapter 4); and the forms that the artist discovers or extorts from his chosen medium (chapters 3 and 9). There are also links with the forms that the analyst discovers as he tries to hold the patient's unspoken utterance in his reverie, and the forms that Winnicott (the analyst) gives back to the patient as a late derivative of maternal mirroring. I attempt to make these links more explicit later in the chapter.

## Retrieving experience

The enterprise of poetry suggests that a person's most important feelings are often the hardest to communicate. They seem to lie in the non-verbal domain and somehow beyond the reach of ordinary language. It seems that one of the functions of poetry is to put us in touch with such feelings and this is one of the reasons for valuing it so highly.

Heaney's account of the poet's activity suggests that it has both active and passive aspects. On the one hand, the poet is like an underground miner who has to sink shafts into the place where images are stored and made; on the other, he is a kind of suppliant, waiting and hoping for the image, the word, the phrase to come of its own accord. On the one hand, he raids the inarticulate like a ruthless baby, on the other, he patiently waits for an adaptive mother to bring him the form ('breast', attuned shape) that he needs.

One of the most graphic accounts of memory retrieval that I know is that of Marcel Proust, near the beginning of his long autobiographical novel *Remembrance of Things Past* (Proust 1922). He tells us that for a long time his childhood memories of Combray were confined to a single tableau revolving round the time when his mother would put him to bed and read to him. It seemed that everything else from that time was beyond recall. Proust reflects on the phenomenon of memory and thinks it is like in the Celtic belief in which the souls of those we have lost are held captive in some object, plant or animal – imprisoned in their forms 'until we happen to pass by the tree, or to obtain possession of the object which forms their prison. They then start to tremble, they call us by our name, and as soon as we have recognized their voice, the spell is broken. We have delivered them: they have overcome death and return to share our life' (ibid.: 57).

It is like this, Proust says, with our own past – it is no use *trying* to recapture a lost memory (the active stance) – we have to wait and hope that some chance event or association will come our way (a more passive waiting) and release the memory from its chains. And this is what happened for him. One day, he came home and his mother, realizing he was cold, gave him a cup of tea. She ordered him some little cakes called *petites madeleines*, plump and scallop-shaped like a pilgrim's shell. At first he declined to have one, and then absent-mindedly changed his mind and dipped a little bit of the cake in his tea. As he put it in his mouth, 'a shudder ran through [his] whole body'. He felt invaded by pleasurable sensations and a sense of something immensely significant taking place, but could not say what it was. He tasted the cake again . . . and again . . . and again . . . Each time he had a similar experience, a sense of something tantalizingly near but then gradually fading with each attempt. He knew there was something he was trying to remember – something waiting to be created, some experience 'which [did] not so far exist' (ibid.: 59). Nothing was of any avail, and he was close to giving up. Then suddenly the memory came flooding back – it was the taste of a little crumb of the *madeleine* that his Aunt Leonie used to give him, dipped in a cup of lime-flower tea, when he would visit her in bed on Sunday mornings as a child. And on the back of that memory, the whole vista of childhood Combray came flooding back in all its vividness.

For Proust, taste and smell had a privileged place in this process, but in some respects his description is similar to what I have described – an internal structure 'finds' an external 'form' which brings it into being. His reference to the Celtic belief in captive spirits is reminiscent of the Aboriginal creation story I refer to in chapter 4, and the idea that these spirits 'start and tremble' and 'call us by our name', strongly suggests a non-verbal communicative process between form and experience of the kind I have suggested.

There are, of course, neurological accounts of how and where in the brain memory is stored, and interesting as these are – for example, the idea that embodied memory is held in the right side of the brain and verbal memory in the left – I intend to stay in a psychological frame and ask what other ways there might be of understanding such sensory memories. Winnicott's theory of the transitional object provides a possible starting point, for although not presented as a theory of memory, it can in fact be seen in this way.

From a certain perspective, the transitional object can be regarded as an external phase of infant memory. As I explained in chapter 4, the efficacy of the object depends on its use in retrieving an experience of the mother during her absence (Winnicott 1953). Touching and stroking the object brings her back: it *is* the infant's way of remembering her.[3] From an external perspective, the object might seem to be only a reminder of her, its sensory qualities offering a *semblance* through which she can be remembered. From the baby's point of view, however, the object *re-creates* her, and for a while at least *contains* her softness and smell. In the words of MacLeish and Lu Chi, we could say that through the object, the infant has 'caged, captured, the whole of [the needed] experience, [the] experience as a whole, in a meaningful form or shape [the bit of blanket], to which the emotions answer' (ibid.: 16–17).

At first then, memory is contained in objects and it is not difficult to see how Winnicott extrapolated from this to think of cultural experience as an outreach of the earlier situation (Winnicott 1967b). If the baby could retrieve and hold on to cherished experience by caging and containing it in

3 I am reminded of Freud's statement that the transference is the patient's way of 'remembering'. From this point of view, the transference object could be regarded as a transitional structure that re-creates (embodies the 'memory' of) a loved figure from the past.

a resonating object, the bit of blanket, perhaps the adult could do something similar. From this perspective, the adult's transitional objects are the telling phrase or artefact, the poem, piece of music, or work of art. All of them retrieve and hold on to precious elements of experience.

Cultural transitional objects do more than this, however – they allow such experience to be enacted and displayed, and we are able to approach them as a resource. At the start of life, embodiment in external objects will be the norm, and attachment to them will be almost as intense as with the original object. With increasing tolerance of separation and the associated development of symbols, it becomes possible for experience to be held in *immaterial* objects – in other words, within the developing mind. Maternal mirroring and attunement, which I discussed in chapters 1, 2 and 4, enable intermediate steps to be envisaged; both belong to a stage in which intangible but preverbal forms begin to replace material objects as containers of experience. However, while symbolic development as a whole is able to follow this pathway to the limits of abstraction, the *evocation* of experience can never fully dispense with containment in sensual (i.e. bodily) forms. Relinquishing such forms is possible, but it leads to a more distanced kind of representation which views experience in relatively detached and dispassionate ways.

## Containment and self-realization

Although the theory of the transitional object suggests a means through which needed elements of experience might be preserved, it does not tell us how the infant begins to grasp the 'shape' of his experience: the pattern of emotions, sequence of moods or the vital rhythms that punctuate his daily living. Such reflexive apprehension of the self, whether in infancy or later life, inevitably involves the perspective of another person. This is because I can only apprehend myself by becoming other to myself – in other words, by adopting the other person's point of view.

However, such apprehension of the self comes in two forms, one objective and relatively distant, the other based on identification. Thus, the detached view, which describes me from *your* perspective and is often an appraisal, says: 'This is how you look from where I stand. This is what I think about you, how I see what you are doing, how I think you should behave, and so on.' The second view is more 'sympathetic': you envision me as though from my perspective. This involves identification – putting yourself in my shoes and giving voice to what you imagine to be my experience. It forms the basis of empathy and underlies both mirroring and attunement.

The first view yields a picture that feels distinct from the subject's own experience and may be at odds with it. It often focuses on external behaviour and may include the moral judgements of the viewer: 'You're a messy child!', 'You look really stupid when you do that!' etc. Because it treats the other person as separate from the viewer, it accentuates feelings of distance. For example, when Sartre imagines himself caught by a third party spying through the keyhole of a room, he describes the moment as one of catastrophic *objectification*. Sartre believes that this feeling is not primarily a function of guilt but depends on the feeling of ceasing to exist as a subject: a feeling that the world subtends from him as the field of his own experience, is suddenly overthrown by a sense of being an object in the other person's world (Sartre 1957; Wright 1991).

The second perspective, based on identification, is quite different from the first, because while the view still comes from the outside, and provides an external dimension, it has the effect of making me feel more intensely the subject that I am. It does this by providing *an external form for my inner experience* so that somehow I perceive the essence of my subjective self in something that lies beyond me. In empathy, for example, the other person attempts to put my *experience* into words; in mirroring, the mother's expression reflects her perception of the infant's *feeling state*; and in attunement, she likewise provides an enactment or portrayal of what she imagines the infant to be *experiencing*. In a certain way, the viewer in each of these scenarios has temporarily obliterated their own perspective. This means that *they do not transform the subject into their object, but give form to the subjectivity of the subject*. This enables the subjectivity 'to grow towards articulation', as Heaney puts it, to become more fully itself. While he is immersed in his own experience, a person has little sense of what it is like; only when the other person plays it back to him ('an echo coming back to you', to use another Heaney idea) does he have the opportunity to apprehend its 'shape' and texture.

The effects of these two 'feedbacks' are very different. The first contextualizes the subject within another person's frame of reference, and objectifies the self-image in acute and often painful ways; the second offers an external portrayal of the subject's experience. The first provides a sharp dose of reality (the world of other people); the second an external form for the experiencing self, and simultaneously a means of apprehending it.

Winnicott's theory of maternal adaptation is based on the idea that an infant cannot bear very much reality and needs the mother to cushion its impact. More than this, the infant needs to feel he can mould the tangible world before having to deal with its brute resistance. Winnicott's developmental theory thus puts maternal adaptation first (holding, containing and supporting), with *gradual* exposure to reality second. As a corollary, it follows that infant experience must be first articulated in ways based on identification (mirroring, attuning and empathic modes), and only after this can it tolerate the hard shaping of a separate view. Indeed, Winnicott suggests that deficiency in earlier modes of reflection may permanently impair the capacity for creative action. In essence, the person's capacity for spontaneous gestures will risk being lost, the self becoming a reactive structure based on compliance to impingement.

Reflections based on identification are one variety of adaptive maternal behaviour; they provide resonant external forms which hold and support the fragile structure of infant experience. Thus, in mirroring, a transient mood is held and intensified in the mother's responsive expression; in attunement, her more varied 'objective' forms punctuate the infant's experience into recognizable affective sequences; eventually, in empathy, her words offer a differentiated and consensual external vehicle for self-experience.

A closer look at attunement suggests a developmental sequence. First the mother enacts a form that reflects the shape of the infant's most recent 'experience'; then, like a primitive word, this becomes associated with the experience; next, the form is internalized as a containing structure for the experience; and finally, as separateness is more firmly established, it comes to represent the experience in a more truly symbolic way.

It seems likely that as the infant develops, preverbal experience is progressively held within a fabric of such maternal forms and I want to consider Bion's 'container-contained' structure in the light of this idea (Bion 1962a, 1962b, 1965).

Bion's theory of the 'container-contained' is an integral part of his theory of thinking which begins with projective identification. The infant projects an unbearable psychic content into the mother and the mother modifies it through her mental processing ($\alpha$-function). The infant re-introjects this modified content which is now a 'container-contained' structure. The unbearable infant element has become bearable (a first stage of thinking) because it is now linked to a containing maternal element that in some sense 'recognizes' what the unbearable content is. Containment, in Bion's schema, is the beginning of K, knowledge (Bion 1962a: 89–94).

Bion's formulations in this area are dense and abstract and closely linked to Kleinian theory. They are, however, suggestive and I have used them for my own purposes. Thus, we can think of the 'container' as a maternally adapted, resonant form (see above), the 'contained' as remembered sub-strate of experience. Already, however, such a formulation departs from Bion, for whom the concept of containment is linked with unbearable experience which the infant is unable to handle. Transposing Bion's terms into the context of attunement, they lose this link, since attunement is closer to play than instinctual agonies. Rather than preserving the infant from disintegration, as in Bion (a negative function), containment in the sense I give it becomes a means of preserving and recognizing experience (a more positive goal). It is closer to the transitional object than the bad breast.

A 'container-contained' structure conceived of in this way bears a close resemblance to what Langer, in the context of art, called a *presentational symbol*, which presents, or shows forth, that which it represents (or contains)

(Langer 1942, 1953). Such a symbol evokes and resonates with the experience stored within it, and from this perspective, the 'container-contained' is a 'living' structure consisting of intercommunicating elements.

This way of thinking enables one to see how maternal reflections could eventually underpin the infant's sense of being creatively alive (Winnicott 1967a). Within the 'container-contained' as an *internal* structure,[4] elements of experience would be 'held' in reverberating circuits of non-verbal 'communication' that reproduced the reflecting and enhancing relations previously enjoyed with the mother.[5]

To think of containment in this way does not mean that all containing structures have been fashioned by the mother, nor does it mean they are primitive or inferior. It is rather that the mother's contribution establishes a process which then becomes part of the infant's mental equipment (here again there is overlap with Bion). Just as the infant originally learned that a physical structure (the mother's 'breast') could be 'moulded' into a subjective 'shape', and went on from this to create the transitional object (by 'moulding' the bit of blanket), so now, the skill of discerning the *pattern* of experience will be gradually internalized. The transitional object offers a glimpse of this transition to greater self-sufficiency.[6]

In this sense, containment in adult life involves a growing capacity to generate (or find) containing structures (symbols) for oneself, and sustain oneself within their forms. This is a way of describing the capacity for imaginative, creative thought. However, such thought can also be described in communicational terms as a type of thinking in which there is lively communication between experiential substrate and representing form; the basic unit of imaginative thought is a dyadic structure of intercommunicating, resonating elements. By extending this argument, it is possible to see that the *symbol* itself is a sophisticated structure of this kind. In creative thought there is dialogue and communication *within* the structure of the symbol itself. This can be most clearly seen in metaphor, in which there is

---

4  I am contrasting the container-contained as a structure of the infant mind with the transient external 'structure' (from the infant's point of view) created by the mother's reflection or enactment where 'containment' is within the fleeting reflection itself.

5  An element of experience 'held' in this way within a 'container-contained' structure can be regarded as a $\beta$-element (Bion) that has been partially transformed by $\alpha$-function. It is this that gives it the potential to be used in a purely mental arena – in other words, that puts it on the way to becoming symbolic.

6  Within this self-sufficiency there is, nevertheless, a kind of communication, in the way that I have described for the 'container-contained'. Thus we could say that when the infant reaches for his bit of blanket and holds it to him, he is in a real sense communicating non-verbally with the mother (the mother's presence). There is dialogue with the mother in the transitional object, just as there is dialogue between the containing form and the contained experience in the mental structure of the 'container-contained'.

communication between the images in the sensory core of the structure, as well as between these images and the words that bring them together (Wright 1976).

## Poetry and technique

In the last part of this chapter I want to discuss the implications for technique of the ideas I have explored. This is the most difficult task because it concerns the manner of saying things rather than the content of what is said.

I began by considering poetic speech and what Heaney calls the craft and technique of poetry. The essence of poetic speech is to find ways of resurrecting and containing 'deep' experience; it has to make words and phrases resonate with forgotten life and thus to create forms within which that life can be safeguarded and held. I have suggested that this is also part of the psychoanalyst's (and psychotherapist's) task.

However, opinion on this would depend on how one views the purpose of psychoanalysis: is it to explain and find reasons, or is it to resurrect the pulse of forgotten life? Is it to make the unconscious conscious, interpret the transference and reconstruct the past? Or is it to revive the past in a more Proustian way, thus enriching and giving meaning to the here and now? Is it a technique, or is it an art – in Heaney's terminology, a 'craft' where you learn the tricks of the trade, or what he confusingly calls a 'technique' that can only be discovered through the struggle of the work? We can learn to craft an interpretation, and perhaps how and when to use it; it is much harder to make our language sing and resonate with the patient's experience (and indirectly with our own).

Such questions were hardly an issue in the classical heyday of psychoanalysis. In the eyes of its enthusiastic practitioners it was a budding science, and its probing tool, its subtle knife, was interpretation. To make good interpretations you had to be a translator of symbols. You had to know how to decipher unconscious content and the 'bible' was classical Freudian theory: instincts and their vicissitudes, defences, neurotic symptoms, sexual symbolism, compromise structures and so on. In the heady certainty of this new way of thinking, doubts about the major direction of technique had little place.

In the last fifty years or so psychoanalysis has become less certain about everything: its theories, its techniques and even its aims. There is a plurality of view about every aspect of the discipline and no 'bible' that is universally believed. Both theory and practice have evolved to meet changing clinical problems and equally have been shaped by the very different personalities of a few creative figures. One of the important issues to emerge from this flux, and the one that concerns me here, is the balance between interpretation, on the one hand, and containment and holding, on the other.

The concepts of containment and holding emerged out of psychoanalytic work with a more disturbed patient group than that which shaped the first psychoanalytic ideas. Whether such patients are called narcissistic, border-line or psychotic, the ordinary parameters of clinical work with them could no longer be taken for granted. This clinical challenge created practical interest in containment/holding and a theoretical interest in how these processes developed. It led Winnicott, among others, to modify his tech-nique with such patients in a way that privileged regression and holding over interpretation.

It was argued that this group of patients seemed to have suffered a deficiency of reliable holding in infancy, and given their difficulty in using interpretation (I give a clinical example in chapter 8), it seemed reasonable to modify the balance of analytic technique in favour of holding, at least for extended periods.

From this evolved Winnicott's later position that something other than interpretation was often the most important part of his work. Towards the end of his life, he wrote that 'psychotherapy[7] is not making clever and apt interpretations; by and large it is a long term giving back to the patient what the patient brings. It is a complex derivative of the face that reflects what is there to be seen' (Winnicott 1967a/1971: 117). In similar vein, he considered that unless the patient could first play, therapy, in the traditional sense of making interpretations, was little better than indoctrination.

Many analysts saw these views as heretical and did not accept them, arguing that interpretation, especially transference interpretation, remained the analyst's major tool for effecting change. If, however, we allow room for these newer ideas and hold rather than interpret, we soon discover that the nature of holding is far from clear. Winnicott provided general guid-ance: the analyst 'mirrors', and gives back to the patient what the patient brings. Yet how this is accomplished, and how the therapist now speaks to the patient, is far from obvious.

In this and earlier chapters I have examined holding and containing in a developmental context, focusing on mirroring and attunement. I have singled out these maternal activities, not because I consider them the only formative processes from this period, but because they can be visualized in some detail, and related in analogical ways to the analyst's activity. For example, if we realize that attunement 'works' through the matching of shapes, and the answer of form to feeling, we can look at different kinds of analytic intervention in the light of this idea. Similarly with resonance: if resonance is the mode of contact between form and experience in attune-ment, we can look at language and consider which forms of language are

---

7 I do not think Winnicott was distinguishing psychotherapy from psychoanalysis when he made this statement.

most likely to be resonant. It was this that led me to think about poetry and the way poets think about their activity.

Because *ordinary* language is essentially practical and concerned with external, shared reality – because it is *object*-related – it needs considerable adaptation before it can embody subjective phenomena. As I have discussed, it is a language of reference that views and points to phenomena within a shared contextual field. It classifies, orders and explains the multiplicity of phenomena and is not well suited to portray the individual essence of things. Yet this is precisely what counts when it comes to individual experience. In the same way that with people, we love their unique characteristics, so is it also with feelings and experience. What matters is their individual nature and quality (portrayal); we only sometimes need to know what they are 'about' (explanation).

Psychoanalysis and poetry share a concern with the deepest springs of human life and struggle with the same constraints of language. But while psychoanalysis has officially privileged explanation, poetry has openly espoused the life of feeling, and learned to bend language to this expressive end. Successful poetry *reveals* experience through *patterns* of words, and through words whose patterns create images. It communicates feeling through words used in a special way – through the resonance of metaphor and the cadence of form answering to form. While traditionally and officially, psychoanalysts have cultivated an unruffled language of prose, the poets passionately remind us that the imagery and music of language are key elements in its success.

To exemplify this in detail is beyond the scope of this chapter and intrinsically difficult, but one way of highlighting a quality is to give an example of its absence.

When I was doing my training, it was part of our assignment to watch psychotherapy groups through a one way screen, and one of the things I most vividly recall is the frustration I often felt. This was not because I knew better than the therapist what to say – I am sure I did not. My discomfort was more intuitive, a feeling that the natural flow of the group was often interfered with by the 'therapeutic' interventions. 'Why', I would ask myself, 'does the therapist keep interrupting what is going on? Surely there must be a way of intervening that goes more with the flow?' I now realize that I was listening to the music of the interaction more than the content – the prosody of speech, the rhythm of lines, and the way people interacted and spontaneously adopted the shapes and images of each other's comments. So why did the therapist have to be different? I now realize that it stemmed from his focusing on content and its explanation to the exclusion of everything else.

One group in particular stays in my mind; it was run by a senior and respected analyst. It was part of this analyst's style that he would remain silent for as much as the first three-quarters of an hour. He would then uncross his legs, sit up in his chair, take a big breath and speak for maybe ten minutes. While he did this, his eyes would roll around and he would look at the ceiling or the floor. He had a mellow voice – I liked the music of it – and in so far as I could understand and follow him, I thought that what he said was impressive. I say 'in so far as', because I would sometimes think: 'What about the patients? I wonder if they followed what he said?' And I felt that often they could not, because after the rent in the fabric of the session made by his speech, there would be a slow and desultory picking up of the threads, with little evidence that what he had so brilliantly crafted had been noticed at all.

With some justification, it could be said that this analyst was a master of interpretation, yet his interventions often appeared to derail the progress of the session. In focusing on the content of what the patients said, he seemed to cut across the organic evolution of the group and dislocate it from its own being. I wondered then, and still do, how therapeutic this was.

In making this observation, I recognize that interpretation may inevitably involve a degree of dislocation in the ongoing process – I discuss this more fully in chapter 8. I suggest, however, that working *with* the natural formations of the group or session, fostering and enhancing them by reflection and elaboration, is more likely to bring them to fruition. By fruition, I mean a greater realization of their own nature (self-realization and containment), not a greater understanding of what they are about (knowing the reason why).

The controversial analyst Ronnie Laing once wrote about a psychotic patient, who, when she came out of her psychotic state, said to him, as though by way of explanation: 'I wove a tapestry of symbols and have been living in it' (Laing 1961). This remark always intrigued me for it seemed to me that just the reverse was the case: before breaking down she had *no* tapestry of symbols ('container-contained' structures) in which to live (i.e. to 'hold' her experience) and this was one reason she was mad. In the terms I have been developing, she lived in a place of *un*-reflected objects (Bion's $\beta$-elements), yet to be given maternal containment, and I like to think that Laing, as a brilliantly intuitive therapist, may have helped his patient with this task.

The group therapist I described earlier was preoccupied with interpretation as naming and explaining. His work reflected ideas, current at the time, that this was the *primary task* of the therapeutic *work*. In this model, the therapist was supposed to keep his distance and occupy a place apart; if not a blank screen, he was at least a commentator who stood back and described what was going on.

It may be that this model is now less popular, and that Winnicott's metaphor of *play* (Winnicott 1971) has transformed the therapeutic scene. I think, however, that this is unlikely. The traditional stance is reassuring, and to stay with the written score is safer than embarking on improvisation.

I choose this word carefully because *improvisation* on an infant theme is a way of talking about attunement, and the notion of reflective improvisation on the patient's theme might help to recapture the vividness of Winnicott's insight.

Psychoanalysis and psychotherapy are not completely defined by interpretation, and understanding the reasons for behaviour is only part of the process. For interpretation to be possible there must be something to interpret; for an explanation to be meaningful, there must be experiences that are deeply felt and personal. *When* this is so, interpretation creates *cognitive* structures – a web of reasons and a thread of narrative – that join these experiences together. If, on the other hand, true 'experience' has never been established, interpretation is a futile exercise and experience must first be brought into being. This is the task of holding and containing – to build structures of feeling rather than narratives of thought. In these circumstances, the analyst's primary task, to quote Heaney, is to foster 'the first stirring of the mind round a word or an image or a memory (so that it) grow(s) towards articulation' (ibid.: 21). Only when it has reached fruition, and been contained in a fabric of imaginary forms, will it be resilient enough to weather the distanced perspective of interpretative scrutiny.

# Chapter 8

# Embodied language

The psychoanalytic relationship offers a unique kind of intimacy. Although asymmetric, it demands intense involvement from both parties and a willingness to share thinking and feeling to a degree unparalleled in other kinds of relationship. Such unprecedented sharing is mediated principally, though not exclusively, through language, and while analytic debate considers every aspect of this curious engagement, I shall focus on talking, in particular the way the analyst talks to his patient. My thoughts are a further development of chapters 2 and 7.

Historically speaking this is a relatively neglected topic. Clinical discussions have usually focused on the *content* of the patient's communications and the way these are understood by the analyst. The emphasis has been on whether, when and why the analyst makes an interpretation and which aspect of the material he 'takes up': for example, whether he focuses solely on the here and now of the transference or whether he also includes reconstructions of the past.

Discussions of this kind make two assumptions: first, that the analyst's main task is to make coherent sense of the analytic material, including the transference and countertransference; and second, that interpretation, however defined, is the most important analytic intervention. These assumptions underpin an approach to analysis in which the primary aim is to draw the patient's unconscious organizations of experience into the realm of conscious thought, and within this view, interpretation is the analyst's main tool.

This way of thinking reaches back to the beginning of psychoanalysis when Freud discovered that hysterical symptoms had unconscious meaning. The approach flourished unchecked for more than fifty years and threw light on every aspect of mental functioning from dreams and neurotic symptoms to religious practices and artistic creativity. In every case, the analyst sought out the unconscious content of the structure in question, and attempted to make this conscious and explicit. Interpretation was the principal tool of this endeavour, and at least implicitly, the major factor in promoting psychic change. Within this framework, discussions of technique (interpretation) aimed to clarify different kinds of interpretation in terms of content (anxiety, defence, transference, extra-transference, reconstruction etc.) in order to pinpoint those that most reliably led to mutative insight. The *way* the analyst delivered his interpretations – his tone of voice, use of words and images, the resonance of what he said with the utterance of the patient – found little place in such accounts.

## Finding a voice

From a present day perspective this view of analysis is simplistic because theory and practice, especially in recent decades, have evolved in complex ways, and *pari passu* with the realization that insight on its own is often insufficient, the emphasis has shifted from explicit interpretation to more subtle background factors such as holding (Winnicott) and containment (Bion). But whereas theories of *interpretation* are relatively detailed and coherent, operational accounts of *holding and containing* are harder to come by. Constituting an unobtrusive background to the analytic frame they seem to have eluded clear description.

It can be argued that the analyst's way of speaking to the patient is part of this background holding. I refer to this as the analyst's 'voice', meaning both the voice and words with which he speaks, and his inner relation to what he says. For example, it would include whether the analyst speaks with his own voice or that of someone else – perhaps his own analyst or supervisor – and whether his utterances are professional and safely distanced, or more recognizably personal, and issuing from his own affective core.

At some time or another every analyst has to confront questions of this kind in relation to his own work, and arguably the passage from professional to personal voice is interwoven with achieving an integrated analytic identity.[1] Beyond this, however, the issue has interpersonal dimensions, it being mainly through his voice that the analyst makes affective engagement with the patient, and equally through his voice that the patient gauges his analyst's integrity.

Finding a personal voice, however, is not the exclusive concern of the psychoanalyst; it is an issue for any creative person, not least for the patient who frequently discovers an authentic voice during the course of an analysis. It is certainly an issue for the poet. 'Finding a voice,' writes Seamus Heaney, 'means that you can get your own feeling into your own words and that your words have the feel of you about them' (Heaney 1974/2002: 16). Heaney

---

1 I imagine that every analyst, at one time or another, finds himself speaking with someone else's voice. For a long time after I had qualified there were occasions when I could hear my own analyst speaking as I made interpretations. These were probably times of increased anxiety, for in such circumstances it is reassuring to be one's analyst rather than oneself. For an inexperienced analyst, the voice of one's own analyst offers a reassuring façade behind which he can hide his uncertainty and emotion.

refs to the poet's voice but his statement has relevance for analysis, for it indicates maturity in the analyst when his words develop his own personal stamp, and equally in the patient when he finds a voice that genuinely expresses his inner being.

How then does the *poet* find his voice? Heaney tells us that:

> in practice, you hear it coming back from someone else, you hear something in another['s] . . . sounds that . . . enters the echo chamber of your heart and excites your whole nervous system . . . In fact . . . this other writer *has spoken something essential (that) you recognize . . . as a true sounding of aspects of yourself and your experience.*
>
> (ibid.: 16, italics mine)

The notion of finding oneself in another's speech is clearly pertinent to the psychoanalytic enterprise which also involves a sense of being profoundly recognized by another person (the analyst) who makes 'a true sounding of aspects of (oneself) and (one's) experience'. Heaney implies that through such recognition a new ability is formed, the ability to make 'true soundings' of *oneself* and to capture these in authentic, personal language. We could thus surmise that the analysand too develops an authentic voice through being first 'spoken' by the analyst. This would be a further form of the general truth that we only become fully ourselves through being 'recognized' in an authentic way by another person.

In Heaney's account, this process is far from intellectual: the other's words enter one's heart and 'excite [the] whole nervous system'. However, not all words have this ability; only some have the capacity to 'carry truth alive into the heart', as Wordsworth put it.[2] If we transfer this insight to analysis, which depends equally on words, we can see how the analyst's words, and the way he uses them, could be centrally important to the analytic process. It thus becomes meaningful to consider different ways of speaking, and to ask which forms of speech might best convey the analyst's 'true soundings' of the patient's states of mind, and thus offer a transforming 'recognition'.

## Creating a language

I do not want to explore the complicated process through which an analyst becomes more truly himself when he works with his patients in an authentic way. There may, however, be a direct relationship between his capacity to do this and that of the patient to find his or her own identity; as Searles (1973) first described, there must be a therapeutic symbiosis before there can be separation with enhanced maturity. I believe that such symbiosis

2 Wordsworth: *Preface to the Lyrical Ballads.*

involves, among other things, the creation of a joint and living language within which the pulse and feel of the patient's experience can be shared. If, in Heaney's account, we substitute 'analyst' for 'this other writer' – the *analyst* 'has spoken something essential . . . that you recognize as a true sounding of . . . your experience . . .' (ibid.: 16) – it is possible to glimpse the interpenetration of language and experience that genuine analytic discourse requires. For while it is true that *explanatory* interpretation may enlarge a patient's understanding, it frequently fails to 'excite the whole nervous system'. The ability of words to 'enter the echo chamber of (the patient's) heart' depends on some other quality. As Ogden writes:

> The analytic discourse requires of the analytic pair the development of *a metaphorical language* adequate to the creation of sounds and meanings that *reflect what it feels like* to think, feel, and physically experience (in short to be alive as a human being to the extent that one is capable) at a given moment.
>
> (Ogden 1997: 3, italics mine)

Inevitably, the analyst must be prepared to lead in this process, but unless he can find his own analytic voice and learn to speak in his own embodied and metaphorical way, he will hardly be a useful guide.

## Discursive and metaphorical language

In suggesting that the analyst should cultivate the art of metaphorical speech (a language of images), I am adopting a view that goes beyond the classical idea of interpretation as explanation. As I have already described, the task of the interpreting analyst was to make the unconscious dynamic explicit. His work was a process of explanation and clarification that gave sense to every psychic phenomenon, however bizarre or unintelligible. Classical interpretation had an explanatory form that aimed to create insight: 'You are doing this, feeling that, because of *a*, *b*, or *c*, perhaps to avoid *x*, *y* or *z*.' An extreme statement of this position was that of Ezriel (1956) who believed that every interpretation should be able to show how the present behaviour (the required relationship) was a defensive avoidance of some other state of affairs (the avoided relationship), the occurrence of which would lead to specific consequences (the calamity). Indeed, he thought that the analyst should remain silent unless he could offer to the patient such a complete tripartite structure.[3]

Ezriel's attitude was extreme, but softer forms of his position were endemic until the last few decades. As a position, it required a relatively

3 See chapter 2, footnote 4.

silent analyst whose active participation was limited to occasional interpretative utterances (explanations). Characteristically these would be
delivered in a level and logical way which left little room for ambiguity. It
was also perhaps part of this model that the analyst should be a blank screen
(in terms of his behaviour, though not in terms of his countertransference
receptivity), it making sense that the analyst should not disturb his professional façade or the development of the transference with lively, emotional
contributions of his own. I am not suggesting that in practice analysts always
behaved in such a distanced way, but describe a model that existed in the
back of the analyst's mind which in some degree would have influenced his
practice.

Whether or not this description strikes any chords, it can be argued that
the *act* of interpretation necessarily incorporates distance. Precisely because
it offers a discursive survey of the patient's feelings and behaviour, it
requires at least a temporary standing back from involvements based on
identification, with consequent loss of vividness. As Spencer Brown (1969)
put it in a different context, to 'explain', to set things out in discursive form,
is 'to take a view away from its prime reality or royalty, or to gain knowledge and lose the kingdom'. In this formal sense, knowledge inevitably
implies loss of verisimilitude; formal relationships are grasped at the
expense of living detail.

There could therefore be said to be two ways of knowing an object which
complement each other. The first is experiential, sensory and engaged and
includes identification with the object; the second involves standing back
from the object in order to obtain a totalizing but more distant view. We
can think of the first as providing sensory, lived knowledge of the object (or
subject), the second as yielding a more distanced external schema (Buber
1937; MacMurray 1957; Wright 1991).

These forms of knowing can also be described in terms of relational
structure. Thus, the engaged type of knowing is *dyadic*, knowledge being
gained from identification and interacting with the object; the second is
*triadic* and involves locating oneself outside the dyad in the position of a
third. From this more distanced observer position, the dyad can be seen as
a totality – it acquires a coherent and more external form.[4]

If we think of interpretation in these terms, it clearly involves standing
back from the dyad (e.g. the lived transference relationship), in order to 'see'
it (understand it) more clearly; the interpreting analyst is the third, the
totalizing, distanced observer. Through this operation the dyadic relationship acquires an 'objective', quasi-visual form through which it can be
grasped and held in the mind. However, in making such an interpretation the

---

4 Cf. Sartre (1960/1976: 116): 'The unity of a dyad can be *realized* only within a totalization
  performed from outside by a third party.'

analyst is asking the patient to engage in a series of moves that shadow his own – in other words, it requires the patient also to separate and stand back from his lived experience and suffer the loss of its 'prime reality or royalty'.

It is my contention that the way the patient negotiates such separation from sensory immersion will depend on his earlier experience of separation within the original dyad. A clinical example will illustrate this.

Shortly after beginning my psychotherapy training, I inherited a near psychotic man who over several years had been seen in weekly sessions by a succession of psychotherapy registrars. I quickly decided that he lacked the capacity to use psychotherapy, and with all the enthusiasm of a beginner, I broached the subject of termination. He did not appear to take much notice, so the next time I saw him, I again raised the topic in a more determined fashion. I said I thought we should have a good look at the situation and consider if it was really useful for him to continue. We might perhaps decide that working towards an ending was the best option. At this, the patient got up and left the room. The next thing I knew, he had returned and hurled a tea mug at my head and before I could react, he had launched himself on me in what I am convinced was a homicidal attack. At the time, I literally did not know what had hit me and was too busy preserving my life to think about what was happening. Forty years later, I perhaps begin to understand the episode. My omnipotent belief in my new-found powers as a psychotherapist had led me to make a poorly timed and, from his point of view, catastrophic interpretation, that he was inherently ill-equipped to handle. It is probable that his visits to the department, with whom he had developed a kind of symbiotic relationship, were the only times in his life when he felt in any degree safe, if not alive and he thus experienced my asking him to 'stand back' (in the observer position) and 'look at' the possibility of stopping his therapy as a murderous attack. His only way of dealing with this was to try and annihilate me.[5]

To summarize: My argument suggests that interpretation leads to a relatively distanced kind of knowledge which codifies experience and places it in a larger context. It involves a person seeing himself as an object in relation to others and offers an explanatory account of his feelings and behaviour. It uses a form of language that is poorly suited to capturing the uniqueness of individual experience and in this sense can be felt as diminishing. Some patients react to this interpretative process badly, feeling observed and dislocated from themselves in a way that transforms them into objects or specimens; they feel scrutinized and looked at, and robbed of their subjective individuality. In such cases the observer/analyst is at best experienced as un-empathic, at worst as a mortal threat to the self.

---

5 An alternative explanation would simply be in terms of dyadic rupture – the threat of ending a dyadic symbiosis. The rupture of interpretation involves standing back from the dyad – i.e. becoming a third in relation to it – which recapitulates an earlier loss of dyadic closeness.

Not all patients, perhaps relatively few, react in this way and this implies that in 'normal' scenarios personal experience is less vulnerable. To account for this, I make the hypothesis that protection is afforded by pre-existing containing structures which offer a kind of barrier to the analyst's objectifying gaze (interpretation). These would be transitional, non-verbal structures that 'hold' experience and keep it alive by resonating with it (see below and chapter 7). They would be related to, though not the same as, metaphorical language and constitute the source – the 'image cellar' (Heaney 1974/2002) – from which metaphor and incipient understanding would arise.

One of the most striking features of metaphorical language is its closeness to sensory experience; it is a form of embodied language. If I try and explain to another person what an experience is *like*, my only verbal recourse is metaphor. I might say: 'I feel as though I'm in a dark tunnel' or 'I feel broken' or 'I feel as happy as a bird on a summer's day.' In each case I invite the other person to imagine himself into a certain situation (in other words, to occupy the metaphorical image) and trust that through creative extrapolation from that situation he will gain some inkling of how I feel. I thus lead the other person to my feeling through an analogical, imagined structure which resonates in some crucial way with the 'shape' of my own experience. This structure then acts as a bridge which evokes in him a feeling state that echoes my own.

Being able to use images in this way empowers me with a language through which I can communicate my feelings. It implies that in some degree I know what my feelings are, though I may not understand them or know what they are about. And it means that I can 'have' feelings and experience them as 'mine'. In this sense I am a person and a going concern, and I cannot easily be robbed of my feelings because I have at my disposal a means of holding on to, containing, and accessing them within myself. I think of this 'holding' as mediated by *non-verbal*, perhaps transitional, symbolic structures that replicate the 'shape' and/or quality of the relevant experience; and I imagine that when I speak metaphorically in order to convey my feeling, I draw on this substratum of available symbolic forms. I shall not at the moment discuss this substratum except to say that it seems to be a developmental achievement that depends on prior maternal provision. From this point of view, my ability to 'speak' myself through images[6]

6 Dreams and metaphorical language are two ways in which a person may 'speak himself' through images but I also have in mind the great variety of artistic forms of expression: painting, sculpture, music etc. I believe that the non-verbal forms employed in these different media are in some degree derivatives of, and dependent upon, an earlier experience of having been 'spoken'/reflected by the mother or other caring figure. I mention mirroring and attunement later in this chapter but have discussed them more fully in relation to artistic creation in chapters 3, 4 and 9, and also in a number of previous publications (Wright 1998, 2000, and 2006).

depends on having first been 'spoken' in this way by another person (originally the mother).

If, as counterpoint, we think of the state of affairs in a psychotic patient, a critical difference becomes apparent: the power of using images to symbolize experience is severely impaired. For example, I once had a patient who informed me that his spinal cord was fused with that of another person. He suffered greatly because of this as it gave 'the other person' (his delusional figure) extraordinary power over him, so that he felt constantly controlled and influenced by him in a persecutory way. As I got to know him better it became increasingly clear that this other person was a derivative of his mother, from whom he had never been able to separate sufficiently. Of course, when his medication 'worked' his delusion would diminish its hold on him, but frequently he stopped taking it and his sense of persecution would then return. During one such period he got a can of petrol, sprinkled it around the parental home and set light to it. Fortunately the parents were not killed but his murderous intent was plain.

Clearly this patient had divined in some degree what his difficulty was. There was rudimentary 'knowledge' in his 'image cellar', but he did not possess this in a form he could hold in his mind (i.e. in symbolic form). He had never learned (or perhaps lost the capacity) to 'speak' his experience to himself – i.e. to tell himself in metaphorical mode 'what his situation was like'. He thus *suffered* the 'sense' of his situation in a concrete way (i.e. in the realm of things), and tried to get rid of the problem in a similar concrete fashion. Thus the only way he could rid himself of his 'fused' mother was by killing her – presumably he felt that his spinal cord (the core of his being) would then become free. It can be seen from this that his delusion contained a seed of knowledge, but he had been unable to free that knowledge from the experience itself – in other words, to 'speak' it in metaphors. According to my thesis, this stemmed from his having been insufficiently 'spoken' by others during a formative stage of his development – including the mother he tried to kill.[7]

---

7 It could be argued that this patient's primary difficulty was his inability to 'triangulate' experience – in other words, he lacked the capacity to move to an observing third position. However, this capacity is a relatively late achievement and it seems likely that the psychotic defect stems from an earlier phase of symbolic development at the dyadic level. This could be linked to a difficulty in perceiving the separateness of a non-verbal pattern from the patterned experience itself. I have argued that this separation is facilitated by maternal attunement, which brings patterned forms to experience from the outside. This approach would fit with Hobson's view of symbolic development outlined in Hobson (2000). Equally, however, intolerance of separation could be invoked as an explanation, a possibility that would equate better with Bion's (1962b) views.

## Learning to speak

Interpretation, in the sense I am using the term, is relevant and meaningful to a person who can already 'speak' his feelings. It can then help him understand and organize those feelings in a new way. If a patient is not able to 'speak' his feelings, if he does not 'have' them, or 'know what they are like', the task of analysis, in my view, is to help him develop a way of 'speaking' that will enable him to know them. In other words, he has to be helped to discover his feelings experientially and contain them,[8] *before* they can be discussed and interpreted. This requires that the analyst discover ways of speaking to the patient that are markedly different from traditional interpretation. As Danielle Quinodoz (2003) says, the analyst himself must 'learn to speak' – by which she means to speak in a sensory and metaphorical language.[9] This view is close to Winnicott's teaching that interpretation in the absence of a capacity for play is indoctrination, because it pressures the patient to inhabit a set of external forms that have little connection with his own experience. In such circumstances, analytic 'insight' can only create a 'false self' structure.

To link this with what I said earlier: if the language of interpretation is a post-separation language that takes for granted what is sometimes termed 'triangular space' (Britton 1998), the new language that the analyst must learn is a language of 'dyadic space'. In this language, embodied imagery is the prime symbolic currency and identification the main tool of 'knowledge'. With such dyadic patients, the primary aim is not so much to understand what everything is about; it is more a question of making room for something to be there, and helping it to find a voice (i.e. an expressive language). This voice will not in the first place be centred on talking *about* the self but will use words and images *to bring the self to life* and *foster the development of feeling and experience*. In this process, image and metaphor will be more important than ideas, and enrichment and development of images more important than explanation.

Approaching the patient's material from this perspective is likely to bring the analyst into conflict with everything he has been taught. In this arena, attunement and spontaneous response are more important than 'correct' behaviour, and explanatory interpretation will often be counterproductive. Thus, while conventional teaching urges the analyst to *use* his counter-

---

8 In a certain sense, 'discovering' and 'containing' are the same thing.

9 Quinodoz (2003) writes: 'Enabling a patient to relive personal experiences . . . and make links between the present moment and past emotional experiences . . . cannot be done with explanations or with purely logical language that appeals to the patient's rationality alone. [It] needs a form of language that evokes fantasies, that is close to poetry, and centred on affects . . . [It] is a form of language that resembles artistic and poetic discourse . . . that makes use of metaphors, images and analogies' (p. 1475).

transference in the making of interpretations but not to express it, the new perspective would argue for greater spontaneity, and some sharing of one's responses directly with the patient. There is probably no way of arguing this point that would convince its opponents – its justification lies in the 'feeling' of the session, the need to respond freely to evolving imagery, and the evidently beneficial effects of behaving in a less constrained fashion. For example, if a patient's material evokes in me an image or a line of poetry, I will *sometimes* offer this as a more or less un-vetted response. I might do this quite literally, or preface it with something like 'listening to you talking makes me think of this . . .' (line of poetry, image etc). This form of response, which could be seen as a verbal equivalent of Winnicott's squiggle game, involves both trust in one's intuitive reactions and a relative freedom from paranoid anxiety in relation to the patient – in other words, the analyst has got to feel reasonably 'safe' with the patient, *as well as* the patient feeling reasonably safe in relation to the analyst. I suspect, in fact, that such activity would not normally suggest itself unless the ambience of the session was sufficiently relaxed and mutually trusting.

As a way of responding, this could be seen as deriving from early forms of relatedness between mother and baby. I have discussed mirroring (Winnicott 1967a) and attunement (Stern 1985) and in both these processes, the mother's response is shaped by her identification with the infant's affective 'experience' (as sensed by her) and offers the infant a resonating 'form' that portrays (embodies) its essence. Such responses may be similar to what Ogden had in mind when he spoke of the necessity for the analytic pair to develop '*a metaphorical language* adequate to the creation of sounds and meanings that reflect *what it feels like to think, feel, and physically experience* (in short to be alive as a human being to the extent that one is capable) at a given moment' (Ogden 1997: 3, italics mine).

Winnicott (1967a) believed that maternal reflections (e.g. the expression the infant sees in the mother's face) give experiential reality to the infant's spontaneous gestures, and probably the forms generated by maternal attunement are even more effective (see chapters 1 and 4). He saw them as consolidating the sense of self and agency, the feeling of being an 'I' who can influence (create) the outside world. Beyond this, however, such forms can be seen as the mother's way of 'speaking' her child into existence (see my discussion of Rilke, chapter 4), by providing containing images for *potential* experience that has yet to be. Such forms would provide a first counterpart of the experience described by Heaney in which the other person's words are felt to be 'a true sounding of aspects of oneself and one's experience'. The mother 'sounds' the infant experience and that sounding 'creates' the experience and makes it 'real' (i.e. fully alive). I have suggested that in time, such maternal forms are internalized as containers of infant experience – incipient non-verbal symbols that reflect its unique patterns. Through their contour, shape and rhythm, for example, such forms 'recognize' (authenticate) the corresponding experience and provide a 'place' for it within the developing inner world.[10]

I have suggested that patients with fragile self structures have suffered a deficiency in such early responses, and if this is so, it seems appropriate that analysis should address this deficit through a comparable reflective process. In such circumstances, *discussing* with a child or patient their inability to play is unlikely to be helpful; *showing* the child or patient *how* to play is more likely to be effective. I will illustrate what I mean with a clinical vignette.

## Clinical illustration

This patient, who taught me a great deal, was important in crystallizing the thoughts and feelings I explore in this chapter. She was a woman in her fifties, separated, lonely and unhappy. I saw her three, sometimes four times a week for several years. She was emotional and volatile, with extremely limited capacity for reflection, and she often taxed me to the limit. She saw things in stark terms as 'black or 'white', 'good' or 'bad', and for much of the time I was 'bad', at least on the surface. On the other hand, she came to sessions regularly and found breaks extremely difficult. She lay on the couch in sporadic and sometimes unconventional ways; at times she lay on her stomach, and fixed me with her eyes at point blank range. She would pace the room or move from chair to chair. She made extensive use of the cushions (she called them '*my* cushions'), taking them away during breaks and sometimes throwing them when she was angry. Usually she held 'her cushion' close to her and sometimes hid her face in it.

In the early stages of therapy she was polite and compliant, even at times seductive, but once that early stage was over, she reacted negatively and contemptuously to practically everything I said. I felt this was not so much because she thought I was wrong – it was more the fact that she experienced all my interpretations as a form of control that threatened her very existence. She often tried to shut out my words by putting her hands over her ears and telling me to stop talking.

I suffered her onslaughts for a year or more and tried to interpret what she was doing in a more or less conventional transference way. She was the middle of three siblings with an older brother and younger sister, and always felt she was the one who was not really wanted. Her life was ruled by a strict and overbearing mother who continually told her off, while her

10  I have discussed the notion of an inner maternal 'place' in Wright (1991) and compared it with a 'no place' which lies beyond the corral of maternal holding and influence and is 'unconscious'. I would now say that the notion of maternal 'place' refers to experience that has been contained and 'spoken' (i.e. reflected) by the mother.

weak and gentle father stayed out of trouble in the background. These 'facts' provided ample material for my interpretive efforts, but eventually, in the face of her unabated hostility and a sense of complete stalemate between us, I began to change my way of working.

At the time this was more or less an intuitive response and I could not have formulated very clearly what I was doing, or why. However, I gradually found myself becoming less interpretative in a formal sense, and more responsive and interactive. No doubt I was reacting to the frustration and sense of helplessness she induced in me, a feeling that seemed to reflect what she had felt with her authoritarian mother. However, having tried every way of interpreting to no avail, I felt that *any* improvement in our relationship would be more therapeutic than the unremitting repetition and destructiveness that characterized the sessions.

The changes that slipped into what I did were largely non-verbal: the way I sat forward in my chair, the amount of eye contact and the frequency of my interventions. My voice became more responsive to the tenor and tempo of her moods and I found myself laughing, and probably sighing, more freely. The pattern of the interaction became more conversational; I was more genuinely involved and less the level interpreter occupying the observer position. In short, I came down from my analytic 'high horse' and as a result felt more 'human'.

Perhaps inevitably, I worried about my change of stance and my analytic superego tried to chastise me for acting out; in spite of this, however, I continued with what I was doing and gradually became more confident that the changes were beneficial. I seemed to be discovering ways of being with the patient that enabled the therapy to move forwards.

Until this point the pressure to react to her outbursts was intense, and though for the most part I resisted, and hoped in this way to provide a still point in the midst of her emotional storms, I often felt exhausted at the end of a session. Sometimes I felt like an instrument on which she played her tunes, and while I knew that I did not have to dance to them (in the sense of doing what she wanted me to do), it took me longer to realize that interpretation was not my only option, and a different kind of 'dancing' might be possible. It was this different way of responding that gradually evolved.

The main idea that supported me at this time was Winnicott's distinction between holding and interpretation and his growing emphasis on holding.[11] At this time, I did not really know what holding involved, but it seemed to me that this patient was pushing me, in the only way she knew, towards a

---

11 This theme runs through Winnicott's work, making it difficult to pinpoint one source that is more important than another. It underpins the way he increasingly worked and he clearly describes the approach in Winnicott (1967a).

different approach.[12] I can now see that this meant my allowing, and at times fostering, a more transitional form of relating; I use the term in a Winnicottian way as designating a state and/or time in which separation between self and other is not clearly established and illusory presences can be sufficiently vivid to soften the reality of absence.

I have already mentioned how she made use of the cushions to help her cope with unmanageable feelings at breaks and weekends, but in similar vein, she would sometimes fax me to ask me if I was there. This, too, I 'allowed' and would briefly answer her messages when I found them: 'Yes, I *am* here, and I'll see you on such and such a day' (her next appointment). Because I intuitively felt that such token actions and responses helped her survive the breaks without falling apart, I went along with what was happening without trying to interpret it.

I will give just one example of an intervention that illustrates in some degree the shift from ordinary interpretation to something more transitional and containing (and also more playful). It revolved around my introducing a different chair into the consulting room. The patient arrived at a session one morning to find that I had replaced a large upholstered Victorian armchair by one of lighter weight with black wooden arms. Always sensitive to changes in the setting, and scrutinizing things closely as she came into the room, she asked immediately where the chair had gone. At first I did not answer. Then she said: 'I don't like *that* chair (the replacement chair)! It's horrible!' I could have remained silent, as previously I would have done, but knew from experience how unproductive this could be. So I said: 'What don't you like about it?' She repeated again: 'It's just horrible', but then went on to elaborate – what she most disliked were the black wooden arms. At this moment the session felt interactive and emotionally engaged.

---

12 'Holding' (Winnicott) and 'containing' (Bion) are terms with distinct meanings given by the different theoretical matrices in which each is embedded. Ogden (2004) has provided a sensitive analysis of the terms from this perspective. His conclusion is worth quoting: 'Winnicott's holding and Bion's container-contained represent different analytic vertices from which to view the same analytic experience. Holding is concerned primarily with being and its relationship to time; the container-contained is centrally concerned with the processing (dreaming) of thoughts derived from lived emotional experience. Together they afford "stereoscopic" depth to the understanding of the emotional experiences occurring in the analytic session' (p. 1362). I use the concepts in a more fluid and imprecise way that includes their ordinary meaning. This enables me to develop my thinking about such issues with less constraint from established theories. Nevertheless, I agree with Ogden that holding has a more generalized 'feel' than Bion's containment (e.g. the way the setting 'holds' the patient), while the latter concept more readily carries the sense of specific maternal (or analytic) operations, even though Bion himself was unforthcoming about their detail. Paradoxically, Winnicott, with his detailed accounts of maternal responsiveness, gives a better sense of what 'containing' might actually involve than Bion.

During this exchange, the thought came to me that the large armchair I had moved out of the room was somehow connected with her father (the more approachable and containing parent). This suggested that the arm-chair with black arms might be connected with her mother, a figure of hatred, even a kind of witch. Earlier in the therapy I would probably have made a formal interpretation, but having learned from experience, I merely nodded towards the new armchair (which was black like a witch) and said: 'That must be your mother's chair then!' She said nothing, but screwed up her eyes and looked at it closely; she then shrunk back, at the same time covering her eyes with her hands in dramatic fashion. It was almost (but not quite) as though the chair in question *was* her mother. So I said to her: 'Maybe the other chair was your father's, then?' She considered this in the same quizzical way, neither confirming nor contradicting my surmise. This in itself was unusual, as disagreement was standard. She then said, in a lighter and livelier tone, as though cottoning on to the fact that this was a game: 'Whose chair is *that*, then?' – pointing to a smaller armchair sitting in its normal place. Quite spontaneously, she then exclaimed: 'Maybe that's *my* chair! It's small, like a child's!' To which I replied: 'Yes! That's what I was thinking! Did you have one like that at home?' She now became reflective and hesitant – extremely unusual for her: 'No . . .,' she said, then added excitedly: 'Yes I did! It was a little wicker chair!' She then continued in a lively way to tell me further memories from her childhood, and the more engaged, at times playful mood persisted for much of the session.

## Discussion

From a content point of view, the exchange over the chairs is hardly momentous but in spite of this it marked an important change in the work. The interaction was light and playful and I was drawn into her experience in a way that was unusual. Although my thinking continued, at least in the background, I responded spontaneously; I stayed close to her feelings about the change of chairs and she responded in a different and lively way. The transformation was especially striking for someone who usually complained about everything.

It seemed to me that this difference depended on the different way in which I had responded. Whereas previously I would have made an inter-pretation around the idea of the 'black' and 'horrible' mother/analyst, I made a more playful remark: 'That must be your mother's chair then!' She then responded by *play acting* her horror at this 'mother' (embodied in the chair), her playful reaction being in marked contrast to the un-modulated hatred she normally expressed towards her mother, and frequently towards me. This 'game' then developed to include 'her chair', and through this we moved further into her childhood experience. There was a genuine moment of sharing and trust.

If I had made a formal interpretation about her blackening attacks on her black and horrible mother/analyst/black chair, we would soon have been back in the old pattern. She would have felt I was attacking her, and I would again have *been* this horrible mother, locked in a transference enactment from which there was no escape. By responding playfully and staying close to the immediacy of her experience, it was possible to avoid this unproductive *cul de sac*.

Measured against interpretation in the formal sense, my intervention was incomplete and possibly collusive. I could be seen as avoiding a negative transference (being the hated mother) and colluding with the patient to keep things sweet (being the nice father). There were things we did not talk about (on this occasion the analyst/mother link) and we sidestepped things that were still too difficult. All these criticisms could be true but would miss the main point: namely that *the way I reacted facilitated the work and allowed me to engage more directly with the patient's experience*. It enabled her to handle a sudden change without being overwhelmed by it, and to stay with her experience rather than getting rid of it in her usual manner. This benign development was linked with a more flexible use of objects (the three armchairs) which in this exchange both embodied her experience and remained separate from it. She was beginning to make use of illusion and transitional space.

## Transference interpretation

I suggested earlier that classical interpretation is a divisive process. By encouraging the move to an external (third) position (Wright 1991), it separates the patient from the immediacy of their experience and the correlative sense of being one with it. In this sense, interpretation is like a 'subtle knife' (Pullman 1997) that divides the patient from their own self. In its zealousness to create a structure of thought, it creates a gap in the fabric of being. The patterns of thought are then offered in place of the felt shapes of living, a 'no-breast' in place of a 'breast' (Bion 1962b).[13]

When we speak of containment in analysis (Bion 1962b, 1965) we imply a more maternal function, and just as containment precedes symbolization in development, so might a similar sequence be necessary in analysis. In assessing a patient's response to interpretation, it is thus necessary to consider his early experience of separation and, crucially, whether this emerged from a background of adequate containment or was arbitrarily imposed, without regard for his ability to cope with it. If it was smoothly negotiated, in a way that safeguarded the continuity of experience, we might expect that interpretation would be tolerated. If, on the other hand, it

13 Bion, W. (1961) 'A theory of thinking', *International Journal of Psycho-Analysis* 43: 306–10.

was harshly imposed with trauma to experience and the self, we might expect interpretation to revive that trauma.

In discussing the fate of the transitional object, Winnicott (1953) says that it normally fades away, gradually losing its emotional investment. The need for a near delusory sense of the mother's body becomes unnecessary, and is replaced by newly developing capacities that enable the mother to be kept alive internally. The concrete external object (the transitional object) which first holds the memory of the mother is replaced by mental structures ('internal images') that hold her memory in more attenuated form. In the normal situation, this development would take place under the mother's coverage (Winnicott 1960a) while she herself was sufficiently available to meet the baby's continuing need, and with her absences mitigated by continuing use of the transitional object. In this normal 'journey' towards symbols (i.e. mental structures) (Winnicott 1953/1971: 6), the potentially traumatic loss of bodily possession is hardly noticed *provided* the mother furnishes the right conditions. The loss of the object is cushioned by inter-mediate and illusory forms of possession (transitional forms).

Interpretation can be thought of in a similar way. When the experience being interpreted can be 'held' within pre-existing transitional forms, the potential trauma of loss does not materialize. The separated symbol (inter-pretation) can then be experienced in a helpful way as *completing* a pre-existing psychic structure, not as a 'cold' and distanced substitute for it.

## Containment and maternal forms

The maternal contribution runs through every aspect of Winnicott's theory of development and in order to understand my position, it is necessary to recall the nature of this contribution. Essentially it involves the provision of containing forms that realize or complete an infant need. In the beginning, such forms are embodied and sensual but as development proceeds, this quality becomes less marked. It is thus possible to envisage a sequence beginning with the maternal 'breast' that realizes a concrete infant anticipa-tion – 'primary creativity' (Winnicott 1953); then the mother's facial expression that mirrors and reflects an infant emotional state (Winnicott 1967a); a little later, her attuned enactments that provide perceptual ana-logues of infant 'vitality affects' (Stern 1985); and finally words, that com-plete and name specific segments of experience, *at least in those situations where the mother is able to be in touch with it*. Within this sequence there is progressive attenuation of the maternal response, a growing distance from concrete bodily realization.

For Winnicott, the importance of such maternal forms has little to do with wish-fulfilment or instinctual satisfaction. He is more concerned with the way the maternal form (response) corresponds to infant need or gesture. This relationship is one of formal similarity, and from this point of view, it is not so much the *fact* of being fed that is important – the fact of instinctual satisfaction – as the patterning and timing of the feed. Similarly, in relation to the infant's emotional state, it is not so much what the infant conveys in terms of specific need that catches his attention but the patterning of the mother's response to it, and the way this portrays her identification with the infant's experience through its similarity of form.[14]

Winnicott's work, extended particularly by Stern, highlights a form of mother–infant communication that depends on iconic resemblance of forms (pre-symbolic images) rather than conventional vehicles of meaning (fully fledged symbols, verbal or otherwise). Winnicott saw this as the primary mode of communication between mother and infant and realized that it played an essential part in laying the foundations of the self. He saw how the adaptive presentation of the breast allows there to be an experience of creative omnipotence (primary creativity), and how maternal mirroring draws the infant self from potential to actual being (i.e. your response gives 'reality' to my experience). Stern's work on attunement can be viewed in a similar way, the mother's portrayal of an infant state providing an external 'form' or dwelling place for nascent experience, which can then be internalized as a fitting container of it.

Fundamental to this way of thinking is the idea of *resonance* between forms. Resonance can be thought of in terms of primitive communication – it is based on the recognition of formal similarity and mediated intuitively (non-verbally) rather than intellectually (through words). Thus in attunement, the mother's portrayal is similar in 'shape' to the infant's embodied experience (Stern 1985), and in this sense, external form and *potentially* inner state could be said to 'recognize' each other. Through such 'recognition' ('true sounding' – Heaney) of the infant state, the *potentially* inner becomes an *actual* 'experience' which the infant can now recognize through the provided form. In this sense, the maternal form can be seen as a way stage in the development of symbols, the mother's 'speaking' (singing, acting) of the infant showing the baby a way of knowing and recognizing himself.

## Interpretation and image making

It follows from my argument that interpretation is only one form of analytic intervention and not necessarily the most important. Although the first to be described, and often regarded as defining the analyst's activity, it could be seen as a finishing tool rather than a basic implement; its

---

14 Patterning, timing and a resonant isomorphism are some of the characteristics of therapist response that I have tried to single out in attempting to describe what is meant by containing and mirroring.

successful use depends on there being an 'object' of experience that requires finishing. Work with narcissistic and borderline patients forces the realization that this is not always the case and that basic structures may be deficient. In such patients there is a hole or gap where 'experience' should be, and as Enid Balint surmised (in the case of Susan, chapter 5), this may not so much result from massive projection as deficient maternal recognition (Balint, E. 1963/1993).

In the terms of this discussion, the hole in experience implies deficient containing structures – a state of affairs in which elements of *potential* experience have never been matched to resonating forms (images) and as a result have failed to enter the (symbolic, or pre-symbolic) register of the self. The containing fabric of images is incomplete, leading to a sense of scarcely existing as a self and living under constant threat of annihilation.[15] From this point of view, the annihilation feared by such patients is not physical extinction but *experiential* death – the fear that subjectivity will be overwhelmed by the other's objectifying 'view'. To such a person, the analyst's interpretation can be a threatening structure of this kind.

With such patients, the analytic task is different from that in normal (neurotic) patients and requires different technical skills. For extended periods, interpretation may have little to offer because it is experienced in such a traumatic way (as in the patient I described above). In these circumstances a different approach is required. This could be characterized as *a form of relating that fosters the discovery and development of personal experience*. I have given some indication of what this may be like. It involves above all the provision and drawing out of images that will strengthen and repair the containing fabric of experience – in other words, that will make a 'place' for it to 'be'. Whereas in interpretation, the analyst's task is to draw together and explain the dispersed elements of the patient's material so as to make a coherent story – 'I think this is what is going on at the moment: you are doing this, feeling that, because of such and such . . .' – the task of containment is to hold and foster the inner development of image and experience. The stance is one of close identification; the need is to give back to the patient the embodied images that such identification engenders.

Some readers may feel that this kind of responsive tracking and imaging is a major characteristic of how they work and a way of describing the analyst's countertransference reaction. Ogden, for example, often describes in great detail his flow of 'dreamlike' responses to the patient. There are, however, two main differences in what I am describing. The first is an

15 I once had a patient who felt so non-existent that she thought her husband would come home one day and sit in the chair she was occupying because he would no longer see her. Her sense of self was so tenuous that she felt herself to be almost invisible.

attitudinal set – when the analyst is engaged with the patient in a more containing way, he is perhaps less likely to be searching for material to interpret, and more 'capable of being in uncertainties, mysteries, doubts, without any irritable reaching after fact and reason . . .' (Keats).[16] The second difference concerns the use the analyst makes of his responses. In the case of the interpreting analyst such responses are merely the raw material that he ultimately processes into an interpretation. In the case of the containing analyst, they may be used in a more immediately reflecting way, with less concern about their part in the larger picture. This does not mean that such an analyst ignores the larger picture. He is merely less concerned about it at that moment and in so far as he is thinking about it, he is more likely to keep it to himself.

The containing, as opposed to interpretative, model is one of pre-separation mother and infant rather than post-separation oedipal child; it evokes a picture of *conversation* between quasi-merged analyst and patient rather than overlapping *monologues* between separate individuals. I am thinking particularly of the rhythm of the interaction which differs significantly in the two cases.

However, to speak of rhythm is again to evoke poetry with its ability to make 'deep soundings' of the self with powerful containing imagery. Through this capacity, poetry can suggest the kinds of speech that best capture and evoke the deepest levels of feeling. It cannot teach us how to speak as analysts, but it can make us more sensitive to the way that feelings lie in the rhythm and cadence of words as much as their content, and in the concreteness of images rather than the logic of discursive description (see Ogden 1997; Padel 2002).[17] The poet Rilke in his *Duino Elegies* (Rilke 1923/ 1960) described how the poet had to speak for all the things of the world that had no voice, and in so doing bring them into full existence. In a similar way, the analyst's speech must be impassioned (i.e. coming from his own feelings) and embodied (metaphorical), for like the poet, he has to 'speak' the patient's experience into existence and until he has achieved this, there is nothing to interpret.

16 Letter from Keats to his brothers George and Thomas Keats dated 21st December 1817. *Oxford Dictionary of Quotations*, Oxford: OUP, 1979: 293: 19.
17 Padel (2002: 13) writes: '(In a good poem) the sound becomes the meaning while it expresses it. (It is) a love affair of sound and sense.' This is similar to Heaney's notion of 'seek[ing] the contour of a meaning within the pattern of a rhythm' (Heaney 1988/2002: 34). Perhaps the same could be said of a containing intervention, that it evokes in its verbal form the experience of which it speaks.

# Chapter 9

# The search for form

## Self-realization and external form

In this chapter I make a further attempt to develop a theory of artistic creation informed by Winnicott's work. It builds on chapters 3 and 4, and although inevitably there is some overlap, I have tried to extend my earlier ideas in a number of ways.

Winnicott's theories were more often suggestive than comprehensive but at least an implicit theory of art can be found in his writings. There are hints, for example, in his statement that 'cultural experiences are in direct continuity with play, the play of those who have not yet heard of games . . .' (Winnicott 1967b/1971: 100), and also in his reference to 'a third area, that of play, which expands into creative living and into the whole cultural life of man' (ibid.: 102). More cogently, perhaps, he writes of the infant's innate potential for creativity ('primary creativity') that depends for realization on the mother's adaptive responses. According to this view, the roots of creativity lie at the very start of life in the feeding situation, where the adaptive mother gives the infant an experience of 'creating' the breast by providing it in the right way, at the right time (Winnicott 1953). This way of thinking subtly transforms the classical concept of wish-fulfilment by stressing its object-relational aspect: primary creativity does not merely involve libidinal satisfaction but *the finding by the baby* (and provision by the mother) *of a form that corresponds to its own inner state*. This formulation suggestively prefigures certain theories of art.

One such theory is that of the philosopher, Susanne Langer, who regarded the art object as a structure of non-verbal symbols that portray the forms of emotional life (Langer 1942, 1953). Her theory was complex and far reaching but its definition of art was simple: 'Art is the creation of forms symbolic of human feeling' (Langer 1953: 40). In Langer's way of thinking, *the artist* (like the baby) *finds external form for inner states*, thus echoing the transaction of primary creativity. In both scenarios an inner 'something' is realized through a shaping, transforming process.

In what follows, I attempt to construct a meaningful bridge between these two areas: the *self*-created forms of the artist and the answering forms provided by the mother in infancy. I shall start by considering Winnicott's theory of transitional phenomena (see also chapters 3 and 7).

For Winnicott (1953) the transitional object is the infant's first 'not-me' possession – a part of the external world that lies beyond the infant. It also constitutes a discovery, something the infant has *found*. From another point of view it is *created* by the infant – by a process that transforms an ordinary bit of blanket into something more than an ordinary bit of blanket. What then is this 'something more' that the bit of blanket now contains? It is, says Winnicott, *a subjective part of the infant*, the memory of earlier experiences with the mother. He likens it to the transubstantiated Host that for the Catholic *becomes* the body and blood of Christ; in similar fashion, he says, the bit of blanket *becomes* for the baby the (experience of) the mother's body.

However, this transforming process has a history and is made possible by the mother having given the baby a similar experience of finding an anticipated form (her actual breast) in the feeding situation. This initiates a line of development in which external objects can be invested with personal significance rather than simply accepted as they are. From this point of view, the transitional object is not a one off occurrence but prototypical of a creative relation to the world. Winnicott writes: '[If the mother can supply the right conditions], every detail of the baby's life is an example of creative living. Every object is a "found" object [just as the breast was in the feeding situation]. *Given the chance*, the baby begins to live creatively, and *to use actual objects to be creative into and with*' (Winnicott 1967a/1971: 101, italics mine).

Winnicott extrapolates from this to suggest that creative living always involves commerce with the object of this kind. First we put ourselves *into* the object, then realize ourselves *through* this object which has become significant for us.[1] 'Found objects' are always significant because of this

---

1  It would be possible and more usual to discuss this kind of exchange in terms of projective processes. Projection, however, has never completely lost its original sense of getting rid of something unwanted, and projective identification implies a sense of boundary that is lacking in Winnicott's formulation. In his account of mirroring, for example, the infant just gets on with things and the mother identifies, responds and reflects in an equally spontaneous way. Neither mother nor infant tries to get rid of anything and neither 'puts anything into' the other, at least in this sense. Throughout this book, I try and develop a more communicational framework in which the gap between subjects is bridged by non-verbal communication (i.e. through non-verbal signals). This renders less necessary the use of a projective model which sees projection by one person into the other as the primary means of bridging the gap. The non-verbal communication model is based on the idea that a potential for communication is a primary given in the human being's equipment, so that when the baby cries or smiles, for example, such action carries with it a built in expectation of response from the environment/mother. I discuss this in relation to projective identification in chapter 6.

subjective investment. This applies not only to the baby's transitional object, but to any object that in later life arrests our attention through its having this special aura.[2] Pebbles, pieces of driftwood, images provided by the natural world, even people can be thought of in this way. All are 'found objects', in which we simultaneously 'find' parts of ourselves. Artists are particularly likely to collect 'found objects' that resonate with personal or 'aesthetic' significance, and the wider notion of *finding oneself in, and through, an objective medium* is central to understanding the artistic enterprise from this Winnicottian perspective.

However, in order to develop this idea, I must mention a further piece of his theory, namely *maternal mirroring* (see chapter 2). Mirroring too is a form of *transitional* functioning but it heralds a development, because it marks an evolution of the concrete mother–infant transaction at the breast into a social and quasi-symbolic exchange. It remains a transitional process because it retains features of the pre-separation state but it draws trans-actions with the infant into a less embodied arena. Thus the image of the self reflected in the mother's face (a non-verbal signal) is not experienced as separate from the infant and 'belonging' to the mother, nor can it be physically apprehended by the infant; it is more that the infant feels realized within the containment of her animated response (see chapter 2, footnote 10, p. 34). In Balint's phrase, there is a 'harmonious mix-up' (Balint, M. 1959) in which the maternal reflection is merely an external phase (external from the observer's point of view) of the infant's sense of being.

In mirroring, the mother's face, like the baby's bit of blanket, functions as a responsive *medium* for the infant.[3] In other words, we can think of this 'medium' as an extension of the infant from which he draws out the *significant forms* of the mother's responsive expressions. These are significant, not only because they are an aspect of the caring figure, *but because they echo and give form to the current feeling state*. It could be said that they are the *anticipated response* to it.[4] Each discrete expression resonates with a discrete infant state and provides an image of it. In this sense, the infant *discovers himself* in the mother's response, and to misquote Langer, finds in the medium of her face an external form for his own feeling.

2 I have already suggested that transference objects can be thought of in this transitional way as examples of 'found' objects – a person 'finds' their father, mother, sibling or some aspect of these original figures in the analyst, or other figure in their present day life.
3 I developed the idea of the mother as responsive *medium* in a previous paper (Wright 1998) which in modified form appears as chapter 3 of the present volume. To think of the mother in this way not only captures the sense of the baby acting on the mother and playing on her sensibilities – it also makes a link to the artistic process and the medium out of which the artist creates his forms.
4 The same considerations apply here as in footnote 1. To conceptualize events in terms of 'anticipated response' invokes a communicational frame of reference ('two body') rather than a projection/introjection frame ('one body').

To put things in this way begins to make the link with art more apparent: there is an emotional reaching out towards the object, with perhaps the expectation of a response; a medium that allows itself to be transformed; and a 'finding' or creating within that medium of significant forms that reveal the subject to himself. Winnicott's model thus readily transposes into the language of art. My use of the phrase *significant form* is deliberate, for like the term *found object* it moves easily between the languages of infant development and aesthetics.

## Picture surface as maternal face

Connections of this kind between art and infancy have been noted before. The art critic Peter Fuller perceived the relevance of Winnicott's work to an understanding of art and discussed the work of the American painter Robert Natkin from this perspective (Fuller 1980). He suggested that the picture surface could be thought of as a face-like structure with which the artist communicated in ways that reached back to earlier experience with the mother's face. Significantly, he pointed out that while the maternal response is largely beyond the infant's control, the artist can modify his picture surface until it gives back to him the 'responses' that he 'needs'. These are the colours, forms, shapes, and relationships of one part to another that constitute the elements of his painting – the forms that resonate with the *inner* structures he intuitively attempts to realize in his work. 'The canvas surface,' wrote Fuller, '[becomes] a surrogate for the good mother's face' (ibid.: 211) and a more reliable provider of responsive forms than the mother of infancy. Natkin's own account of a chronically disconfirming childhood supported this idea: his mother was erratic, emotional, and punitive, slapping him whenever he showed emotion.

Natkin was preoccupied with faces throughout his career. Starting as a portrait painter (a painter of faces), he later turned to more abstract painting in which colour and texture were paramount – he could not stand the 'limitations and fixity which the physiognomy of facial features imposed on his [portrait] work' (ibid.: 210). Fuller took this to mean that portraits replicated for the artist the rigidity of his mother's face, so that in painting them, he felt prevented from freely interacting (communicating) with his canvas. It was as though the constraints of portraiture recreated the rigid and un-confirming dialogues of childhood, and to get beyond these he needed a freer and more abstract medium. With the move into abstraction his paintings sprang to life; through brilliant colour and varied textures, his picture surfaces began to give back an increasingly rich display of resonant feeling. At long last he had discovered a medium that responded to his emotional gestures.

Fuller sometimes watched Natkin painting and noted how intensely he was focused as he made his marks on the canvas:

> He dabs the pigment on in layer after layer using indented cloths wrapped around a sponge . . . The rhythms of his body inform the way in which he gradually builds up the image . . . controlled and seemingly instinctive . . . There is . . . a real sense in which every painting he makes is imprinted with his touch and movement: it cannot but stand in an intimate close relation with his body, and be expressive of the emotions and sensations he uses in his body.
>
> (ibid.: 233)

It seems then that abstract painting offered Natkin a new responsiveness that the portraits (and the mother's face) were unable to provide. Through experiment and struggle, he had found a way of producing for himself the expressive surface ('face') he needed, the materials he used, and ultimately the canvas itself, being drawn into the service of this need. He told Fuller that 'everything he had ever painted from the early portraits on was, in fact, a face' (ibid.: 210), and he 'found' himself as an artist at the point when these 'faces' began to give back to him the shapes and rhythms of his own emotional self.

The significance of this understanding transcends the particular case and raises the possibility of a more general statement: The artist, we could say, operates in dialogue with his canvas, and creates an illusory and expressive surface through his technique. With all the varied elements of that technique, he learns to draw from his medium forms that reflect and recreate the pulse and rhythm of his inner life. According to this view, the new relation between artist and medium parallels, but also improves on, an earlier preverbal relation with the mother, whose facial expressions mirrored, or failed to mirror, the emotional gestures of the artist as infant.

From this, it would seem that artistic creation may have a therapeutic function for the artist. Winnicott believed that when the mother's face fails as a responsive 'mirror', the infant 'look[s] around for other ways of getting something of [himself] back from the environment' (ibid.: 112). I suggest that artistic creativity is a later means of achieving the same ends, and from this perspective, the artist's medium is a new version of the maternal face. It too functions as a responsive extension of the artist – as an external medium in which he struggles to resume an unfinished earlier dialogue. *Creating forms for human feeling* (Langer's definition of art) is, in Balint's terms, a 'new beginning' on a more sophisticated level (Balint, M. 1952). It revives a process of self-creation (and transformation) that was insufficiently established in the medium of the first relationship.

## Maternal attunement

Winnicott's work has been seminal for psychoanalysis: in emphasizing the communicative dimension of early experience, and in placing the maternal face at the centre of early relatedness, he made a new kind of vision possible. However, one reaches a limit in using his insight to explore creative activity. For while the principle of mirroring offers a new conception of self-development, the tools it provides seem insufficient. The shortfall lies in the limitations of the face as expressive object, for while it provides a limited range of reflective expressions for emotional states and a number of 'qualifiers' in the shape of discreet 'looks' and facial gestures, it is not versatile enough to reflect the expanding variety of infant vitality. This is where Stern's work on attunement is so important (Rose 1996; Stern 1985).[5]

According to Stern, 'attunement is a recasting . . . of a subjective state' (ibid.: 161). But so too, in a slightly different way, is maternal mirroring and so too is art: each 'recasts' subjective feeling states into more or less objective form. Mirroring 'recasts' the infant's spontaneous affect into the visible form of the mother's facial expression; art 'recasts' human feeling and experience into the objective forms of the art object.

So what is attunement and why is it such a relevant concept? I have already discussed this in chapters 1, 3 and 4 but will outline the essentials of the concept again. The term is used by Stern for the many different ways in which the mother recasts her infant's experience. Peaking in the late preverbal period, its expressive forms are varied and make use of both sight and hearing. Eventually, as verbal comprehension develops, it gives way to language. How then does it work, and what does the mother do? What kinds of infant states provide the material for her recasting?

As I have described, the essence of attunement lies in the mother's ability to identify with the 'shape' of the baby's experience as revealed in its manifest behaviour. She 'reads' the changing rhythm of its interest – its way of being-in-the-world – in the contour of its body tensions, the speed and variation of its activity, the patterning of its vocalizations. Stern calls these the infant's 'vitality affects'. Without thinking, the mother internalizes these contours and transforms them into expressive patterns of her own. She shares these with the baby, spontaneously giving back a stream of 'performances' that reflect the baby's 'experience' as she has perceived it. Often such enactments transform the baby's expressive behaviour into a *different* sensory modality; they also modulate and vary it, much as a musical theme on one instrument may be taken up and repeated, with subtle differences, by another. Such recasting distinguishes the mother's response from mimicry: she does not copy the baby's *behaviour*, but grasps its *experience*,

5 Gilbert Rose, in a number of different publications, has explored the relevance of Stern's ideas for a psychoanalytic perspective on aesthetics. He has also made extensive use of Langer's theory of art in his synthesis. His work is couched within the framework of classical American psychoanalysis with its own idiom of expression, but in so far as I can understand his position, there is much with which I would agree. His most recent publication is Rose (1996).

which she then replays in a way that bears her stamp. Stern believes these variations and transformations are important because they give the enactment an aura of otherness.[6] Looking towards the later transformations of art, it could be said that in passing through the *medium* of the mother, the baby's lived emotional pattern is creatively changed and begins to confront him as an objective form in the gestures which the mother has 'shaped'.

In this way, attunement envelops the baby in a fabric of images (maternal responses) which recast its quirky vitality into (potentially) objective forms. The baby thrives within this imagined space and feels enhanced by feelings of resonance.[7] But the process goes further than mirroring, for while mirroring reflects the major patterns of affective arousal in a limited range of expressive forms (the mother's facial expressions), attunement has the potential to capture the essence of the baby's living in all its developing richness and diversity. The variety of forms (visual, vocal and kinetic) that attunement furnishes are more suited to match the increasing complexity of infant expression and arguably pave the way for language which will soon become the overriding form of exchange.

What is the relevance of this for artistic creativity? It is the possibility that the richness of the artist's imagination and his skill in finding forms for inner feeling states is a later development of the mother's intuitive skills – or perhaps a compensation for her relative lack of them. In mastering the techniques of his art, the artist has taken over the mother's form-making capacity, and brought it to fruition in his work. Not only does he now

6  In this nascent phase of symbol-formation, the *difference* between the mother's response and the infant's expression is probably important, helping to differentiate the maternal pattern from the experience itself. This might help the infant to grasp the notion, which at some point has to be grasped, that the pattern *stands for* the object (symbolic function) rather than indicating the presence of the object itself (signal function). In the transitional stage, such separateness is not an issue: patterns are important here as a means of *re-evoking* experience and providing containers for it (cf. the bit of blanket). If, however, recasting and mirroring prefigure language, it is possible that a growing separateness of pattern and experience might nudge the infant towards more symbolic modes of relating.

7  Maternal enactments present the baby with a portrayal, which in effect is the baby that the mother has imagined. If her imagining is reasonably accurate, we can suppose that the baby happily inhabits the form provided, and as with mirroring, feels enhanced by the feeling of resonance. If the imagined baby is skewed by the mother's own phantasies, the outcome will be different, for the mother's portrayal will then *dis*confirm the actual baby. This was probably the situation with which the poet Rilke had to contend (see Wright 2000 and chapter 4), his mother calling him by a girl's name (Maria) and dressing him like a girl in his early years. In such circumstances, the struggle to escape entrapment by the mother's image and find new ways of affirming one's true nature becomes a major life task, though conceivably one in which the creative arts can help. I have argued in the above paper that for Rilke, transformation (confirmation) through his own poetic forms was a central part of his struggle as both man and artist.

make the spontaneous and vital gestures that express his individuality; he also finds in his chosen medium the answering forms that bring them to reality in the objective world (Wright 1998, 2000).[8]

## Aesthetic experience

In exploring the artist's involvement in the objects he creates, it becomes clear that the creative process is a kind of dialogue in which he struggles with his medium until it gives back to him the resonating forms for which he is searching. I have assumed (following Langer) that these are the elusive shapes of his own subjective life, which only achieve realization in the aesthetic objects he creates.[9]

For the viewer of art, the situation is different because the work confronts us as a finished product, and the making dimension, so important to the artist, recedes into the background. As spectators we have no say in the creation of the object's forms; it confronts us as finished and given. Yet in spite of this, the work remains a responsive object that lends itself to the viewer. Whenever anyone connects with it in a meaningful way, there is dialogue between its forms and the viewer's emotional being; in spite of the constraints, its finished shapes allow themselves to be inhabited by the viewer's sentience and it then gives resonant form to these emotional intuitions, just as it did for the artist. This leads to the much discussed question of the *aesthetic* response – the feeling of often unspecified *significance* that a work of art engenders in the sensitive viewer. What is this significance and how can it be illuminated by psychoanalytic ideas?

As I have outlined in chapter 4, Freud himself was deeply interested in art but tended to focus on the specifics of its *content*. He approached the work of art as though it was a dream or neurotic symptom, asking what it was 'about', what unconscious fantasies it expressed and what it revealed about the psychological make up of the artist. He thought the meaning of art lay in its unconscious symbolism and failed to grasp the more elusive

---

8  Stern (1985: 158) has one paragraph where he mentions the work of Langer and the possible relevance of attunement to artistic creativity. I am not aware that he has elaborated on this further.

9  Langer coined the term 'presentational symbol' for a type of non-verbal symbol that 'presents' or portrays that to which it refers in iconic form. Such symbols are quite different from 'discursive symbols' such as words which merely *refer* to what they represent in an arbitrary but conventional way. Discursive symbols can be formed into languages because they have fixed, conventional referents; presentational symbols cannot be so deployed because the reference is entirely personal and arbitrary, being based on analogical similarity. It makes no sense, therefore, to argue that artistic forms constitute a *language* of feeling. A presentational form will portray the 'shape' of a feeling, but there can be no lexicon of presentational forms.

issues to do with its form. In short, he never sufficiently addressed the all important question: 'What kind of thing is a painting?' but assumed it was similar to other psychic productions that had yielded to his method of investigation (Freud 1908, 1910, 1914).

From an aesthetic point of view, this was a fateful decision and psychoanalytic investigations based on Freud's model have generally failed to illuminate aesthetic experience. This is because it was assumed that the work of art was essentially a vehicle for repressed or forbidden wishes, and from this point of view, the impact of Shakespeare's *Hamlet*, or the *Oedipus Rex* of Sophocles, for example, lay in the fact that they expressed forbidden oedipal fantasies. Strictly speaking, however, such considerations lie outside the aesthetic question which relates to formal characteristics of the work of art; while the content of the art object may affect us deeply, it remains distinct from the question of artistic value. This at least is the formalist assumption.

I shall now discuss how an understanding of *formal* structure (as opposed to content) can begin to illuminate the aesthetic question. The literature is vast but I draw on only three non-analytic sources (Bell 1914; Fry 1924; Langer 1942, 1953) and two recent psychoanalytic contributions of particular relevance (Segal 1991; Bollas 1987).

I begin with the formal approach of Clive Bell and Roger Fry, which centres on the idea of 'significant form'. These writers were both concerned with *significance* in art, and they asked: 'What is it that makes art significant, and is there something unique in our response to it that is different from our response to ordinary objects?' Bell was the first to say there was.

> That there is a particular kind of emotion provoked by works of visual art, and that this . . . is provoked by every kind of visual art . . . is not disputed, I think, by anyone capable of feeling it. This emotion is called the aesthetic emotion; and if we can discover some quality common and peculiar to all the objects that provoke it, we shall have solved what I take to be the central problem of aesthetics. [He asks what this 'essential quality' might be and replies that] . . . Only one answer seems possible – significant form. *In each [instance], lines and colours combined in a particular way, certain forms and relations of forms, stir our aesthetic emotions.* These . . . aesthetically moving forms, I call 'Significant Form'; and 'Significant Form' is the one quality common to all works of visual art.
>
> (Bell 1914, in Harrison and Wood 1992: 113, italics mine)

Bell's analysis referred only to the visual arts but Fry extended his theory more widely and attempted to define the *aesthetic emotion*. The concept, however, proved difficult to pin down. The aesthetic emotion was not, he said, like ordinary emotions that are linked to particular objects or situations, but is stirred in us when we recognize *significant form*. This concept too was hard to define but seemed to depend on the 'the recognition of inevitable sequences' in the art object: in other words, on a certain perception of pattern and form that felt 'right' to the viewer, and in that sense 'had to be' the way it was. Fry's argument was self-enclosed and circular, and in some ways lacking in substance: We experience the aesthetic emotion when confronted with significant form; we deem a form significant when it arouses our aesthetic emotion.

Within this approach, aesthetic experience is not linked to any particular motif – to what is depicted – but to some more general characteristic of the art object. Our *aesthetic* response to *Hamlet*, for example, does not depend on the *content* of the story but on other elusive aspects of the play that we struggle to define. To approach their nature, we have to turn to some overall *quality* of the depiction.

In this context, the work of Bollas (1987) is helpful. Discussing the aesthetic emotion from a broadly Winnicottian perspective, he suggests that objects triggering such a response are connected in our minds with early 'transformational experiences' in which the mother's care was felt to transform the infant's being in a profound way. Such ministrations would not have been special events but part of the baby's normal experience of the mother in the early stages: 'Whenever we desired, despaired, reached towards, played, or were in rage, love, pain or need, we were met by [the] mother and handled according to her idiom of care' (ibid.: 36). Thus she transformed our experience – for example from hunger to satiation – but in her own unique way, with her own particular style. This style he called her 'idiom of care' and suggested it was inscribed in our being in a pre-symbolic way that we can recognize but not remember. In his terms, it constituted part of 'the un-thought known' (Stern calls it the 'structural unconscious'), and he referred to it as a 'maternal aesthetic'.

From this perspective, aesthetic experience depends on the revival of such early feelings:

> The uncanny pleasure of being held by a poem, a composition, a painting, or for that matter, any object, rests on those moments when the infant's world is given form by the mother, since he cannot shape them or link them together without her coverage. . . . The transformational object [from our point of view, the art object] seems to promise the beseeching subject *an experience where self-fragmentations will be integrated through a processing form*.
>
> (ibid.: 32–3, italics mine)

This comes close to the idea of the art object as a source of containing and resonating forms, but for Bollas, the revival of early memory – the sense of being *in the presence of* a transformational object – seems more important than the value of the forms themselves as integrating agents in the contemporary life of the subject. This slant on aesthetic experience seems to make the work of art a nostalgic object, inducing recollection and hope of transformation but downplaying its contemporary therapeutic possibilities as a repository of needed forms. In this sense, Bollas' views differ significantly from my own.

I shall now consider the work of Hannah Segal, a Kleinian psychoanalyst who has written cogently and sensitively on aesthetic issues. Taking the criticisms of Freud's 'content' approach seriously, she believes aesthetic experience is linked to wider issues than the depiction of specific content. Foremost is what she calls the 'truthfulness' of a representation: a form is 'significant' when it 'truthfully' portrays an emotional structure or situation (Segal 1991). Thus, while we might respond to *Hamlet* emotionally because of *what* it depicts (e.g. aspects of the oedipal conflict with which we identify), the *aesthetic power* of the play – its capacity to arouse the aesthetic emotion – would depend on the 'truthfulness' with which that content was portrayed. This is a formal consideration which refers to the adequacy of symbolic means, and indirectly, the skill of the creator. In *Hamlet*, or indeed any other play, this would take us into the area of language and the power of imagery and metaphor to reflect the pattern and coherence of emotional life.

With the notion of 'truthfulness', Segal directs attention to the *construction* of the art object – the way it is made and put together, and how this reflects or fails to reflect the structure of our emotional being. However, on a vastly simplified scale, the same question confronts us when we turn to mirroring and attunement: how truthfully does the mother's facial expression mirror the baby's affective state; and how truthfully does her mini-enactment portray the baby's vitality affect which has just unfolded before her eyes.[10]

This way of thinking links aesthetic significance to wider emotional issues. It is no longer a self-enclosed process depending on formal relations *within* the art object (Fry's definition of 'significant form') but now concerns the relation *between* these and the dynamic forms of emotional life. The aesthetic emotion becomes in this way an indicator of *personal* significance, telling us that the forms and organization of a particular work of art correspond truthfully to some felt pattern of our own emotional life. In this sense, every object with aesthetic import is potentially in tune with *some* elements of human feeling, and while any *particular* work of art will be limited by its creator's range of sensibility, every 'truthful' work will have its supporters because it resonates and speaks to them. Finally, this approach

---

10 Perhaps even more pertinent is the accuracy of the mother's labelling when language becomes the predominant form of communication.

enables bridges to be made with early experience (Bollas' 'maternal aesthetic' and Fuller's link to the maternal face), for if *in infancy* the very means to selfhood depend on the truthfulness of representation – in other words, on the accuracy of maternal reflection/attunement (Winnicott 1967a; Stern 1985) – we can understand how art, its distant successor, is able to evoke such powerful reactions.

## Integration, wholeness and aesthetic impact

The concept of truthful representation has considerable heuristic value. For Segal, however, the complexity of artistic creation and our response to its products cannot be fully accounted for in this way, for we feel intuitively that the art object has an *integrative* capacity, an ability to draw together disparate elements of the self into more complex wholes. To explain this, Segal falls back on a 'content' type of explanation, thereby giving the aesthetic emotion a Kleinian twist. Arguing that destruction and re-creation lie at the heart of artistic endeavour, she suggests that significance in art is inseparably linked with the core depressive conflict of destruction and reparation. This conclusion seriously narrows her definition of art and closes the door to alternative explanations of its integrative action.

Segal's Kleinian view focuses on the *object* – internally damaged by the artist's attacks and restored and made whole in the creative act. A Winnicottian perspective raises different possibilities: if the work of art functions in a transitional way as extension of the artist's self, might not artistic creation aim to establish and restore the *self*, rather than perform reparative work on the *object*? This would place the artist's most urgent need at the narcissistic level, the sense of integration we get from a work of art reflecting a new found wholeness of the artist's *self* – and by extension, of our own – rather than the wholeness of a previously damaged and now repaired *object*.[11]

I have already discussed in relation to Natkin's work how the artist's skill in making resonant forms may result from an original deficiency; how through internalizing and developing the deficient maternal function, the artist learns to provide significant forms for himself; and how by treating his canvas as a surrogate maternal extension, he coaxes, cajoles and extorts the responses he needs from a more or less resistant medium. I have

---

11  I have already discussed this idea in relation to the poet Rilke (Wright 2000, and chapter 4). Rilke believed it was the poet's task to give life and voice to all the 'dumb' creatures of the world, animate and inanimate; these creatures had no voice of their own and depended on the poet to proclaim (present) their living essence in his verse. It is clear that for Rilke the poetic medium was equivalent to the artist's canvas (a transitional extension of the poet) and the forms with which he sings the dumb creatures into existence are the very forms he himself needs in order to realize his own self.

sketched how in normal development, a similar process completes the baby's experience, marking and containing it within a maternal form, and how this stands at the threshold of symbolization, offering a first means of drawing experience into objective form, and paving the way for language. Following Winnicott, I have argued that we first become selves through this process, the sense of 'being me' *depending* on experience being 'held' in this fashion.

Within this framework, attunement and mirroring can be seen as core processes that literally bring the self into being. In this sense, un-mirrored and non-attuned elements have yet to be realized; with no objective form, they are unavailable for self-enrichment and cannot be organized into larger patterns of experience. *Until emotional life can be marked and symbolized there is no real experience, and no way of handling it* (see chapter 12).

From this perspective, the artist's pressing need is to bring his own self into being through his creative work. By providing forms for latent elements of his affective life, he draws them into being and gathers them within his own purview and jurisdiction.[12] Such unmarked elements are those that have been ignored, whether through the imperviousness of an un-empathic mother or a kind of selective inattention that is probably more normal.[13] Stern (1985: 160) has suggested there may be an *inherent* problem in attuning to certain negative affects, and if this is so, the shortfall the artist addresses is universal.

This perspective displaces reparation of the object from its central role in artistic creation and replaces it with self-creation and discovery. From this point of view, the primary task of the artist is not to repair the *object* but to draw the *self* into a fabric of resonating forms. Once corralled within the

12  Cf. Heaney's 'jurisdiction of form' in chapter 7, p. 109.
13  Bion's theory of containment (Bion 1962a, 1962b; 1965) overlaps with Winnicott's (1967a) mirroring and also provides an approach to the transformation of infant experience. However, Bion's concept is subtly different from Winnicott's and fails to capture elements which are central to the mirroring process. To give just one example: Bion's notion of the mother 'processing' her infant's feelings within her 'reverie' and giving them back to the infant in manageable form, undoubtedly draws attention to the dialogic relation between mother and infant. What it lacks, however, is the sense of *making experience feel real through recognition* which was Winnicott's primary concern. To capture the sense of this requires a more interactive or dialogical language – e.g. something out there *resonates with* and *confirms* something in here – and such words are part of a different semantic landscape. Bion's ideas are interwoven with the concept of projective identification, and the idea that the infant communicates primarily through this means. References to such processes are absent from Winnicott's account – indeed, it could be argued that Winnicott's baby has an embryonic communicative potential from the beginning which already anticipates a responsive other. This would place Winnicott closer to Suttie (the infant has a 'primary need for the mother') and Trevarthen (a need for 'companionship' and 'proto-conversation') than to Klein (Suttie 1935; Trevarthen 1979; Wright 2006).

project of the picture, the secondary task is to integrate these forms, and thus the self, into a more coherent whole.[14]

For the viewer of the work of art such creative, *making* phases are inevitably curtailed; he can only *seek*, and find through *looking* creatively. The viewer discovers works of art with special resonance, and these allow him to engage with their forms in a meaningful way as transitional extensions of himself, and as medium for self-transformation. Like the artist, the viewer needs such forms to draw his experience into being, and since his needs overlap with those of the artist, he is an artist by default. For both creator and viewer the art object functions in a similar way – as a surrogate mother, made or chosen as the case may be, which resonates with his own sentient core.

## Conclusion

In approaching artistic creativity, and in particular the process of painting, I have built on Winnicott's seminal ideas. His astonishing understanding of early processes allows one to grasp in an almost concrete fashion the dialogical, relational core of the individual self. He enabled us to see that latent or *potential* elements of the self require completion by a resonant maternal response (mirroring, and later attunement), and he understood the sense of falseness and emptiness that results from failure in this process.

I have argued that the deeper functions of *art* are genetically linked to this preverbal arena and that significant form, in the aesthetic sense, is form that truthfully (i.e. accurately) resonates with subjective elements and brings them into existential being. In Winnicott's terms, they enable a person to 'exist and feel real' (ibid.: 117). The artist has developed the capacity and skill to create such forms and his use of a *medium* as transitional extension of himself is analogous to the infant's early use of the mother. I have suggested that the development of such skills stems from the need to make good an early deficit by drawing into the purview of symbolic containment those aspects of self that were hitherto unrecognized. Such symbolic retrieval is a necessary precursor of integrative tasks, but I take issue with Segal that artistic creation *inevitably* involves restoration (integration) of a damaged object. In my view, the striving of art towards wholeness and integration is better understood as an attempt to realize the wholeness of the

---

14 I do not want to suggest that the Kleinian concept of reparation is unimportant in a theory of mind, only to challenge its supremacy as an explanatory concept, both in general, and more specifically in relation to the creative process. It is quite probable that *some* creative acts are driven by guilt and remorse and directed towards the restitution of the object. It is highly improbable that *all* creative acts are so driven, and even possible that they form a minority.

*self*, a task that is never complete because of the vagaries of early mothering and the constantly changing circumstances of ordinary life.

I have focused on the visual arts but regard the model I have proposed as relevant to creation in other media. I have emphasized non-verbal dialogue but similar processes operate in poetry, for example, where the poet informs language with his own being, and remakes it in the service of his expressive need (chapters 2 and 7).

Finally, I suggest that the interaction between patient and analyst has important similarities to that between the artist and his medium. Whether we think of the medium as the *affective matrix* of the analytic relationship, or the *language* in which this is progressively articulated, analysis too makes 'forms for human feeling' (Langer), and like the artist's forms these must resonate with experience if they are to serve a containing function (I have discussed this in chapters 7 and 8). This view differs significantly from insight approaches which use explanatory language and which too often, in Winnicott's words, make 'clever and apt interpretations'. The artistic mode seeks *resonating* forms for the patient's experience and sees the analyst's activity as 'a complex derivative of the face that reflects what is there to be seen' (ibid.: 117).

# Chapter 10

# The intuition of the sacred

## Religion, law and the father

In this chapter, I explore the idea that the roots of religious experience lie in the preverbal core of the self. I shall argue that religion offers recognition, and a promise of containment, to elements of the self that have been excluded from the developmental process; and that where it exists, the religious quest is fired by a need for containment, and longing for a containing object. Finally, I shall attempt to show that the religious process so defined is part of an axis of love (*agape*, tenderness) in the human personality, distinct from the libidinal axis (*eros*) described by Freud. In making these assertions, I do not wish to circumscribe the field of religion but to draw attention to a neglected area of psychoanalytic theorizing.

Freud himself was deeply interested in religion but for the most part his views were quite negative. His insights were principally concerned with man's unresolved dependence on parental figures and he believed it was the persistence of longing for a strong father that induced belief in an all-powerful god (Freud 1927, 1930). Echoing in part the paternalistic values of his day, Freud regarded this as a failure of development and he might have agreed with St Paul that the 'putting away of childish things' was the essence of becoming a man (1 Corinthians 13: 11).

It is being increasingly recognized, however, that Freud's views were constrained by his own make-up. While he gave brilliant descriptions of those parts of the personality that turned on the axis of the father, the Oedipus complex and its legacy, his formulations concerning the pre-oedipal period, the maternal axis, were far weaker. The argument linking theory to personality was first put forward by a Tavistock psychotherapist, Ian Suttie, who claimed that not only Freud's account of religion, but his whole theoretical opus, was skewed by an anti-maternal bias in his make-up (Suttie 1935). Noting Freud's difficulty in identifying with the *oceanic feeling* (Freud 1930) and his derivation of love and tenderness from the sexual instinct, he postulated a *taboo on tenderness* in Freud's personality, stemming from a blindness to, or repression of, aspects of his early *relationship* with his mother. In a way that pre-figured Bowlby's *attachment theory* (Bowlby 1969), Suttie suggested that the infant was born with 'a simple attachment-to-mother', a primary need for 'companionship' and contact with her.[1] He considered that feelings of tenderness developed from this early matrix, and had little to do with the sexual appetite or instinct *per se*, at least in the way that Freud envisaged.

That Freud's personality was organized along paternal lines (Wright 1991) is further evidenced by his fascination with the figure of Moses. Freud wrote at length about this 'father' of the Jewish people and was deeply fascinated by Michelangelo's sculpture of him with the tables of the Law. This powerful statue relates to Moses' descent from Mount Sinai with 'two tables of testimony, tables of stone, written with the finger of God' (Exodus 31: 18), and the moment of wrath when he discovered that his people were worshipping the golden calf of heathen neighbours (Freud 1914). Freud too was intolerant of those in his circle who advocated 'false gods' in the form of theories different from his own. Indeed, he was so keen to preserve the *paternal* truth of his discoveries that it took two generations to fully instate the *mother* into psychoanalytic thinking. Consequently, psychoanalytic views on religion remained fixed at the oedipal level of understanding – patricidal impulse, incestuous guilt, atonement, and ultimately subservience to the father. Over and above the personality aspect, however, such constructs would have seemed pertinent at the end of the nineteenth century. Not only was the prevailing ethos paternal but the Judaeo-Christian tradition itself was paternally weighted. The God of Abraham was a father ruling over his chosen race and the God of Christianity inherited many of his characteristics: 'Our *father* which art in heaven, hallowed be thy name,' says the Lord's Prayer; '*Thy* kingdom come, *thy* will be done, on earth as it is in heaven' (italics mine).

Within such a patriarchal society it would have made sense to see the function of religion as the maintenance of good relations with this sky-father (see, for example, Suttie 1935: chapter 9), and this involved, as the Old Testament states again and again, conforming to the paternal Law. It is *he* (the father) who has laid down what is right and wrong, what *can* and *cannot* be done, what *can* and *cannot* be thought. And while historically and developmentally such Law involves submissive relations with an external father figure, with internalization, the subject's wellbeing comes more to depend on the link with a father *imago*. Whether the emotional concerns of such an internal organization are those of transgression and punishment,

---

1 Suttie's term 'companionship' may sound quaint and old fashioned to those used to a harder and quasi-scientific terminology. But the term has been reintroduced by Trevarthen (1979) who claims that the infant does not merely need an attachment object but someone with whom to engage in 'proto-conversation' (i.e. preverbal dialogue).

or forgiveness and re-acceptance as in the story of The Prodigal Son, the key figure remains the father. It will be recalled that in that story, the returning son says: 'Father, I have sinned against heaven and before thee' (St Luke: 15: 18). And as he welcomes him back, the forgiving father replies: 'This, my son, was dead, and is alive again; he was lost and is found' (St Luke 15: 24).

The overlapping scenarios I have described present a patriarchal society (nineteenth and early twentieth century Vienna), a patriarchal religion (the Judaeo-Christian tradition) and a patriarchal theory (psychoanalysis) that includes a patriarchal *theory* of religion. There is a son (Freud) rebelling against the canons of his society and against his own father; a theory that spells out many aspects of such rebellion (oedipal theory); and the same son, who, taking on himself the mantle of authority for the new patriarchy, psychoanalysis, strives, like Moses, to keep its (paternal) beliefs (theories) pure. Patriarchies die hard and, as so often, the rebel son becomes the authoritarian father.[2]

## Love, tenderness and the maternal

Rebellion against the father in psychoanalysis led to some early expulsions from the movement, notably Jung and Adler, important disputes, notably that with the more maternal Ferenczi, and, only *after* Freud's death, to an upsurge of creative theorizing about the role of the mother in infant development. From this perspective, Melanie Klein, Michael and Enid Balint and Donald Winnicott in the British Psychoanalytic Society, Harold Searles, Heinz Kohut and the subsequent protagonists of self-psychology in America, were 'protestants' against the paternal bias.[3] They spoke for what had been neglected during the years of Freud's 'rule', and attempted to reinstate the excluded maternal into theory and practice.

Such maternal revisions took different forms. Ferenczi's ideas, for example, revolved round the therapeutic relationship – it was the analyst's *love* that healed the patient (Ferenczi 1926). This theme continues through Michael and Enid Balint to the work of Winnicott and the contemporary Independent Group of the British Society: it was the environment, the caring, adaptive behaviour of the actual mother that shaped the course of development. Kleinian revision, by contrast, gave primacy to instinct and phantasy, while locating such phantasy in an overall maternal frame.

2 An example of this is described in chapter 6. Wittgenstein's father rebelled against *his* authoritarian father, but in turn became despotic. Wittgenstein himself was an odd mixture of despotic and more submissive traits which struggled together within his personality.
3 These are merely the more important names in a renaissance of thinking about the maternal, pre-oedipal phases of development.

The tension between such differing views significantly affected the development of British psychoanalysis. This can be seen, for example, in the way infant aggression is understood. While Klein's followers stressed the *inherent* aggressiveness of the infant – an original 'badness', perhaps – those in the line of Ferenczi regarded aggression as *reactive;* it was secondary to maternal or environmental failure. In this view, closer to Suttie's position, what is stressed is the inherent tendency of the baby to be *loving* – the baby is endowed with an original 'goodness' which prevails as long as the environment does not fail excessively.

In this chapter I shall theorize from within this softer maternal tradition. I shall argue that 'love' is in some sense present from the beginning, and will focus on the nature of this love – on what it involves – in a practical and detailed way. First, however, I shall discuss a problem that has dogged psychoanalytic thinking about religion from the beginning. This concerns the way in which love has been predominantly construed from within a male, paternal frame.

Religion, at least in its higher forms (Symington 1994), is deeply concerned with love. However, such love is not primarily paternal – a love of the Law – but a love of the human person. It is this love that I call 'maternal'. Paternal religion wants the Law (the Ten Commandments, for example) to reign supreme. Jesus, a more maternal advocate, wanted to replace this love of the Law with an empathic love of one's neighbour. Indeed, some of Jesus' strongest words were spoken against the Scribes and Pharisees who lived by the letter of the Law, and he shocked and angered such 'fathers' of the tradition by suggesting that empathic understanding might obviate the need for punishment. One example would be his approach to the woman taken in adultery (St John 7): First identify with the other person, only then judge. Jesus was thus more concerned with a love based on identification than on one that was erotic or lustful: 'We are all human,' he says; 'any one of us could be in this position for we are all adulterers in our hearts.'

But altruistic love (*agape*) is precisely what has troubled psychoanalysis from the beginning. For if you derive such love from a root that is primarily erotic and self-seeking (*eros*, aim-inhibited sexuality), how can it be genuinely other-directed? How can *agape* ever gain ascendancy if it is merely an outpost of self-seeking *eros*?

Suttie's answer was clear: it was the theory – psychoanalytic theory – that needed correction because it shared in the anti-maternal skew of Freud's personality (the taboo on tenderness). If one listened to one's intuition, the problem simply disappeared. Given a *primary* need for contact and social relatedness with the mother, it was obvious that the caring aspects of love were built upon this. Religious love could now be seen as the flowering of a developmental line present from the beginning. Suttie's view of a separate relational axis has been amply confirmed by Bowlby's later work (Bowlby 1969) and within this more empirical framework, a rationale now exists for basing altruistic love, or love of the neighbour, on the earliest mother–infant bond.[4]

## Institutional and revealed religion

Symington (1993), in a short article on religion and psychoanalysis, divided religions into two major groups. *Revealed religions* are more or less institutionalized and impose a set of mandatory beliefs and practices. They coincide in some degree with the type of religion I have termed patriarchal. However, Symington noted another important group that he called *natural religions*, among which he placed the teachings of Socrates, Buddha and at least some of the teachings of Jesus. *Natural religions*, according to Symington, are not so much concerned with conformity to practice and the letter of the Law as with inward questions to do with the meaning of life: How does man find fulfilment? How is a man to find true satisfaction in his life? Such questions are more subjective, but no less real, than questions of whether or not one has sinned according to the Law, but they involve intuitive appraisal of the inner person rather than objective evidence. So within this approach, an action or thought can be said to *feel* right because it *fits* in relation to some inner criterion; another action or thought feels wrong because it does *not fit* and creates a sense of inner discord. It is clear that such judgements are made according to intuitive, *inner* criteria rather than by reference to objective rules.

With their emphasis on inner states of mind and internal criteria of judgement, natural religions place greater emphasis than revealed religions on the wellbeing of the self, and this suggests a structuring round the axis of the mother. Compared with patriarchal religions, they are less involved with *objective* truth and *objective* right and wrong – values of the oedipal period concerned with the 'out there'. They are more concerned with *subjective* truth – the intuitive and empathic appraisal of what is right for the *self* – involving maternal values of the pre-oedipal period. In adult life, the subject himself makes such appraisals; at the start of life, another person would have made them on his behalf. Quite clearly, the person who originally looked

4 I am not suggesting that the earliest mother–infant relationship is lacking in sexual/erotic elements in the wider sense – clearly the infant is immersed in sensual, bodily experience. What I am arguing for, and trying to clarify, is the coexistence from the beginning of distinct threads or strands: one that is erotic, and to some extent corralled within the excited phases of instinctual activity in the traditional sense (e.g. feeding at the breast); another that from the beginning is relational and has more to do with communication and social contact. The smiling response would be an early manifestation of this second axis, as later would the need for mirroring and attunement.

after the self in this caring way would have been the mother, making such appraisals on behalf of the infant.

In this chapter, my concern is with Symington's second group of religions in which self-appraisal and individual experience are paramount. It needs to be noted, however, that revealed religions begin with an individual vision (subjective, maternal), and with the passage of time this is commandeered by a ruling (paternal) group and given institutional (external) form. As Buber pointed out (Buber 1937), the institutionalization of religion ultimately leads to loss of contact with the subjective vision – with god or the sacred – religion then deteriorating into external observance. But then a new cycle may begin, with further breakthrough to the sacred, and at this point religion is spiritually renewed. Buber's account is a reminder that the *fons et origo* of religion is always the *individual's* experience of the sacred.

## Significant moments, preverbal experience and the sacred

While the great world religions were based on the insights of a few outstanding individuals, *an intuition of the sacred* falls within the realm of ordinary experience. I am referring to what the ordinary person might call *a significant moment*, a moment outside of ordinary time, when the world, or some part of it, becomes lit up in a different way. The quality of such moments can be understood by thinking of a person's relation to a piece of music or a line of poetry. The first contact is fraught with significance – there are shivers down the spine and the heart misses a beat – but such physical sensations are merely markers. Subjectively, the feeling is of recognition, of being addressed – the musical or poetic phrase 'speaks' or 'sings' to a part of the subject's soul. There is a feeling of validation and reluctance to let the moment go: 'This beautiful form is what I have been searching for! It is a part of me!'[5]

Similar moments may punctuate a person's involvement with the natural world. A person may love nature and enjoy contact with it; but from time to time, there is a different kind of experience a sense of being *struck* by it in a special way. What is then experienced is no longer ordinary but an epiphany of significance: as with the fragment of poetry or music, the subject has a sense of *living through the forms*, of becoming one with the

---

5 Heaney (1986/2002: 188) writes: 'The lines are inhabited by certain profoundly true tones . . . and they do what poetry most essentially does: they fortify our inclination to credit promptings of our intuitive being. They help us to say in the first recesses of ourselves, in the shyest, pre-social part of our nature, "Yes, I know something like that too. Yes, that's right; thank you for putting words on it and making it more or less official."' Heaney is speaking of poetry, but the same resonance can be experienced in relation to other forms of writing, and indeed any kind of art.

landscape. This kind of experience is one phase of the creative impulse; it has much in common with the artist's vision and his need to *capture* a landscape, or rather his 'vision' of it, within the forms of his medium, thereby making it more real and available to him.

To link such ordinary experiences with explicitly religious areas may seem strange, but I believe there is a continuum between these mini-moments that catch at the heart and the great visions that eventually move mankind. The underlying event is essentially the same: in each case, an outer form, created by a shaping perception, or re-created by the artist's skill, *resonates* with a part of the self as yet unformed, and gives it, in that moment, a kind of being. The landscape that 'takes form' in the seeing eye, the 'forms' created by the artist that are reconstituted by the attuned viewer, and the religious 'forms' that promise salvation – each provides a 'home' or 'habitation' for the self, and simultaneously a richer experience of it. In each case there is contact between the discovered or created form (external) and something deep in the subject's nature (internal); the 'self' (secular) or 'soul' (religious) finds in these moments an external recognition or echo.

In whatever setting such moments occur, a further commonality may be noted – they cannot be called forth on demand. There is always a sense of surprise, and usually a feeling of grace, of having been 'chosen' in some way for something special. With religion, for example, the significant moment may occur in spite of the person's conscious opposition to religious things, as for St Paul on the road to Damascus (Acts of the Apostles 9). Or it may be the fruition of a search, of being drawn towards something *felt* to be important – reading religious texts, going to places of worship, and so on. But when (and if) the moment comes, it always surprises and is felt to be personal and specific: a *particular* form – religious, artistic or natural – grabs and stirs the subject, and touches *him*. Relationship and recognition are essential features of the experience (see chapter 11).

Most important is the non-verbal nature of such experiences – they are seldom mediated through words and are difficult to describe. They are not, however, formless because the perceived form that shapes the experience is intrinsic to it. When the composer Mahler was asked by an admirer of his music what one of his pieces meant, he replied: 'Madam, if I could tell you in words what it meant I would not be writing music.' The significance thus lies within the form itself, the same being true of significant moments – the moment comes, has its effect, and goes, but it has no existence apart from the containing form.

A few examples from Josephine Klein's recent book on psychotherapy and the ineffable (Klein 2004) serve to illustrate some of the features I have described. The first two particularly express the non-verbal nature of the experience; the third illustrates how it may be mediated by, and contained within, a complex of sensory (i.e. non-verbal) forms.

The Spanish mystic, St John of the Cross, in 'Verses written after an ecstasy of high exaltation', wrote (italics mine):

> The gift that leaves men *knowing nought*,
> Yet *passing knowledge* with their thought.

And St Teresa of Avila, writing of one of her mystical experiences, again emphasizes the lack of communicable knowledge:

> There is no sense of anything but enjoyment, *without any knowledge* of what is being enjoyed. The soul realizes that it is enjoying some good thing that contains all good things together, but *it cannot comprehend* this good thing.
>
> > (St Teresa of Avila, *The Life of the Holy Mother Teresa*,
> > ch. XXI, italics mine)

Finally, a more secular example, in which the writer uses her facility with poetic language to convey at least some qualities of the experience:

> It is a sunny fall afternoon and I'm engaged in one of my favourite pastimes – picking chestnuts. I'm playing alone under a spreading, leafy, protective tree. My mother is sitting on a bench nearby, rocking the buggy in which my sister is asleep . . . I pick up a reddish brown chestnut, and suddenly, through its warm skin, I feel the beat as of a heart. But the beat is also in everything else around me, and everything pulsates and shimmers as if it were coursing with the blood of life. Stooping under the tree, I am holding life in my hand, and I am in the centre of a harmonious, vibrating transparency. For that moment I know everything there is to know,[6] I have stumbled into the very centre of plenitude, and I hold myself still with fulfilment, before the knowledge of my knowledge escapes me.
>
> > (Hoffman 1989: 41–2)

## Religious experience, the aesthetic moment and maternal containment

If experiences of this kind are indeed contained within a 'language'[7] of *non-verbal* forms, and if as I have suggested, they belong generically to a

---

6  Hoffman uses the words 'know' and 'knowledge' in relation to her experience, but clearly she is not referring to cognitive knowledge, but immediately sensed apprehension, mediated through non-verbal sensory forms.

7  Strictly speaking, it is incorrect to speak of a *language* of non-verbal forms because such forms are idiosyncratic and created by each individual for their own self. There is therefore no one to one correspondence between form (symbol) and meaning, and meaning is always personal to the individual.

religious domain that is closer to the maternal, it may be possible to link them to prototypical experiences of the preverbal period. This is what Bollas has done in his work on the 'un-thought known' (Bollas 1987). What I have called 'significant moments', he refers to as 'aesthetic moments':

> when a person is shaken by an experience into absolute certainty that he has been cradled by, and dwelled with, the spirit of the object, a rendezvous of *mute recognition* that defies representation . . . (Such moments) are *fundamentally wordless* occasions, notable for the density of the subject's feeling and the fundamentally *non-representational knowledge* of being embraced by the aesthetic object.
>
> (ibid.: 30–1, italics mine)

For Bollas, all such aesthetic moments are a reliving of early experience:

> The uncanny pleasure of being held by a poem, a composition, a painting, or, for that matter, any object, rests on those moments when the infant's internal world is partly *given form* by the mother since he cannot shape them or link them together without her coverage.
>
> (ibid.: 32, italics mine)

They constitute a revival of what Bollas calls 'moments of transformation', brought about by the mother through her ordinary sensitive ministrations of infant care. Not only does she transform painful hunger into comfortable satiation; she changes the diapers, turns the baby on his back, smiles, talks, coos and so on. Bollas dates such experiences from a time before the mother was perceived as a separate object. Her appearances are 'apparitional-like' (ibid.: 33) and each announces a significant and welcome change in the infant's state. But for Bollas, it is not only *what* she does, but her special way of doing it, that becomes part of the infant's experience. Her 'idiom of care', as he calls it, becomes 'the infant's first aesthetic', a pattern of holding, being and relating that is linked to major transformations of the infant's psychosomatic state. He writes:

> Alongside the infant's experience of being transformed is the reality that he is being transformed according to the mother's aesthetic . . . The baby takes in not only the content of the mother's communications but also their form. In the beginning of life, handling the infant is the primary mode of communicating, so the *internalization of the mother's form* (her aesthetic) is prior to the internalization of her verbal messages.
>
> (ibid.: 33–4, italics mine)

For Bollas, the aesthetic moment *recreates* the transformational moment with its unique maternal pattern; the earlier moment is glimpsed and re-embodied within the perceived shapes of the present. The aesthetic moment thus constitutes an irruption of preverbal memory, a sense of being drawn again into iconically remembered maternal holding.

Bollas is aware of the religious resonance of what he writes for his language is redolent with religious expressions. 'Reverential', 'beseeching', 'supplication', 'transported', 'uncanny', are just some of the words he uses. But the word 'sacred' occurs repeatedly and is the closest he can get to this earliest experience: 'The sacred,' he says, 'precedes the maternal' (ibid.: 39).

## Transformation as provision of maternal form

Bollas' ideas are a creative extension of Winnicott's work on the 'environ-ment mother', a term he used for the pre-object mother who facilitates infant development by her adaptive responses. Winnicott's work in this area is well known, but it is pertinent to emphasize an aspect that is relatively downplayed in Bollas' formulations. Although he speaks of the mother as 'giving form' (ibid.: 32) to the infant's inner world, the emphasis lies on her transformation of the baby's experience. Winnicott, on the other hand, emphasized the mother's role as *provider of forms*, though he did not put it in quite this way. It is, however, implicit in some of his most important concepts: primary creativity, the transitional object, and even more in his later work on the mirror role of the mother's face (Winnicott 1953, 1967a).

The concept of primary creativity was Winnicott's way of referring to the baby's experience when the mother provided a 'form' (the 'breast') that the baby needed to complete an experience of searching. The sequence was: 'baby's *anticipation* of breast' in terms of both arousal and specificity; 'mother's *provision* of breast' in terms of both timing and manner of presen-tation. Where these two things (the baby's anticipation and the mother's answering 'form') were sufficiently alike, the baby could feel he had *created* the breast: the 'form' of the maternal response then matched the 'shape' of the infant's anticipation. The infant could then build on this experience and go on to find/create forms for himself which were 'adapted to' (embodying) aspects of his own experience. According to Winnicott, the *transitional object* is the baby's first achievement of this kind: the baby discovers a missing sensory form in the qualities of the bit of blanket, and so uses the bit of blanket to *recreate* an experience of the mother whenever it is needed. In this way the baby becomes able to evoke the mother's presence in her absence – the beginnings of imaginative experience. In a later paper, Winnicott (1967b) suggests a direct line from such early creativity to the larger world of culture (including religion), culture for the most part being based on imaginative illusion. From this point of view, culture is a vast repository of forms for human feeling to be drawn on by individuals as needed in a personal way.

In his work on transitional phenomena, Winnicott was only beginning to appreciate the importance of forms provided by the mother for infant experience. He was still in thrall to the traditional paradigm of the breast as concrete object of instinctual gratification, even while struggling to incorporate into it new insights about the importance of the mother's responsiveness. Sixteen years later (1967a) he is much clearer about the mother's provision; the paradigm shifts from instinctual gratification to preverbal *communication* and the mother's facial expressions. I refer to the mirror role of the mother's face and the way he saw her expressions as reflecting forms for infant experience.

In this new paradigm, the baby uses the mother's *face* as a reflective medium. When he smiles, for example, what he sees in the mother's responsive smile is a visual form of his own inner state. Winnicott is not primarily concerned here with what Bollas termed 'transformation' – the changing of 'bad' experience into 'good' – but with how the mother's response enables the infant to *appropriate* or grasp his own (in this case 'good') experience. Through her emotional reflection the baby acquires the wherewithal to become more fully what he already is. Winnicott puts this in existential terms: 'I am seen, so [now] I exist' (1967a/1971: 114).

## Facial expression as non-material form

The shift in paradigm between Winnicott's earlier and later work has implications for any discussion of religion for it places a non-material experience at the centre of emotional development. While the breast paradigm clings to Freud's original way of thinking in which love derives from feeding at the breast, the face paradigm, which puts the maternal face at the centre of emotional development, makes non-material visual forms (which cannot be touched or physically incorporated) the principal currency.

In typical fashion, Winnicott does not tell us where the new idea fits in to his total scheme of things, but arguably it runs in parallel with the earlier view. As attachment theory and infant research have shown, the maternal face provides a major focus of infant attention from soon after birth. Not only is the facial *gestalt* part of the mother's unique pattern (a focus of her 'apparitional-like appearances' (Bollas); it is also an *expressive surface*, the screen on which her emotional expressions play. Long before words can be understood, *it becomes the centre of communication between mother and infant*, and a major source of responsive forms in the way that Winnicott describes.

It is not difficult, therefore, to suppose that the mother's face occupies a privileged place in the infant's feelings. At a later date, it will become the visual identity of the mother as *object*. At this early stage, however, it can be regarded as the organizing core of the mother's 'apparitional-like appearances' and magical transformations. Moreover, if Bollas is right in suggesting that 'the sacred [transformational object] precedes the maternal [mother as separate object]' (1987: 39), then surely the maternal face must lie at the heart of the sacred.[8]

Where does this new understanding leave us in relation to religion? In my view, it provides a platform from which to approach the nature of spiritual love. Spiritual love is related, I suggest, to what Anna Freud might have called a different 'developmental line' from sexuality, with its early focus on excited feeding. It stems from a different place, a different axis of the infant's equipment, related to the earliest bond with the mother, and thus to the earliest issues of security. According to this view, its central object is the maternal face and its expressions, and its central dynamic to do with maternal empathy and understanding – or the lack of it. Indeed, it could be argued that just as the infant has an in-built propensity to relate to the human face, so also will it have an in-built expectation of response (facial mirroring) that will lead to a search for it. Whether or not that is so, the currency of such response is a distanced 'form', not a tangible object, and this marks a clear divide, even at this early stage, between material and non-material ('spiritual') strivings.

## Containment, attunement and the religious quest

Winnicott (1967a/1971) saw the mother's facial expression as giving a new dimension of being to the infant, enabling it 'to feel real rather than existing' (ibid.: 117). It is possible, however, to see the function of the mother's 'forms' in a variety of related ways. First, it is a *recognition and acceptance* of the baby's emotional gesture; second, it offers potential *containment* of the infant's emotional (psychosomatic) state; and third, it provides an *objectification* of that state, an external form with which to mark it. In this sense, the maternal expression, like the transitional object, constitutes an early symbolic form (iconic, not verbal).

However, to communicate through facial expressions is like speaking a language with few words; the smile and other expressions are relatively unspecific, and poorly suited to convey the increasing complexity of experience that needs to be shared. It might therefore be asked whether and how this 'language' (see footnote 7) might develop in the period *before* verbal

---

8  I have often been asked where I stand in relation to the work of Levinas (1961) who gives the face a privileged position in attempting to understand the essence of being human. There is, to be sure, an overlap with my own position in that he sees the face as a purely expressive 'object' which cannot be grasped in an ordinary sensory way. However, while Levinas writes from the perspective of European philosophy and wants to show that our experience of the face lies at the root of the ethical, my own approach is based on a psychoanalytic understanding of infant development, and aims to make connections between aesthetic and religious experience and early relational experiences with the mother's face.

language makes its appearance. Does it too increase in complexity, thus enriching the possibilities of sharing preverbal experience? Daniel Stern's work on maternal attunement (Stern 1985) offers a way of thinking about this question.

What happens in attunement is this. During the course of her ongoing interactions with the infant (Stern says attunements begin around nine months[9] and continue through the preverbal period), the mother intuitively makes responses that constitute a replay, or mini-enactment, of the way she has just experienced her infant. These responses are replays of sequences in the infant's level of arousal and excitement (Stern calls them *vitality affects*), as intuitively discerned by the mother. In effect, such replays constitute a *specific* sharing of the infant's experience, a *specific* appreciation of it. They are graphic, iconic mini-performances, and although not directly mimetic, they follow quite closely, in pattern and rhythm, the sequences the mother has observed. They follow, in Stern's language, the *contours* of the infant's vitality affects, thus making available to the infant the *profiles* and *shapes* of those patterns. Stern defines attunement as 'the recasting . . . of an affective state' (ibid.: 161), a recasting in perceivable, but essentially non-verbal form. The mother's attunement performance thus shapes and punctuates the infant's flow of experience far more specifically, and within a far greater variety of 'forms', than facial expression on its own can muster. Yet arguably its function is similar: recognition and acceptance, sharing and containment, and incipient objectification. In principle, then, attunements offer to the infant a rudimentary *preverbal language of forms* with which to contain, recall and manipulate experience (see footnote 7). Its richness and usefulness, however, depend upon the mother's sensitivity and responsiveness.

The preverbal era of human development lasts for up to two years. During this time, many important aspects of personality are organized and much early experience is structured within the infant's developing self. It can seem, however, that psychoanalytic discussions do not go into detail about how such structuring takes place. While it is generally accepted that the processes of projective identification and mirroring are important, the actual way they achieve structuring is glossed over. Bion's concept of maternal containment (Bion 1962a, 1962b; Britton 1998) is often discussed in this context but the details remain elusive. To say that 'beta elements' are transformed by the mother's 'alpha function' (Bion 1962b) does tell us

9 It may be surprising to realize that attunement, in Stern's sense, begins so late but this is a matter of definition. For Stern, attunement is linked to the beginnings of subjectivity and the possibility of inter-subjective experience. Rich social exchanges occur throughout the first nine months but according to Stern lack the inter-subjective dimension. Their focus is behavioural and interactive (games, imitations and so on) rather than affective. Attunement is linked to affect recognition and the beginnings of (preverbal) symbolic exchange.

something, but it does not precisely describe *what* the mother gives back, nor the way in which the infant uses it.

Winnicott's concept of facial mirroring goes some way towards addressing this problem because it offers a glimpse of how an internal feeling state might become linked to an external form, the mother's expression. At least potentially, such linkage gives the infant a first handle (primitive symbol) with which to manipulate and mark an inner feeling. At risk of simplification, one could say that the mother's expression provides a visual 'name' for an inner state.

Such considerations become more cogent when one considers Stern's descriptions of attunement. For in attunement, the maternal response is of similar form and shape (isomorphic) to the infant's arousal pattern. That at least is the theory. But without doubt, the mother's activity also *shapes* the infant's experience because the way she sees her infant's experience will inevitably be constrained by her own make-up. If it can be assumed, however, that a sensitive mother can be genuinely in touch with her baby, the patterns she gives back should be sufficiently isomorphic and 'fit' the emerging experience; and because the rhythm (pattern in time) of the responsive form matches the infant pattern of arousal, there will be resonance, enhancement and containment. I am using the term containment loosely for an imagined relation between form and content, based on iconic similarity.

If, however, containment, acceptance and sharing depend on the sensitivity of maternal attunement, there is much scope for the process to miscarry. Stern (1985) even suggests that it may be impossible to attune to certain negative affects such as anger: 'the sense of threat and harm,' he writes, 'places a barrier between the two separate experiences such that the notion of communion is no longer applicable' (ibid.: 160). Even in the best case then, containment may be patchy and incomplete, leading to lacunae in emotional development.

It seems probable that what a person regards as his or her 'self' is closely linked to maternal acceptance and containment. The 'contained' is that which has been given a maternal 'blessing' – in the beginning a maternal smile or attuned enactment. The 'contained' is that which has made *a circuit through the (m)other* – a view that Bion might have endorsed. Through this circuit it acquires a form, a resonating and accepting 'shape'. That which is 'contained' is thus *held* by a maternal form within the mother's ambience (now, of course, as an aspect of experience) – or, as Bollas might say, within the ambience of the sacred.

But what happens, psychologically speaking, to that which has *not* been contained? What is the fate and nature of such un-ratified material? This is a question that concerned Bion who thought of the 'uncontained' as a place of un-transformed beta elements and fragmented bizarre objects. Within the present framework, to be 'contained' is to be wrapped within a maternal form; to be 'uncontained' is to dwell in a limbo of unrecognized selves, away from the shadow of the mother's presence.

To be 'uncontained' is thus to be radically excluded. Moreover, such disinherited 'selves' (or elements of self) may well be fragmented and unusable, for without maternal recognition, they have no 'name' and no form. They may be terrifying because unnamed, and although not necessarily 'bad', they may *seem* unredeemable, like a caste of untouchables doomed to wander forever.[10]

Now, religion is often a quest for redemption, yet as usually understood, the need for it lies in the badness or sinfulness of man. And while it would be foolish to claim that guilt and a sense of badness were insignificant factors in shaping religion, they are not the only cause of man's existential distress. While they may be central in an oedipal world of whole objects, in the preverbal world on which I have focused, they are not the main concerns. In this earlier maternal world, the central issue is containment, and in so far as the religious need has its roots in *this* domain, the quest for redemption is driven by a need to be 'found' (i.e. reflected and recognized). In the existential distress of this domain, guilt and sin play little part. A failure of containment is the 'cause' of the malaise, and acceptance and recognition are its cure.

## Rilke: Transformation and redemption through poetry

In order to give substance to these notions, I shall briefly discuss the Austrian poet, Rainer Maria Rilke, who lived in a state of continual existential angst, yet believed passionately in the possibility of redemption through his art. I previously discussed this poet in chapter 4. It has been suggested (Britton 1998) that Rilke was the young poet, already famous, who once walked in the Dolomites with Freud. Freud (1937) later described Rilke as 'the great poet, who was a little helpless in facing life', and Lou Andreas-Salome, Rilke's one time lover, as 'his Muse and protective mother' (ibid.: 297). Rilke was not only a connoisseur of 'significant moments' – bad as well as good; he was also deeply interested in the nature of poetic activity, and in his later poetry offered a 'philosophy' of the poetic process.

He had a poignant sense of the precariousness of life and the transience of each created thing. Each unique creature had only one chance to live and only one thing could save it from disappearing without trace – the poet giving voice to its unique essence. Rilke experienced all creatures, including man-made objects, as *dumb* and *in need of a speaker; they had no voice of*

10 As Bion has stressed, such uncontained $\beta$-elements are also frighteningly concrete and thing-like.

*their own*. Only a poet had the sensibility to get inside them and thus proclaim their unique and vibrant existence. So it was that each thing turned to the poet in silent supplication, urging him *to speak on its behalf*. Only this would make the creature fully 'real', and fulfilling this need was the poet's vocation: 'Are we perhaps *here* just for saying . . .' he exclaims, listing a whole series of quite ordinary objects. 'But for *saying*, remember, / oh for such saying as never the things themselves / hoped so intensely to be . . .' (Rilke 1960: 224).

Now on one level, the similarities with a mother and her infant are striking. There is a dumb creature who needs the poet's voice to articulate and give form to its unique being, and an infant with no words, who, according to Winnicott and Stern, needs the mother to articulate its 'forms' in order to 'feel real' rather than 'merely existing'. But Rilke is not talking about mothers and babies but about a passionate activity in which he feels *compelled* to engage – so much so that he shuts himself in a tower with his writing for weeks on end. He wrote poetry as though his life depended on it – and probably it did.

I have argued elsewhere in greater detail (Wright 2000; also chapters 4 and 9) that the artist is frequently someone who struggles through his art to make good an earlier maternal deficit. Rilke was no exception, having had an appallingly narcissistic mother who even wanted him to be a girl, a fact enshrined in his second name, Maria. When Rilke speaks of the dumb creatures waiting to be brought into real existence by the poet's 'saying', it is surely the case that on a deeper level he refers to himself. It is surely his own unspoken, un-reflected self that turns in silent supplication to the poet-mother (also part of himself) for redemption.

In pursuing his passionate vocation, the poet becomes his own 'sayer', his own self-reflecting and attuning other. He tackles the problem of deficient containment and the consequent sense of being only half-alive, by becoming his own creator of containing forms. He finds and masters a medium – in this case the medium of poetic language – and brings it under his control; through his skills he now coaxes or coerces this medium into furnishing the forms he needs. Whereas in infancy he was at the mercy of his mother's whim – perhaps in Rilke's case a highly *selective* attunement – he is now his own provider of resonating forms. He becomes his own therapist – or, dare one say it, his own *saviour*.

In writing about Rilke and his redemption of the dumb creatures, I have been drawn, as was Bollas in his discussion of the aesthetic moment, into a quasi-religious terminology. In part this may stem from this particular poet's passionate intensity that blurs the distinction between artistic and religious forms, but I think the reason lies also in the roots of religious need. If the 'environment mother' who brings 'forms' and 'transformations' to the infant is 'sacred', it is easy to see how the longing for such a mother *when she is unavailable* creates the need for a *saviour*. Rilke thus exemplifies in his life, and records in his work, the springs of a certain kind of religious impulse in the ordinary man.

## Conclusions and summary

I started this chapter by looking at certain broad divisions that have a bearing on religious phenomena: institutional and personal religion, paternal and maternal elements of religious life, and patriarchal and matriarchal organizations. I touched on the dominance of patriarchal forms within Judaism and Christianity and a similar dominance in psychoanalytic institutions. I followed Suttie in suggesting that psychoanalytic understanding of religion had been hampered by this patriarchal or paternal bias, both in Freud's own personality, and subsequently within the psychoanalytic establishment.

In trying to redress this balance and open up discussion of maternal elements in religious culture, I have focused on two things: the notion of *forms*, which is closely linked with *mirroring* and *containment*, and the connected idea of *significant moments*. In linking these to a newer understanding of the mother–infant relationship, I have sought to show that a more sympathetic understanding of religion is possible than that provided by traditional psychoanalytic thinking. This has been hampered, not only by paternal bias but by an out-dated view of love that derives the altruistic variety from earlier self-seeking forms (see chapter 11). These things were a legacy of Freud's thinking, and revision is long overdue. I have discussed work by a number of psychoanalysts and psychotherapists, notably Suttie, Winnicott, Bowlby, and Bollas, that makes it plausible to link religion with the attachment/relational axis of human development. This places the early mother – her face and responsive forms – at the centre of spiritual longing; empirical infant research, particularly the work of Stern, has provided concrete detail of the period in which such longing would originate.

In asserting that the deepest roots of religion lie in the preverbal core of the self, I do not claim that everything about religion can be understood in these terms. I suggest, however, that core elements of religious aspiration are linked to a need for containment and recognition; and that religion, like art and psychotherapy, creates new possibilities of redemption by providing self-containing forms. Since the original containment – the mother's *saying*, in Rilke's terms – is always incomplete, the need for a second chance, *a new beginning* (Balint, M. 1932), is universal. Religion, art and psychotherapy offer this chance in different, though related ways.

# Recognition and relatedness

My subject in this chapter is the vast and ancient topic of love. I consider the question: 'What is love?' and although my viewpoint is psychoanalytic, I am sometimes critical of the psychoanalytic perspective. In writing the chapter, I have drawn on my own experience – of having been a child who was more or less loved, an adolescent who thought he was not, a man who found that he could be, a husband and father who loved as well as he could, and a romantic lover who has fallen in and out of love on more than one occasion.

It has surely influenced my position that I was brought up in a strict religious environment and suffered intense conflict as I moved beyond it. I am still interested in religion as a human phenomenon, but having experienced how life-destroying it can be, my days of direct involvement are over. Given that our first experience of relatedness is sensual and bodily, it can only strain our capacity for loving to be told that we have to give up our sensual existence. Offered a choice between life and religion in this sense, there is only one sensible decision to be made.

## Eros and agape

I start with the obvious point that there cannot be a simple definition of love it is not a unitary phenomenon but complex and various. There are many ways of being that are called loving and we must not let language mislead us into thinking that all these states are the same. This was recognized by the Greeks who had two different words for love: *eros* and *agape*. *Eros* was erotic love, *agape* an altogether more spiritual and selfless condition. There are shadows of this distinction in Freud's accounts of loving, erotic love being the natural state with its roots in the bodily being and experience of the child, parental love and friendship being *sublimated* or *aim-inhibited*. This meant that such love had given up the aims of bodily satisfaction and at least on the surface was more altruistic and other-directed.

My second point concerns the relation between religion and love and leads to a strategic issue: how best to approach the topic of loving. By religion I refer mainly to Christianity though what I say may well have relevance to other religions.

The teachings of religion, especially those of the New Testament, are closely interwoven with the idea of love. Many of the teachings of Jesus concern love, and many of the letters to the early churches stress that love is a Christian requirement. We are told that 'God *is* love' (1 John 4: 8, italics mine) and that 'God so loved the world that he gave his only begotten Son, Jesus, that all the world might be saved' (John 3: 16). We are told about 'Faith, Hope, and Love, but the greatest of these is Love' (1 Corinthians 13: 13). And we are told to 'Love one another' (John 13: 34), and to 'Love thy neighbour as thyself' (Matthew 22: 39). Love is central to Christianity; its principal aim is to make people more loving and it tells us that if we imitate Christ, and become like him ('putting on Christ' – Galatians 3: 27), we shall have the best chance of success.

Religion thus instructs us concerning Love and shows us how we can best lead loving (i.e. godly) lives. In Christianity there is an epiphany, or revelation of Love in the person and teaching of Jesus, from whom we can imitate and learn. Within this approach, the nature of Love is given or revealed. It existed first within the Godhead, in ideal form, is mediated to men in various ways but principally through God's Son, Jesus, and these help us to grow towards it. Throughout our lives we are aspirants, or relative failures, on this path towards ideal Love, or God.

This is where our approach to understanding the topic of love becomes important. If we start with religion, we start with something that is given and *a priori*; it is absolute and not to be questioned. The approach is God-centred, gives primacy to God, and the task of human beings is to apply the revelations and teachings of God in their actual lives.

If, on the other hand, we start with Man, the scene looks different. In this case, love is something to be understood within a humanist and natural science perspective. It cannot be understood by reference to anything outside of man but has to make sense solely within the parameters of the human condition. So, for example, we could start as William James might have done – I am thinking of his classic text *The Varieties of Religious Experience* (James 1902) – with many actual examples of human loving, and see if a pattern emerges as we examine them. We could collate and classify these experiences and from them attempt to make generalizations about our subject. Loving, we might then be able to say, seems 'thus' or 'thus'.

These two approaches could be termed the *ideal* and *pragmatic* respectively, and it may be useful to come back to this distinction from time to time. I shall speak from within the pragmatic approach, in other words from that disordered and confused place in which men lead their actual lives. Within this human perspective, we find little flashes of love – patches of light, as it were – interspersed with areas of darkness. We find a person loving one minute and hating the next; being kind on one occasion and cruel on another. We can say: 'Human beings are capable of this thing called loving, but they constantly lose it as other states of mind and ways of being take over. Life as lived is a kaleidoscope of different emotions and ways of being and individuals vary in how much loving they can achieve.'

Religion too might talk about men in this way, so we need to look further for the distinction I am trying to make. It lies perhaps in the explanations we give for such a state of affairs. Religion might say that love is a divine spark put in us by God, but that man constantly falls into error because of the temptations of the Devil. A humanist, on the other hand, would approach the matter from a biological or natural science perspective, as Freud did in *The Future of an Illusion* (Freud 1927). He argued that God, and our love of him, are residues of childhood experience with our own parents and we cling to notions of God out of insecurity. Our loving capacities, even the forms of our adult loving, are shaped by the kinds of love we experienced as children and our propensity to hate and aggression are part of a biological endowment that we share with other animals. These types of explanation are radically different from each other and we have to choose between them. Clearly my own bias is humanist rather than metaphysical.

To opt for a humanist framework, however, does not mean that we have to agree with all of Freud's explanations; we may be able to find something that takes better account of the facts. Any explanation must do justice to the facts and should not do violence to the phenomena we are trying to understand. So, in the case of love, our explanation must respect the nature of the experiences we have collected; there must be no distortion of the phenomenology. Thus, if we feel that love has a certain *quality*, we must not destroy that quality with our explanation but be able to account for it.

A recurring problem with Freud's explanations of the higher human propensities is that they tend to demean that which they purport to explain. In spite of their fertility and power, his explanations are often over-reductive.[1] In the present case too we might think that love is downgraded because Freud presents it as *nothing other than* aim-inhibited sexuality and this seems to diminish the actual experience of love.

To criticize Freud, however, is not to dismiss him. His approach revolutionized Man's view of himself and contributed to relocating him in a naturalistic framework. Together with Darwin (1859), Freud's accounts have decentred Man from his key position in God's universe and placed him fairly and squarely in the natural world. 'Man as an animal' has replaced 'Man as the pinnacle of God's creation'.

Where there are opposing elements in a structure, it invariably splits and polarizes, and this is certainly so in relation to love. Love is easily idealized

---

1 We saw this in relation to Freud's writings on art (chapters 4 and 9) where he attempted to understand the artist's activity as a kind of wish-fulfilment.

and made divine but equally easily denigrated and reduced to animal instinct. At the same time, attempts to bridge the opposing elements, both in imagination and in life, seem to make Man a more remarkable creature. If he is seen *only* as made in the image of God – 'a little lower than the angels' (Psalm 8: 5) – then falling like Lucifer is almost inevitable. If, on the other hand, he is relegated to the level of the animals – and Freud's 're-visioning' of man could be seen as tending in this direction – sooner or later there is an opposite pull in order to redress some inner balance. Extreme views invariably exclude important facts and eventually these reassert themselves: Man is not *just* an animal; he is an animal, but also something more.

It is this 'something more' that I want to address and I want to conceptualize it within a humanist framework. So we might begin by saying: 'There is something in Man's loving that sets him apart from the animals; in spite of his continuity with the rest of creation, there is also a discontinuity, a difference.' Again, this is something with which the religious person might agree but our two explanations would diverge. The religious person would say: 'You are talking about Man's soul – the divine spark that comes from God.' To which I, as a humanist, might reply: 'Yes, you can call it "soul" but I think man's "soul" can be accounted for in different ways – by the peculiar circumstances of human infancy which are unique to the human species.'

It has often been said that Man's difference from other animals is linked with his symbolic capability which enables him to *imagine* the world as well as to act within it. Although I shall not have time to develop this idea, it can be argued that this too derives from the specific kinds of relatedness in which the human infant is bathed. From the beginning, the human mother not only feeds and protects her baby but wraps him in a garment of imaginary forms which furnish a kind of substrate for symbolic development.

## Love and recognition

It is part of the nature of love that you cannot approach it head on; it can only be seen indirectly through the way a person lives their life. This being so, I want to relate a story. I remember a summer afternoon at school. A rare respite from Spartan times – tea on the lawn with my English master, a glimpse of life as it could be. A few of us were there to meet an American professor interested in the poetry of Alexander Pope. I knew nothing of Pope, but as it turned out that did not matter. After a while, the professor started reading from his *Essay on Man* (Pope 1734/1870). There was perhaps irony in his declaiming of this dry and formal English poet in his rich southern American drawl, but this somehow added to the music of what I heard:

Plac'd on this isthmus of the middle state
A being darkly wise and rudely great . . .

> He hangs between; in doubt to act or rest,
> In doubt to deem himself a god or beast;
> In doubt his mind or body to prefer . . .

I was totally captivated and felt the rhythm was bearing me towards some inescapable truth:

> Created half to rise and half to fall
> Great lord of all things, yet a prey to all;
> Sole judge of truth, in endless error hurl'd;
> The glory, jest and riddle of the world.
>                             (Pope 1734/1870: 225)

Something had powerfully connected. The afternoon lit up. What was it that I felt? Surely it was something like love. Did I love this *man* with his rich warm voice? Or did I love the *poet* whom I had never known until now, or the *words* which suddenly captured a whole area of experience and placed it before me as something I needed at that moment? I still do not know but I was deeply moved and excited. Here was a great thought, declaimed in a beautiful way and it touched my heart.

Why have I described this moment? I think because it brings together and crystallizes a number of different strands. There was a moment of feeling cared for: a few people, not a crowd; warmth and personal contact, not the grim impersonality of school; a sense of being singled out and valued – I was there because someone thought I was worth it. All these things combined, I think, to create a moment of love – I was surprised by love in what was normally a strict and loveless place.[2]

This was not all, however; the experience was a moment of discovery and recognition: here was a poet who spoke to *me*. I knew only too well about the middle state, not least because of my religious upbringing. I knew about the struggle with myself, the trying and the failing, the 'half to rise and half to fall'. I knew about the grandeur of the world, about its joy, but also about its awfulness. All these things were part of my experience. But suddenly it was all 'there' in what this unknown professor had declaimed; it was 'there' in these strange new words which went to my heart. No clergyman had touched me like this as he ranted from the pulpit Sunday after Sunday, but here for a moment someone had reached me. I felt for a moment known and understood.

---

2 The school I went to was a traditional English public school which in the post-war period was Spartan in the extreme. There was institutionalized bullying, the boys slept twenty-six to a dormitory, and there was no private space. Many of the masters used fear as a teaching tool, but there were exceptions, and my English master was one of them.

This brings me to an important idea: that *being deeply known and recognized is an important element of loving*. It may be too that it works both ways: not only do I feel love for the person who recognizes me in this way and makes me feel loved; I am, in a sense, loving the other person whenever I engage in an act of true recognition. To say this places love firmly into the *relational* sphere – it is inter-subjective as well as within the person. 'All true living [perhaps loving] is meeting,' wrote Martin Buber (1937: 11). Connecting, recognizing, touching and being touched (being in touch) – from this perspective all true loving is relational.

## Instinctual and relational love

I will now return to Freud's idea that the higher forms of loving – those we might think of as altruistic – are really forms of aim-inhibited sexuality. To understand this we have to go back to his view that the *earliest* forms of human loving are sexual (erotic) and appetitive. This view was central to his instinct theory which always remained a cornerstone of his thinking. Instinct is the basic driving force of human beings as it is for animals, and instinct has an aim and an object. When an instinct is aroused it seeks discharge, and the object, in this view, is only important in so far as it enables discharge to occur. Thus the object of the adult sexual drive is the woman's body, the aim being genital discharge. The object of the baby's instinctual arousal is the mother's breast, the aim being satisfaction of the oral drive.

According to this view the child's feelings of love and dependency are secondary to the instinctual process. Love is *anaclitic* – it 'leans on' satisfactory instinctual discharge: 'I love you *because* you feed me'; or, 'I love you because you satisfy my sexual drive.' Within this framework it is not so much that 'we love him because he first loved us' (1 John 4: 19); it is rather that 'we love her because she first fed us and satisfied our instinctual arousal'.

Instinct theory is relatively simplistic yet tries to explain the phenomena of love which are highly complex. It is not that the theory is inadequate to explain *some* elements of love but as a total explanation it fails to satisfy. Religion draws our attention upwards, towards something that is disembodied and 'spiritual' in love, while Freud's view draws us downwards towards love's embodied and sensual core.[3]

Although Freud's explanations may now seem incomplete in some respects, it is certainly the case that human love is tied to the body, and

---

3 My point is not that Freud was wrong to direct attention to our animal roots but rather to argue that in so doing, and in his anxiety to reinstate those roots into a picture of man that had lost touch with biological reality, he ignored the kernel of 'truth' in the religious position.

often linked with the mouth and images of feeding and drinking. Both elements, 'spiritual' and 'bodily', can be clearly seen in these lines from Marlowe's *Dr Faustus*:[4]

> Was this the face that launched a thousand ships
> And burned the topless towers of Ilium?
> Fair Helen make me immortal with a kiss.

Thus it is the *face* that wars are fought over – I will discuss later why the face – but the *mouth* that consummates with a kiss. The passage continues:

> Her lips suck forth my soul; see where it flies!
> Come, Helen, come give me my soul again!
> Here will I dwell, for heaven be in these lips,
> And all is dross that is not Helena.

For Marlowe, in the condition of being 'in love', 'higher' and 'lower' lie very close together: 'her *lips suck* forth [bodily, oral] my *soul* [spiritual]', and 'Here will I dwell [in this *bodily* kiss] because *heaven* [spiritual] be in these *lips* [bodily], and all is dross that is not *Helena*.' In the state of being in love, the woman's name (the *person* of Helen perhaps) seems to hold together the 'spiritual' and 'bodily' which might otherwise fly apart.

This example highlights the difficulty we are facing: Is kissing, for example, *just* a means of satisfying the oral drive or instinct? Or is it also a form of interpersonal relating that taps into something quite different from the satisfaction of lust? Can it be both? Is it sometimes the one and sometimes the other? Similar questions can be asked of touching: is touching simply part of grabbing hold of the object in order to consummate with it, as instinct theory might suggest, or is it also a form of interpersonal relating, a way of approaching the *person*?

Freud probably overstated his case in disposing of the spiritual, and while he refocused attention in a necessary way on the bodily and sensual nature of our relationship with others, he may have allowed something to escape in the process. This makes for a skewed view of human nature and equally a skewed view of love. Only recently have there been attempts to redress this imbalance.

Correcting the bias is not simply a matter of finding the missing pieces of a jigsaw. In placing instinct at the root of all behaviour, Freud set the parameters of a discourse which created its own limitations. It is true that he started to incorporate in his theories what later became the object-relational point of view but there are limits to how much new wine can be

4 *The Tragical History of Dr Faustus* by Christopher Marlowe, Act 5, Scene 1.

put into old bottles (the bottle of instinct theory) and much psychoanalytic theorizing has suffered because of reluctance to discard theories which have outlived their usefulness. This issue has been eloquently discussed by Mitchell (1988).

What then has been left out of the picture? It is, I believe, the radically relational nature of human reality. In particular, there is no place for the face in its formulations, the face being the relational centre of the person (Wright 1991). The baby's first relationship is not, as object relations theory would suggest, with the mother's breast, or at least not only with her breast; at least equally, and in a different way, it involves her face. Moreover, the infant's relation with the mother's face is evidently based on an inborn disposition to relate to faces in ways that are independent of the instinctual, excited relation to her breast.

The idea that there is something in human beings that is present from the beginning, yet separate from the instinctual relation to objects, is critically important because it suggests the possibility of a different place from which the nucleus of love, in its more altruistic forms, could take origin.

The poet Wordsworth saw in the human infant a remnant of some other-worldly origin, a trace of spiritual ancestry. The baby 'trailed clouds of glory' from a pre-existence in which the 'soul' had been with 'god'[5]:

> Our birth is but a sleep and a forgetting:
> Our Soul, that rises with us, our life's star,
> Hath had elsewhere its setting,
> And cometh from afar . . .

Moving as these lines are, they offer an explanation that is unacceptable to both humanist and psychoanalyst. If we take the poet's insight meta-phorically, however, it becomes possible to think of an 'elsewhere' *within* human development and within psychoanalytic theory, that is separate from instinct in Freud's sense, and within which other-worldly feelings (i.e. altruistic or 'spiritual' feelings) might have their origin. The obvious loca-tion for this 'elsewhere' is the place where mother and infant relate to each other in non-instinctual ways – a preverbal place where 'heaven' lies in the mother's face and presence, and 'hell' lies in her absence.

When Freud discussed religion he saw practically everything in terms of oedipal developments. The religion he wanted to understand was Judaism, with its heavy emphasis on a strict paternal god (see chapter 10). When it came to earlier maternal aspects of religion he got no further than a reference to the 'oceanic feeling' which he admitted he did not understand from the inside. He did, however, link such mystical feelings with the stage

---

5 *Ode, Intimations of Immortality*, Wordsworth (1807).

of primary narcissism, or un-differentiation between mother and infant (Freud 1930). No doubt because he viewed development in a mechanistic way and thought of the baby as essentially an organism seeking instinctual discharge, there was no place in his theory for a type of infant experience which could illuminate the spiritual in a different way. In his thinking, the mystical was necessarily devalued *because* it was infantile.

One of the first and most cogent critics of psychoanalysis from within the field of psychotherapy was Ian Suttie in his book *The Origins of Love and Hate* (Suttie 1935). What most concerned Suttie was precisely what Freud had left out of his theories and the impact this had on his theoretical understanding of love. He argued that Freud did not have a convincing explanation of human tenderness. Indeed, he detected a bias in all Freud's writings which he called a *taboo on tenderness* – a systematic blind spot in his thinking. Yet for Suttie, tenderness lay at the heart of loving, and equally at the centre of the mother's relationship with her baby. He argued that this was not primarily anaclitic – in other words, dependent on the feeding situation – but was basic and primary. The baby, he said, had a *primary need for the mother*, similar to the primary need for *companionship* that the infant researcher Colwyn Trevarthen more recently claimed was central to an understanding of mother–infant relatedness (Trevarthen 1979).

These ideas are important because they postulate an independent line of development, based on a fundamental disposition for relatedness to the mother, which is not directly connected to the appetitive instincts but closely linked to the experience of tenderness and affection. According to this view, altruistic love is not the result of sublimation – in other words, aim-inhibited sexuality. It exists in its own right and its nucleus lies in this primary relational bond.

Suttie pressed his insight further and suggested that the violent emotional expressions of human beings resulted from thwarting of this primary relational need. Hate, for example, was not a manifestation of the death instinct as it was for Freud, and even more for Klein, but stemmed from thwarting and frustration of the desire for closeness and relationship. This idea anticipates Guntrip's later view of greed as love grown hungry and hate as love grown angry (Hazell 1996).

In certain respects, Suttie's ideas prefigure Bowlby's attachment theory, though this is more soundly based on research evidence. Bowlby too regarded attachment as a primary relational bond between infant and mother. He saw it as independent of instinct in the Freudian sense, and his ideas gained support from ethological evidence which demonstrated such an independent attachment propensity in many species (Bowlby 1969).

In this context, it is interesting that Bowlby is among the few psychoanalysts who have underlined the importance of the face in human development (Wright 1991). It mediates attachment between mother and infant, with smiling and facial interaction reinforcing the relational bond. Bowlby emphasizes how quickly the baby becomes able to recognize the mother's face, and citing the baby's preference for face-like stimuli almost from birth, he notes the conversational quality of facial interaction once the infant's smiling response is established. Trevarthen too has documented evidence for such preverbal conversation between mother and infant, calling it 'proto-conversation' (Trevarthen 1979).

To summarize: until recently, psychoanalytic theory has largely ignored the relational matrix of human development and has consequently found it difficult to give an adequate account of human loving. Human loving is above all concerned with relatedness and communication, while psycho-analytic theory has focused on 'objects', and the concrete, instinctual transactions between them (e.g. feeding and sex). Even the more recent developments of object relations theory have emphasized the object aspect (particularly the school of Klein), and until Winnicott's seminal paper on maternal mirroring (Winnicott 1967a), the object (in a theoretical sense) did not have a face. Having a place for the face in the object transforms the object, and as I have previously suggested (Wright 1991), it transforms theory by allowing the relational core to be explored in its own right.

## Love and the relational

My intention has been to reinstate the face at the heart of human loving, which can be done without discarding love's *body*, which Freud recaptured with such difficulty from the domain of idealized love. It is, however, necessary to assert the *primacy* of the face and the non-derivative nature of the relational in love and human development.

What does it mean to say that love is relational? It means that love is not just about my desire (lust), about what I want to do to the object, or the object to me. Nor is it only about the good feelings I or the other person have when we are 'in love', nor only about the concrete satisfaction of desire, though clearly it includes all these things. To say that love is relational is to find a place for the 'something more' I have spoken about: the less tangible things that go on between objects, or better, between subjects, that are equally important, and from certain points of view, more so. Finally, to say that love is relational is to speak of a certain kind of communication and understanding in which one person strives to hold the subjectivity of the other person in the forefront of their mind.

I have discussed the importance of the mother's face in the preceding chapters and also in a number of previous publications (Wright 1991, 2005, 2006). In the present context, the mother's face is significant because *it is the only object in the infant's world which can never be appropriated concretely*. I do not mean that it cannot be touched – indeed touching and stroking the face can be a way of expressing love. I mean that even at the level of the facial *gestalt* – that very specific constellation of features which is essential to the infant's bond with the mother – what is crucial can only be apprehended visually, in other words, in a non-appropriative, non-tactile mode. The face *in its essence* is a visual object and it always surprises me that this fact has been virtually unnoticed in the psychoanalytic literature.

What is true of the facial *gestalt* is equally true of the expressions which play across the maternal face. They too are a visual display, and given the infant's preferential attention to the face, soon become, like a first television screen, compulsive viewing, a pageant of changing configurations whose 'meanings' will gradually be felt and grasped.[6]

These considerations are striking, but more fundamental is the 'biology' of facial expressiveness. At least since Darwin wrote *The Expression of the Emotions in Man and Animals* (Darwin 1872), it has been known that the face plays a central part in the communicative behaviour of primates. In monkeys and apes, which have no language as such, it is one of the principal vehicles of social communication and cohesion. Moreover, recent research suggests that the face is 'pre-wired' to express certain emotional configurations, these being recognizable across cultures. In other words, the emotionally expressive patterns of the categorical affects – rage, joy, grief and several others – do not seem to be learned by cultural transmission. This probably means that the infant has an innate potential to 'read' their significance.

To some extent this is conjectural. We do not know when the baby begins to grasp the significance of the mother's expressions, but we do know that it gazes at the mother's face from shortly after birth, and increasingly interacts with it, particularly through smiling. *This suggests an in-built communication channel, linked to the emotions, that is not directly tied to instinctual satisfaction but exists independently of it.* It does not preclude the face and its expressions acquiring links with states of satisfaction but that is a different matter.

Again to summarize: I have attempted to stake out an area of human experience which from the beginning is relatively distinct from the field of instinctual satisfaction. I have suggested a biological underpinning for such a state of affairs and argued that the mother's face is a primary focus for it. Its privileged position is relatively safeguarded by the fact that facial expressions cannot be apprehended through the same sensory channel (oral/tactile) as instinctual experience. Interfacial communication is a zone of experience confined to the visual channel from the beginning.

This separate status can be used to support the argument that 'higher' forms of love are not merely derivatives of instinctual-appropriative modes. *Agape*, we could then say, is distinct from aim-inhibited *eros*; it is present

---

6 Stern (1990) has attempted to imaginatively enter into a baby's experience, including the experience of the mother's face, in his *Diary of a Baby*.

in an embryonic way from the start and has its origins in the non-appropriative strand of early relatedness to the mother.

## Love, recognition and attunement

In St Paul's first letter to the Corinthians, there is a famous passage on love – the Bible calls it 'charity'. In a rather beautiful way, St Paul describes the many qualities of love, and in effect, the passage constitutes a summary of Christian virtues. At the end of his speech, in a rather obscure though evocative section, St Paul looks forward to the time of Christ's second coming. He tells us that while at the present time our vision of God is incomplete and clouded, when that time comes we shall know him without reservation: 'For now we see through a glass, darkly; but then face to face: now I know in part; but then shall I know even as also I am known' (1 Corinthians 13: 12).

This statement can be read in the light of my previous discussion. Now 'we see through a glass, darkly' – the image in the glass is clouded, but the true revelation will be a direct encounter, 'face to face'. Towards the end of the passage he makes a further statement that the complete revelation of the Godhead – of Love – involves a kind of *knowledge*: 'Then shall I know even as also I am known.' St Paul seems to be saying that the ultimate revelation is a *mutual* knowing, in which each party, God and Man, will know the other through their face. This could be linked to the mother–infant relationship in which the infant eventually learns to know the *mother* and her feelings through the expressions on *her* face, just as the mother has always, like God, known the infant through the expressions on his face. We could call this the Pauline view of love – the idea that love involves *mutual* knowing and *mutual* recognition.

I suggested earlier that we feel loved when we feel recognized and known and will now speculate as to why such things are felt to be so important. Biologically speaking, we can think of the *specificity* of the mother–infant bond and the importance of this for survival. It is *this* mother animal, and no other that will look after *this*, her *own* offspring, and no other. For this to work, there has to be a mechanism for each to recognize this specific other. We are in the realm of attachment theory. In some animals we have imprinting; in man, in keeping with his greater freedom from instinctual necessities, there is learned specificity. However, to think in this way is to look from the outside, and in human life, the external, biological perspective is somehow transformed into the complex inter-relations of subjectivity – the *experience* of being recognized and known.

As I have discussed, it is coming to be accepted that such experience is centrally important in the process of becoming a self (e.g. Hobson 2000; Target and Fonagy 1996; Winnicott 1967a). I can only fully *become* the self I am through your *recognizing* me as that self. I am not talking here of the

Descartian *cogito* – 'I think, therefore I am' – in which the guarantee of my existence lies within myself and my own subjectivity; I refer to something that depends more radically on the social process. A metaphysical version of the idea was expressed by the eighteenth-century philosopher Bishop Berkeley who wrote: '*Esse est percipi*' – 'to be is to be perceived': we only exist in so far as we are perceived by God. However, a developmental statement of this idea underscores Winnicott's later work – the infant's sense of existing depends at the start on seeing himself in the mother's expression (Winnicott 1967a). Stern's concept of attunement develops this idea in ways I have already discussed (see chapters 1, 3, 5 and 10; and Stern 1985). In each case the mother reveals the infant's being in the forms through which she recognizes his subjectivity, and in the terms of my argument, this simultaneously reveals that his mother loves him.

As in the case of the mother and baby mammal, such recognition is highly specific but now concerned with states of being, and the inner profile of the person, rather than with external characteristics. It is the mother's knowing and recognizing of her baby in all its quirky specificity, and her communication back to the baby of this knowing, in her own quirky and specific fashion, that ultimately gives the baby a maternal (i.e. accepting and containing) place in which to be. It is here that links can be made with the religious notion of being accepted by a loving God who knows every hair of our head, and every thought of our hearts, and equally with the notion of true lovers, who feel there to be a total mingling of their lives, and a sense of complete knowing and acceptance of this other they each know, however illusory this may be.

# Chapter 12

# The silver mirror

In the untitled poem which stands at the beginning of this book, Rilke (1960) presents the stark image of a 'creature there has never been'. As the poetic drama unfolds, and this not yet existing 'creature' begins to emerge into life, it seems to become a metaphor for the psychoanalytic enterprise and a means of drawing together the themes I have discussed.

The poem, probably based on a famous mediaeval tapestry depicting a lady with a unicorn,[1] movingly describes how a purely imaginary creature was loved and nurtured by a shadowy female figure(s): 'They never knew it, and yet, none the less / they loved the way it moved, its suppleness, / its neck, its very gaze, mild and serene.' The poignancy of the poem lies in the way such loving was able to draw the creature from non-existence into life: 'Not there, because they loved it, it behaved / as though it were.' Slowly it came to inhabit the space imagined for it: 'And in that clear unpeopled space they saved / it lightly reared its head, with scarce a trace / of not being there'. Through the imaginative embrace of the woman's mind, the creature was imperceptibly transformed from non-being into being.

As I described in chapter 4, Rilke was deeply preoccupied with the creative process, and saw his poetic vocation as an existential necessity. It was central, not marginal to his way of life, and from his personal biography, it is clear that the 'creature' he struggled to bring into existence was his own unrealized and never fully reflected self.

Emotionally deprived as a child, and arguably emotionally abused, he must have longed for someone to perform for him what these shadowy 'others' had done for the creature in his poem, namely to feed him 'with the possibility of being'. With a few exceptions, however, he more or less

---

1 I refer to the series of six mediaeval Flemish tapestries referred to as *'La Dame à la licorne'*, representing the six senses. In the third tapestry which represents vision, the lady is seated, holding a mirror in her right hand. The unicorn kneels on the ground with his front legs in the lady's lap and gazes at his reflection in the mirror (see paperback cover image).

despaired of finding this in his ordinary life[2] and strove to satisfy the need in the process of creation itself.

In a different context, Winnicott too was concerned with the 'possibility of being', and his theory documents the conditions within which the *potential* being of the infant could come to be realized. Standing over this process and guardian of it was the good enough adaptive mother, who shielded the infant from impinging reality and gave external form to his searching gestures.

Winnicott believed that the infant's emotional development depended on the availability of the mother's adaptive provision. She *was* the infant's first environment – not only in the sense of reliably being there, but in a more active, intuitive way as creator of what the infant needed. Her task was not confined to providing warmth, affection and food; it entailed a more imaginative activity, based on intense identification with, and non-verbal understanding of her baby. In Winnicott's view, the mother created and re-created her baby within the space she envisaged for him, and as in the Rilke poem, she fed him not only 'with corn' (milk and physical care) but also with 'the possibility of being'. In the holding of her 'facilitating environment', the baby 'reared its head, with scarce a trace of not being there' – in other words, it came to inhabit the space prepared for him in the mother's mind, and in the process emerged as a real being.

In this context, one of Winnicott's most striking metaphors was that of the mother's face as the infant's first mirror (Winnicott 1967a). This vividly portrays the non-verbal emotional connection between mother and infant and highlights the precariousness of the interaction on which emotional and mental development depends. Winnicott saw that the infant needed the mother's emotional reflections at least as much as her breast and milk, and if there was breakdown in the reflecting process, the results were pervasive and serious. He realized that in the stage of absolute dependence, the infant could only feel fully alive within the 'holding' of the mother's mirroring, and he saw that the infant's first sense of potency depended on being able to light up the mother's face. The philosopher Merleau-Ponty (1962: 146) understood this when he wrote: 'I live in the facial expressions of the other'; and Rilke knew from its absence, the power of such reflection to bestow life on the recipient. It is thus significant that Rilke's poem ends with an image of the mirror in whose reflection the creature's 'brow put forth a horn . . . / Whitely it stole up to a maid, – *to be* / Within the silver mirror and in her'.[3]

2  It may be that Lou Andreas-Salome, his one time lover and longer term Muse, provided such attention in some degree.
3  Given that Rilke's mother wanted him to be a girl, the imagery of the horn and stealing up to the maid 'to be' within her is clearly significant. However, in the context of this chapter, I am more concerned with the nature of the process than the content of the imagery.

Winnicott was not blind to the fact that mental processes possess innate developmental thrust which guarantees a basic level of progression. However, he was more concerned with how the *quality* of development depended on the *quality* of maternal care. Thus, he believed that if the mother failed to accurately mirror the infant's emotional states, as for example in maternal depression, the infant's creative capacity would 'begin to atrophy' (ibid.: 112). This view implied that the infant's potential for creative activity was mediated through the channel of the mother's identification and the 'possibility of being' in any full sense of the word depended on reflection in the 'silver mirror' of her mind.

As I have discussed in earlier chapters, Winnicott's concept of mirroring was ground-breaking but also tantalizing, for while the sense of being affectively 'held' in the mother's expression is relatively easy to grasp, the way in which longer term structural development could be affected is less clear. One factor, as Winnicott himself implied, might depend on the power of the reflection to give external reality to the infant's subjective state. However, this potential is restricted by the range of responses available to the human face, and this is where Stern's concept of attunement enriches the picture; by extending the reflecting process into the late preverbal period, it opens the way to a richer variety of maternal forms with greater range and specificity (Stern 1985). Since in attunement the mother portrays (mirrors) the infant's experience in each and every sensory modality, her responses take on a varied and playful quality that is likely to engage the baby as a willing spectator. This is important, for if the infant is to make the connection between the mother's enactment and its own preceding experience, it will have to register the similarity of pattern between them. The outcome of attunement will thus depend on the mother's imaginative and expressive capacity in giving external form to the infant's bodily based experience.

It is here that I have made links between three different areas of activity: the attuning mother who reflects the forms of the infant's subjective experience; the artist, who compensates for deficient attunement by making reflecting forms of his own; and the psychoanalyst, who helps the patient into being by fostering a new provision of attuning forms. In exploring these links, I have tried to feel my way into the experience of each area: to *be* the baby and feel myself held by the mother's enactment; to *be* the artist and experience the emergence of significant form within my medium; and to *be* the analytic patient who not only feels understood, but held within a shared and resonant image. In each case I have tried to feel from the inside the sense of resonant connection which derives from recognition (or being recognized) through form.

From the perspective I have taken, attunement emerges as the bedrock of non-verbal communication, and reveals in a highly visible way the relationship between shapes and patterns which underpins the preverbal ability to make links between objects and experiences. It can thus be seen as the primary mode of relatedness between infant and mother, providing the building blocks for later mental development. This view helps one to understand how deficiency in this area can have such devastating consequences; and it links with my work on artistic creativity in which I have argued that the artist is mainly concerned with non-verbal connections, and is (often, sometimes, perhaps always) driven to pursue his creative activity in order to make good an earlier deficiency in the area of mirroring and attunement.

To approach psychoanalysis from this perspective has been illuminating because it shifts the emphasis from cognitive understanding ('interpretation') to emotional structuring by means of images and forms ('holding' and 'containing'). Such altered emphasis is not new but is usually framed in the language of countertransference reactions, projective identification and enactment. When viewed in these terms, attention remains focused on *understanding* the analytic event and *explaining* it through interpretation. However, mirroring and attunement suggest new ways of approaching this area and highlight the role of creative image-making in the analytic process. From this perspective, the analyst can be seen as provider of resonant forms which reflect, and even create experience – he is the attuning mother rather than the explaining father, the artist who *creates* images rather than the scientist making theories about them.

Winnicott was explicit that his mirroring metaphor provided a different model of therapeutic practice. He saw 'psychotherapy' (and, I think, analysis) as 'a long term giving the patient back what the patient brings . . . a complex derivative of the face that reflects what is there to be seen'. Moreover, he thought that if he did this 'well enough, the patient [would] find his or her own self, and . . . be able to exist and to feel real' (1967a: 117). However, in saying this he gave no clear indication of what his model implied other than to make less 'clever and apt interpretation(s)'. Nor did he indicate – perhaps because it did not interest him – the way in which such maternal holding of the patient could mediate its longer term effects. In addressing these questions, I have found Stern's concept of attunement (Stern 1985) to be a better guide.

The mother–infant relationship provides a highly visible medium within which to study the interactions that Stern draws together under the term 'attunement'. The mother 'recasts' the infant's affective state, but in a real sense, her recasting is a form of non-verbal *representation*. She creates her enactment (and thus her psychological infant) through imaginative *symbolic* activity at a preconscious level and thus offers the infant a non-verbal *presentational symbol* (Langer) of his preceding affective state.

In considering how this facilitates mental development, we have to imagine that at some point the infant glimpses his 'experience' within the maternal symbol (the mother's enacted pattern), and thereby realizes that the structure represents, or strictly speaking *re*-presents, his own experience. This can be seen as the beginning of the infant's symbolic understanding, and from this perspective, the mother's attuning activity is a necessary forerunner – a preliminary external phase – of the infant mind. Until the infant makes the connection, he lacks an essential mental tool; as soon as he 'sees' what the mother is doing he will attempt to do it for himself. Seeing the connection marks the beginning of internalization through which the infant will take possession of vital mental equipment.

To think in this way gives attunement a formative role in the development of mental infrastructure and makes it possible to see this infrastructure as a quasi-symbolic organization. The mother's attuning form *becomes* the internal holding structure and the means through which the infant can begin to access his own experience and hold it 'in mind'. In this sense, the preverbal mind can be seen as a structure of inner forms and patterns that 'recognize' the patterns of ongoing experience and perpetuate 'in the mind' the mother's attuning recognition. The model also suggests that the relation between preverbal symbol and 'contained experience' in the infant mind consists of an ongoing *inner* attunement in which the sense of having personal experience and 'being a self' can be sustained.

Since holding an experience in mind involves recalling something that is no longer present, it requires a tool capable of evoking the experience it represents in a vivid way. This is precisely what characterizes the maternal symbol that reflects, or *re*-presents the shape of infant experience in attunement. *Such formal resemblance is the essence of preverbal representation*; it differentiates it from discursive language in which the link between word and referent is dissimilar and conventional. Ordinary language points to experience rather than evoking it, and this distinction is important in considering the varieties of therapeutic discourse. Discursive language, and arguably the language of interpretation, will generally lack the capacity of imagery to evoke and hold experience.

In claiming that attunement plays a critical role in infant mental development, I base myself on a widely held view about the origin of mind in interpersonal processes (e.g. Target and Fonagy 1996; Hobson 2000). This view is compatible with Winnicott's assertion that emotional development depends on the quality of early relatedness, in particular the availability of mirroring (and attunement) during a critical period. The internalization model suggests that in favourable circumstances an infant nearing the end of this phase will have in place a system of preverbal 'thinking' in terms of which he can make sense of himself and his environment. The tools of such 'thinking', derived from attunement, would be non-verbal forms that operated through iconic matching. They would allow the infant to *sense* the connection between form and experience (resonance) and in essence would reproduce the earlier interactive process with the mother. The degree of playfulness in this process – the degree to which the infant is able to utilize his inner forms in a provisional way – would perhaps reflect the playfulness with which the mother had related to the infant's experience through attunement at an earlier time.

The attunement model is important in understanding the relation between words and non-verbal experience which is central to language acquisition (chapter 6). It is also relevant to the psychoanalytic interface where words are the principal medium of expression. In both cases, the important question is how words relate to whatever was there before. A model of preverbal development which depends on the quality of maternal reflection makes it possible to see that the quality and nature of the mind's preverbal foundation will vary according to the quality of earlier experience. It is thus possible to understand how in some cases words will relate to underlying structure as a kind of completion – in Merleau-Ponty's (1964b) terms as answering a 'speechless want' – while in others they will present as alien forms bearing little relation to the individual's earlier experience. In one case, the voiceless 'creature' of the self will discover new 'possibilities of being' (i.e. new symbolic possibilities) through words, in another, the individual will be unprotected from the power of language to usurp the self with its own meanings, and in danger of false self development by adapting to its definitions. As Bakhtin (1981) put it: 'The word in language is half someone else's' and has to be 'populated' with our own 'intentions' before we can use it in our own way. When there is a deficiency of pre-existing 'intentions' (preverbal structures derived from attunement) the mind will be colonized by alien words, the words of others which carry their own definitions and expectations. In such a scenario, the 'creature there has never been', the *potential* self, will be overlain by the (false self) web of other people's words; it will speak with their voice and not its own.

The implications of this for the analytic situation are important and relate to the idea (Winnicott 1968b) that unless the patient can play, interpretation is little better than indoctrination. The capacity to play implies a currency of non-verbal forms, acquired through attunement and playful interaction with the mother. When this is in place (in Freud's terms, when there is a currency of 'thing presentations') the analyst's words can be seen as new forms ('word presentations') to be tried on for fit (Freud 1915). There will be a *sense* of what fits, even in relation to unconscious experience, and an inner strength, deriving from the preverbal level, to resist the alien element. If, on the other hand, the patient lacks such inner structure, there will be nothing to put against what the analyst says. There will be no structure for the analyst's words to complete, and even if the interpretations form a coherent garment, it will not become the patient's own. Without a 'body' of (preverbal) 'intentions' waiting to be clothed, analysis simply reinforces the false self (verbal) structure.

In this context, I have tried to define a different kind of analytic activity modelled on mirroring and attunement (chapters 7 and 8). Inevitably the vehicle of this remains language, but language used in evocative and image-based ways. If interpretation is seen as a language of explanation, the alternative is a language of imagery and containing forms. In attunement, the maternal image captures the 'shape' of infant experience, and through it the infant discovers his experience for the first time. In attunement deficient patients, the analyst must resurrect this process. He must find images that resonate with the patient's experience (experience that does not yet exist) so that the patient may discover his experience within these newly containing forms.

In the absence of this, the patient remains 'dead' and 'empty' and lives in a world of unalterable 'things'. He has no imaginary forms with which to represent himself to himself, nor is he able to 'play with reality' (Target and Fonagy 1996). From this perspective, there is nothing for the analyst to interpret. Only after an attuning process has been revived or initiated will interpretation begin to have meaning, and until this happens, the task of analysis lies in creating such resonant forms. In Rilke's terms, the analyst must offer the patient a new 'possibility of being' in a world of newly created reflections.

To see the analyst as a maker of resonant images draws him closer to the creative artist, and understanding the activity of the artist illuminates an important dimension of analytic work. If the artist uses his creative medium to make containing forms for his own emotional life, then the analyst can be seen as placing his image-making function in the service of the patient. He stands in the place of the attuning mother and attempts to revive a process in the patient that has 'died', or failed to develop. He offers the patient a 'silver mirror', and through this the possibility of emerging from existence into life.

# Bibliography

Akhtar, S. (1991) 'Tethers, orbits and invisible fences: clinical, developmental, sociocultural, and technical aspects of optimal distance', in S. Kramer and S. Ahktar (eds) *When the Body Speaks*, Northvale, NJ: Aronson.

Aristotle (350 BC/1983) *Aristotle's 'Poetics'*, trans. J. Hutton, Dewey Edition, London: Norton.

Ayer, A. J. (1936) *Language, Truth and Logic*, London, Gollancz: 1949.

Bakhtin, M. M. (1981) *The Dialogic Imagination*, ed. M. Holquist, trans. C. Emerson and M. Holquist, Austin, TX: University of Texas Press.

Balint, E. (1963) 'On being empty of oneself', in Balint E. (1993) *Before I Was I. Psychoanalysis and the Imagination*, J. Mitchell and M. Parsons (eds), London: Free Association Books.

Balint, M. (1932) 'Character analysis and new beginning', in Balint, M. (1952).

Balint, M. (1952) *Primary Love and Psychoanalytic Technique*, London: Hogarth.

Balint, M. (1959) *Thrills and Regressions*, London: Hogarth Press.

Balint, M. (1968) *The Basic Fault: Therapeutic Aspects of Regression*, London: Tavistock.

Bateson, G. (1985) *Mind and Nature: A Necessary Unity*, Flamingo Edition, London: Fontana.

Bell, C. (1914) *Art*, Oxford: Oxford University Press.

Bion, W. R. (1959a) *Experience in Groups and Other Papers*, London: Tavistock.

Bion, W. R. (1959b) 'Attacks on linking', *International Journal of Psycho-Analysis* 40: 308–15; reprinted in E. B. Spillius (ed.) (1988), *Melanie Klein Today*, vol. 1, London: Routledge.

Bion, W. R. (1962a) *Learning from Experience*, London: Heinemann; reprinted London: Karnac, 1984.

Bion W. R. (1962b) 'The psychoanalytic study of thinking', *International Journal of Psycho-Analysis* 43: 306–10; reprinted in E. B. Spillius (ed.) (1988) *Melanie Klein Today*, vol. 1, London: Routledge.

Bion, W. R. (1965) *Transformations*, London: Heinemann Medical Books.

Black, D. (ed.) (2006) *Psychoanalysis and Religion in the 21st Century: Competitors or Collaborators?*, New Library of Psychoanalysis, London: Routledge.

Bollas, C. (1987) *The Shadow of the Object – Psychoanalysis of the Unthought Known*, London: Free Association Books.

Bollas, C. (1989) *Forces of Destiny*, London: Free Association Books.

Bowlby, J. (1969) *Attachment and Loss, vol. 1, Attachment*, London: The Hogarth Press.

Britton, R. (1998) *Belief and Imagination. Explorations in Psychoanalysis*, London: Routledge.

Buber, M. (1937) *I and Thou*, trans. R. Gregor Smith, Edinburgh: T & T Clark.

Caldwell, L. (ed.) (2000) *Art, Creativity, Living*, Winnicott Studies Monograph Series, London: Karnac.

Chatwin, B. (1987) *The Songlines*, London: Picador.

Darwin, C. (1859) *The Origin of Species*, London: John Murray.

Darwin, C. (1872) *The Expression of the Emotions in Man and Animals*, London: John Murray.

Diamond, N. and Marrone, M. (2003) *Attachment and Intersubjectivity*, London: Whurr.

Eliot, T. S. (1944) *Four Quartets*, London: Faber and Faber.

Ezriel, H. (1956) 'Experimentation within the psychoanalytic session', *British Journal of Philosophical Sciences* 7: 29–48.

Ferenczi, S. (1926) *Final Contributions to the Problems of Psychoanalysis*, London: Hogarth.

Finch, H. L. (1995) *Wittgenstein*, London and NY: Element Books.

Freud, S. (1900) *The Interpretation of Dreams*, S.E. (Standard Edition) 4–5.

Freud, S. (1908) 'Creative writers and day-dreaming', S.E. 9.

Freud, S. (1910) 'Leonardo Da Vinci and a memory of his childhood', S.E. 11.

Freud, S. (1914) 'The Moses of Michelangelo', S.E. 13.

Freud, S. (1915) *The Unconscious*, S.E. 14.

Freud, S. (1927) *The Future of an Illusion*, S.E. 21.

Freud, S. (1930) *Civilisation and its Discontents*, S.E. 21.

Freud, S. (1937) Lou Andreas-Salome, S.E. 23.

Fry, R. (1924) *The Artist and Psychoanalysis*, London: Hogarth.

Fuller, P. (1980) *Art and Psychoanalysis*, London: Writers and Readers Cooperative.

Gallese, V., Fadiga, L., Fogassi, L. and Rizzolati, G. (1996) 'Action recognition in the premotor cortex', *Brain* 119: 593–609.

Gallese, V., Eagle, M. N. and Migone, P. (2007) 'Intentional attunement: mirror neurons and the neural underpinnings of interpersonal relations', *Journal of the American Psychiatric Association* 55: 131–76.

Green, A. (1975) 'The analyst, symbolisation and absence in the analytic setting – In memory of D. W. Winnicott', *International Journal of Psycho-Analysis* 56: 1–22, in A. Green (1986) *On Private Madness*, London: Hogarth; reprinted London: Karnac, 1997.

Grotstein, J. S. (1981) *Splitting and Projective Identification*, New York: Aronson.

Harrison, C. and Wood, P. (eds) (1992) *Art in Theory 1900–1990. An Anthology of Changing Ideas*, Oxford: Blackwell.

Hazell, J. (1996) *H. J. S. Guntrip. A Psychoanalytical Biography*, London: Free Association Books.

Heaney, S. (1994) BBC Television Interview.

Heaney, S. (2002) *Finders Keepers. Selected Prose 1971–2001*, London: Faber and Faber.

Hobson, R. P. (2000) *Autism and the Development of Mind*, Hove (UK) and Hillsdale (USA): LEA.

Hoffman, E. (1989) *Lost in Translation – Life in a New Language*, London: Heinemann.

Hopkins, L. B. (2006) *False Self. The Life of Masud Khan*, New York: Other Press.

James, W. (1902) *The Varieties of Religious Experience*, London: Longmans Green.

Joseph, B. (1987) 'Projective identification: clinical aspects' in J. Sandler (ed.) (1988), *Projection, Identification, Projective Identification*, London: Karnac.

Klein, J. (2004) *Jacob's Ladder. Essays on the Experience of the Ineffable in the Context of Contemporary Psychotherapy*, London: Karnac.

Klein, M. (1946) 'Notes on some schizoid mechanisms', in M. Klein, P. Heimann, S. Isaacs and J. Riviere, *Developments in Psycho-Analysis*, London: Hogarth; also in *The Writings of Melanie Klein*, vol. 3, 1–24.

Lacan, J. (1949) 'The mirror stage as formative of the function of the I', in *Ecrits: A Selection*, trans. A. Sheridan, London: Tavistock, 1977.

Lacan, J. (1953) 'The function and field of speech and language in psychoanalysis', in *Ecrits: A Selection*, trans. A. Sheridan, London: Tavistock, 1977.

Laing, R. D. (1961) *Self and Others*, London: Tavistock.

Laing, R. D., Phillipson, H., and Lee, A. R. (1966) *Interpersonal Perception: A Theory and Method of Research*, New York: Springer.

Langer, S. (1942) *Philosophy in a New Key*, Cambridge, MA: Harvard University Press.

Langer, S. (1953) *Feeling and Form*, London: Routledge and Kegan Paul.

Laplanche, J. and Pontalis, J. B. (1973) *The Language of Psycho-Analysis*, London: Hogarth Press.

Lecours, S. (2007) 'Supportive interventions and non-symbolic mental functioning', *International Journal of Psychoanalysis* 88: 895–915.

Lee, A. R. (1963, September) 'Levels of imperviousness in schizophrenic families'. Paper presented at Western Division Meeting of the American Psychiatric Association, San Francisco. Quoted in Watzlawick *et al.* (1968).

Levinas, E. (1961) *Totality and Infinity – An Essay on Exteriority*, trans. A. Lingis, Pittsburgh, PA: Duquesne University Press.

Loewald, H. (1978) 'Primary process, secondary process, and language', in *Papers on Psychoanalysis*, New Haven: Yale University Press, 1980: 178–206.

MacLeish, A. (1960) *Poetry and Experience*, Peregrine Edition, London: Penguin Books.

MacMurray, J. (1957) *The Self as Agent*, London: Faber and Faber.

Mahler, M. S., Pine, F. and Bergman, A. (1975) *The Psychological Birth of the Human Infant*, London: Hutchinson.

Mead, G. H. (1934) *Mind, Self and Society*, ed. C. W. Morris, Chicago: University of Chicago Press.

Merleau-Ponty, M. (1962) *The Phenomenology of Perception*, trans. C. Smith, London: Routledge and Kegan Paul.

Merleau-Ponty, M. (1964a) 'Indirect language and the voices of silence', in *Signs*, trans. R. McCleary, Evanston, IL: Northwestern University Press.

Merleau-Ponty, M. (1964b) 'On the phenomenon of language', in *Signs*, trans. R. McCleary, Evanston, IL: Northwestern University Press.

Mitchell, S. (1988) *Relational Concepts in Psychoanalysis*, Harvard: Harvard University Press.

Monk, R. (1990) *Ludwig Wittgenstein. The Duty of Genius*, London: Cape.

Morris, C. (1946) *Signs, Language and Behaviour*, New York: Prentice Hall, Inc.

Ogden, T. H. (1979) 'On projective identification', *International Journal of Psycho-Analysis* 60: 357–63.

Ogden, T. H. (1994) *Subjects of Analysis*, London: Karnac.

Ogden, T. H. (1997) 'Some thoughts on the use of language in psychoanalysis', *Psychoanalytic Dialogues* 7, 21.

Ogden, T. H. (2004) 'On holding and containing, being and dreaming', *International Journal of Psychoanalysis* 85: 1349–64.

Padel, R. (2002) *52 Ways of Looking at a Poem*, London: Chatto and Windus.

Pope, A. (1870) *The Poetical Works of Alexander Pope*, ed. H. F. Cary, London: Routledge.

Proust, M. (1922) *Remembrance of Things Past, Part 1, Swanns Way*, London: Chatto and Windus.

Pullman, P. (1997) *His Dark Materials, Vol. 2, The Subtle Knife*, London: Scholastic Ltd.

Quinodoz, D. (2003) 'Words that touch', *International Journal of Psychoanalysis* 84: 1469–85.

Rayner, E. (1991) *The Independent Mind in British Psychoanalysis*, London: Free Association Books.

Rilke, R. M. (1960) *Selected Works, Vol. 2, Poetry*, trans. J. B. Leishman, London: Hogarth.

Rodman, F. R. (2003) *Winnicott. Life and Work*, Cambridge, MA: Perseus Publishing.

Rose, G. J. (1996) *Necessary Illusion: Art as Witness*, Madison, CT: International Universities Press.

Rosenfeld, H. (1971). 'Contribution to the psychopathology of psychotic states', in E. B. Spillius (ed.) (1988) *Melanie Klein Today. Developments in Theory and Practice*, vol. 1, London: Routledge.

Rosenfeld, H. (1987) *Impasse and Interpretation*, London: Tavistock.

Rycroft, C. (1958) 'The nature and function of the analyst's communication to the patient', *International Journal of Psycho-Analysis* 37: 469–72; reprinted in C. Rycroft (1968) *Imagination and Reality*, London: Hogarth Press; reprinted London: Karnac, 1987.

Sandler, J. (1988) 'The concept of projective identification', in J. Sandler (ed.) (1988) *Projection, Identification, Projective Identification*, London: Karnac.

Sartre, J.-P. (1957) *Being and Nothingness*, trans. H. Barnes, London: Methuen.

Sartre, J.-P. (1976) *Critique of Dialectical Reason*, trans. A. Sheridan-Smith, London: New Left Books; first published as *Critique de la Raison Dialectique*, Paris: Gallimard, 1960.

Searles, H. (1963) 'The place of neutral therapist responses in psychotherapy with the schizophrenic patient', in H. Searles (1965) *Collected Papers on Schizophrenia and Related Subjects*, London: Hogarth Press.

Searles, H. F. (1973) 'Concerning therapeutic symbiosis', *Annual of Psychoanalysis* 1: 247–62.

Segal, H. (1986) *The Work of Hannah Segal. A Kleinian Approach to Clinical Practice*, London: Free Association Books.

Segal, H. (1991) *Dream, Phantasy, Art*, London: Routledge.

Spencer Brown, G. (1969) *The Laws of Form*, London: Allen and Unwin.

Spillius, E. B. (ed.) (1988) *Melanie Klein Today. Developments in Theory and Practice, vol. 1, Mainly Theory*, London: Routledge.

Stern, D. (1985) *The Interpersonal World of the Infant*, New York: Basic Books.

Stern, D. (1990) *Diary of a Baby*, New York: Basic Books.

St John of the Cross (1542–1591) *Poems*, trans. Roy Cambell, London: Harvill Press, 1951.

St Teresa of Avila (1515–1582) *The Life of the Holy Mother Teresa of Jesus*, trans. E. Allison Peers, London: Sheed and Ward, 1946.

Suttie, I. (1935) *The Origins of Love and Hate*, London: Kegan Paul; reprinted Pelican Books, 1960 and Peregrine Books, 1963.

Symington, N. (1993) 'Is psychoanalysis a religion?' in *Is Psychoanalysis Another Religion: Contemporary Essays on Spirit, Faith and Morality in Psychoanalysis*, London: Freud Museum.

Symington, N. (1994) *Emotion and Spirit: Questioning the Claims of Psychoanalysis and Religion*, London: Cassell.

Target, M. and Fonagy, P. (1996) 'Playing with reality: 2. The development of psychic reality from a theoretical perspective', *International Journal of Psychoanalysis* 77: 459–79.

Trevarthen, C. (1979) 'Communication and cooperation in early infancy: A description of primary intersubjectivity', in M. Bullowa (ed.) (1979) *Before Speech*, pp. 321–49, Cambridge: Cambridge University Press.

Vivona, J. M. (2006) 'From developmental metaphor to developmental model: The shrinking role of language in the talking cure', *Journal of the American Pychoanalytic Association* 54: 903–17.

Watzlawick, P., Beavin, J. H. and Jackson, D. D. (1968) *The Pragmatics of Human Communication. A Study of Interactional Patterns, Pathologies and Paradoxes*, London: Faber and Faber.

Whitman, W. (1881/1995) *The Complete Poems of Walt Whitman*, Ware (UK): Wordsworth Editions.

Winnicott, D. W. (1945) 'Primitive emotional development', in Winnicott (1958).

Winnicott, D. W. (1953) 'Transitional objects and transitional phenomena – a study of the first not-me possession', *International Journal of Psycho-Analysis* 34: 89–97; reprinted in Winnicott (1958); and also in Winnicott (1971).

Winnicott, D. W. (1956) 'Primary maternal preoccupation', in Winnicott (1958).

Winnicott, D. W. (1958) *Collected Papers – Through Paediatrics to Psychoanalysis*, London: Tavistock.

Winnicott, D. W. (1960a) 'The theory of the parent-infant relationship', *International Journal of Psycho-Analysis* 41: 585–95; reprinted in Winnicott (1965).

Winnicott, D. W. (1960b) 'Ego distortion in terms of true and false self', in Winnicott (1965).

Winnicott, D. W. (1963) 'The development of the capacity for concern', *Bulletin of the Menninger Clinic 27;* reprinted in Winnicott (1965).

Winnicott, D. W. (1965) *The Maturational Processes and the Facilitating Environment*, London: Hogarth Press; also London: Karnac, 1990.

Winnicott, D. W. (1967a) 'Mirror role of mother and family in child development', in D. W. Winnicott (1971) *Playing and Reality*, pp. 111–18, London: Tavistock.

Winnicott, D. W. (1967b) 'The location of cultural experience', in D. W. Winnicott (1971) *Playing and Reality*, pp. 95–103, London: Tavistock, 1971.

Winnicott, D. W. (1968a) 'Communication between infant and mother, and mother and infant, compared and contrasted', in W. G. Joffe (ed.) (1968) *What is Psychoanalysis*, London: Institute of Psychoanalysis/Balliere, Tindall and Cassell.

Winnicott, D. W. (1968b) 'Playing: its theoretical status in the clinical situation', *International Journal of Psycho-Analysis* 49: 591–7.

Winnicott, D. W. (1971). *Playing and Reality*, London: Tavistock.

Winnicott, D. W. (1987) *The Spontaneous Gesture: Selected Letters*, ed. R. Rodman, Cambridge, MA: Harvard University Press.

Wittgenstein, L. (1922) *Tractatus Logico-Philosophicus*, trans. D. F. Pears and B. F. McGuiness, London: Routledge and Kegan Paul, 1974.

Wittgenstein, L. (1953) *Philosophical Investigations*, trans. G. E. M. Anscombe, Oxford: Blackwell.

Wright, K. (1976) 'Metaphor and symptom: a study of integration and its failure', *International Review of Psycho-Analysis* 3: 97–109.

Wright, K. (1991) *Vision and Separation. Between Mother and Baby*, London: Free Association Books.

Wright, K. (1998) 'Deep calling unto deep: Artistic creativity and the maternal object', *British Journal of Psychotherapy* 14: 453–67.

Wright, K. (2000) 'To make experience sing', in: *Art, Creativity, Living*, ed. L. Caldwell, London: Karnac.

Wright, K. (2005) 'Have "objects" got faces?', in *Ten Lectures on Psychotherapy and Spirituality* (2005), ed. N. Field, London: Karnac.

Wright, K. (2006) 'Preverbal experience and the intuition of the sacred', in *Psychoanalysis and Religion in the 21st Century: Competitors or Collaborators?*, ed. D. Black, New Library of Psychoanalysis, London: Routledge.

# Index

Locators for headings with subheadings refer to general aspects of the topic.
Locators in **bold** refer to major entries.
Individual names used as subheadings (e.g. Freud) refer to their contributions to the topic.